Cambridge IG

Development Studies

Wendy Taylor

CAMBRIDGE
UNIVERSITY PRESS

CAMBRIDGE
UNIVERSITY PRESS

University Printing House, Cambridge CB2 8BS, United Kingdom

One Liberty Plaza, 20th Floor, New York, NY 10006, USA

477 Williamstown Road, Port Melbourne, VIC 3207, Australia

4843/24, 2nd Floor, Ansari Road, Daryaganj, Delhi – 110002, India

79 Anson Road, #06–04/06, Singapore 079906

Cambridge University Press is part of the University of Cambridge.

It furthers the University's mission by disseminating knowledge in the pursuit of education, learning and research at the highest international levels of excellence.

www.cambridge.org
Information on this title: www.cambridge.org/9781107670778

First published 2014
20 19 18 17 16 15 14 13 12 11 10 9 8 7 6 5

Printed in Great Britain by CPI Group (UK) Ltd, Croydon CR0 4YY

A catalogue record for this publication is available from the British Library

ISBN 978-1-107-67077-8 Paperback

Contents

Introduction

Millions of people are unable to access basic needs such as enough food and clean water, but across the world countries are seeking ways to improve the living conditions of their people. The Development Studies syllabus gives an understanding of this process and of how politics and economics, together with social and environmental issues contribute to the reduction of poverty. Although the various sections of the syllabus deal with different aspects of development, it is important to understand the interrelationships between these issues and to consider a holistic approach to the development strategies studied in the text.

The political process

A government makes decisions on how a country's natural resources are to be used, where industries will be sited and how the environment will be protected. It decides how taxes will be spent. Conflicts with other countries may result in more money being spent on weapons than on providing clean water. Palaces for the leader may be built instead of hospitals and schools. A government may pass laws to improve the rights of women and abolish child labour, or it may ignore these and other important development issues.

The economic process

Economic growth from industrial production and commercial agriculture will make a society wealthier but it can make the living conditions worse for some local people. If people have an income from work, they pay tax to the government and they can purchase goods and satisfy their basic needs. They can make sure their children get an education and all the benefits that this brings. Companies trade goods, earn foreign exchange and also pay tax. However, industries use up resources such as oil and they produce waste which can damage the environment where people live.

The social process

Development is a process of change that usually improves the living standards of the people of a country. Education, health care, clean water and good sanitation, a varied diet as well as human rights are all social aspects of development. These need funding from economic growth and the political will to provide them. If people are educated and healthy they are able to contribute to the economy and so drive development forward.

Population growth means more resources will be used up which makes it difficult for governments to provide services for everyone.

The environmental process

Economies and societies depend upon natural resources provided by the earth, whether it is raw materials for industry or clean air to breathe. Waste produced is often dumped in the environment on which people depend for their survival. Governments determine whether resources are exploited for short term gain or conserved for use by future generations. Biodiversity must not be destroyed, minerals must not be exhausted, soils must not be eroded and water must not be polluted if people's quality of life is to improve. In general terms, all natural resources must be used responsibly.

Through a combination of these processes poverty is reduced, living standards improve and countries develop. The international community is working to achieve the Millennium Development Goals which are a means of measuring this progress. Partnerships between nations, charities and community groups promote development so that people in developing countries can access the services that people in developed countries take for granted. The world is a dynamic place with people and goods constantly moving around it. Information about anywhere and anything is available, almost instantly, almost everywhere. Globalisation continues to bring countries together.

Sustainable development

Development is also influenced by local decision making and often different strategies have to be considered in order to solve local problems in the best way. To meet the needs of people now as well as in the future, policies must be developed which balance economic growth with rises in living standards for all people in society as well as the protection of the environment. To achieve this is one of the biggest challenges facing mankind.

Case studies which illustrate sustainable projects are used to show how people around the world are tackling this issue. Improving living standards today with consideration for the quality of life of those in the future is certainly possible if governments and a country's people care enough to use the planet's resources wisely. The following is a quote from the website of The Green Belt Movement which shows the importance of protecting the natural environment if improvements to people's quality of life are to be made and sustained.

How It All Started
The Green Belt Movement (GBM) was started in 1977 by Dr Wangari Maathai, the first African woman and the first environmentalist to receive the Nobel Peace Prize (in 2004). What began as a grassroots tree planting program to address the challenges of deforestation, soil erosion and lack of water is now a vehicle for empowering women.

The act of planting a tree is helping women throughout Africa become stewards of the natural environment. But that's just the first step.

By protecting the environment, these women are also becoming powerful champions for sustainable management of scarce resources such as water, equitable economic development, good political governance, and ultimately..... peace.

Our Achievements

Today, more than 40 million trees have been planted across Africa. The result: soil erosion has been reduced in critical watersheds, thousands of acres of biodiversity-rich indigenous forest have been restored and protected, and hundreds of thousands of women and their families are standing up for their rights and those of their communities and so are living healthier, more productive lives.

Yet, so much remains to be done. Forests are still being lost, democracy is fragile, and poverty is still widespread.

Our Vision for the Future

Our goal in the next decade is to plant one billion trees worldwide. A healthy natural world is at the heart of an equitable and peaceful society. And protecting the environment is something every individual can take part in.

Source: http://greenbeltmovement.org/a.php?id=178

The Millennium Development Goals

Wangari Maathai has long supported the aims of the MDGs, and believes that environmental conservation must play a central role if the MDGs are to be achieved. Unless there is adequate food security, based on the care of ecosystems, poverty and hunger cannot be eradicated (1), children will die (4), and education (2) will be impossible, as children are pulled out of school to work in the fields or are too malnourished to learn.

There can be no development (8) or combating of tropical diseases or HIV/ AIDS (6), or healthy (5) and empowered women (3) unless we stop polluting and destroying the environment in which we live and begin to relieve the burden of women, who have to walk so far to get firewood or spend so long gathering food. Only when we acknowledge the centrality of the environment (7) will we have a hope of reaching the Millennium Development Goals.
(The numbers 1–8 refer to the Millennium Development Goals)

Source: http://www.greenbeltmovement.org/w.php?id=40#mdg

Unit 1   Poverty and development

Poverty and education

> **Learning Objectives**
> •) To understand the meaning of poverty and basic needs
> •) To understand how a country's wealth can be measured
> •) To consider the Millennium Development Goals as a global action plan
> •) To realise the importance of education to development
> •) To be able to describe the different levels of education
> •) To consider ways to achieve universal primary education.

🌐 The meaning of poverty

People who live in poverty are unable to provide themselves with basic needs such as food, water, clothing and shelter and therefore suffer from hunger and illness. Access to health care and education may also be regarded as basic needs. Basic needs are essential if someone is to have a reasonable quality of life. 'Wants' are not necessary for living but make life easier and more enjoyable. People who are poor spend their whole day trying to survive and they have little time, energy or knowledge to try to improve their situation.

task A

List the six basic needs and draw up your own list of six 'wants'. Rank these in order of importance. Compare your list with others in your class.

Poverty is usually seen in monetary terms and may be defined as the situation for people who live on less than US$1.25 per day. This figure refers to the equivalent amount of goods and services that would be worth $1.25 in the United States. People who live on less than US$1.25 per day are said to be below the poverty line. Of the 1.4 billion people in the world that live below the poverty line, the majority live in rural areas. People who live in rural areas often grow their own food to survive and the success of the harvest may be the difference between life and death. Tens of thousands of children die each day and many of these are in remote areas, far from medical services and far away from the eyes of the world's media.

Definition

Rural: describes the countryside including its villages and isolated settlements

Living on waste – an example of urban poverty

Children live in oil drums on the edge of one of Manila's huge rubbish dumps in the Philippines. Each time a truck arrives with a fresh load of stinking waste from the city's 15 million inhabitants, there is a rush to find scraps of food to eat and items to collect and sell for recycling. The children suffer from diarrhoea caused by rotten food, polluted water and lack of sanitation. They get injuries from having no protection against sharp objects and their little lungs are damaged by gases given off from the rotting rubbish. They rarely attend school or access medical help; although charities are working to help these very poor families. A common sight at these dumps is shown in Figure 1.1.

Figure 1.1 Living on waste

The river has run dry – an example of rural poverty

Mesela has walked for five kilometres to collect water for her family. Now she is in despair as the river is dry as seen in Figure 1.2. The crops have already failed due to the drought and she will struggle to feed her family. She has no income to buy food, new seeds or any fertilisers for next year. The family will become weak and so work on the land will be even more difficult. There is certainly no money to afford medical care or schooling and in any case the nearest clinic and school are far away in the town and they have no transport.

Figure 1.2 The river has run dry

The vicious circle of poverty

The sort of situations described above may be termed a 'vicious circle of poverty' or a 'poverty trap' such as the one shown in Figure 1.3. Once a family is caught up in this desperate poverty, it is very hard to break out of it, and things just get worse.

In order for people to break out of this vicious circle of poverty it is vital that their basic needs are satisfied. In the short term, aid agencies may offer desperately needed support. In the longer term it is money generated from economic growth, such as improved agricultural production, small craft shops or large factories, which provides the essential wealth for improvements to be made to water supplies, diet and housing.

Education and health care are possible when the government has money from tax revenues to build clinics and schools and people can afford these services when they have an income.

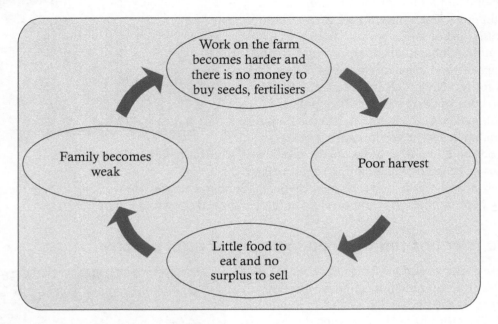

Figure 1.3   A vicious circle of poverty

A country's wealth

A country's wealth is measured in terms of its Gross National Income (GNI). This measurement was previously known as Gross National Product (GNP). GNI is the total income from the goods and services that a country produces each year, including its earnings from other parts of the world. Gross Domestic Product (GDP) is the income from the production of goods and services within a country.

Goods are products such as oil, beans and computers; services include education, transport and shops. Money from the economic activities such as street shoe cleaning is not likely to appear in government data.

For comparisons between countries to be made, the GNI in a country's currency is first converted to American dollars. The more people there are in a country, the smaller the share of the wealth there is for each person. Therefore the size of a country's population also has to be taken into account.

The GNI divided by the population gives a figure for the GNI per person. GNI per person is obviously an average figure for wealth and often hides huge differences in the country's population between those who are very wealthy and those who are in extreme poverty. Table 1.1 shows a list of countries at different levels of development that have been ranked in descending order according to their GNI.

Table 1.1 GNI and Population Data for Selected Countries (2010)

Country	Population (Millions)	GNI (US$Billion)	GNI Per Person (US$)
China	1338	5668	4236
France	65	2746	42,246
Brazil	195	1859	9533
India	1225	1539	1256
Philippines	93	192	2065
Chile	17	184	10,824
Morocco	32	93	2906
Kenya	41	33	805

Source: http://data.worldbank.org/indicator/

task B Rank these countries in descending order in terms of their GNI per person and describe how the list compares with the order in Table 1.1. Explain why Chile has moved up the list and why China has moved down it.

The Millennium Development Goals

In the year 2000, leaders from all countries adopted The United Nations Millennium Declaration and committed themselves to achieve 8 Millennium Development Goals (MDGs). It was the creation of a global partnership to reduce extreme poverty, hunger and disease and to promote gender equality, access to education and sustainable development. Each goal has a number of targets to enable monitoring of progress towards achieving these goals to be made. The MDGs shown in Table 1.2 may be seen as a global action plan to improve the lives of the world's poor by the year 2015. The United Nations development agenda beyond 2015 seeks to build on the MDG framework while at the same time considering other global challenges.

Table 1.2 The MDGs

Goal 1	Eradicate extreme poverty and hunger
Goal 2	Achieve universal primary education
Goal 3	Promote gender equality and empower women
Goal 4	Reduce child mortality
Goal 5	Improve maternal health
Goal 6	Combat HIV/AIDS, malaria and other diseases
Goal 7	Ensure environmental sustainability
Goal 8	Develop a global partnership for development

The measurement of poverty is important if it is going to be eradicated. Governments will know the challenge they face and will be able to target their efforts in those places where the need is the greatest. By measuring progress in reducing poverty, it may be possible to determine which approach has the best results.

MDG 1 Eradicate extreme poverty and hunger

MDG 1 has three targets which are as follows.

1. Target 1A is to halve, between 1990 and 2015, the proportion of people whose income is less than US$1 a day. (US$1 has been altered to US$1.25 since the MDGs were drawn up)
2. Target 1B is to achieve full and productive employment and decent work for all, including women and young people.
3. Target 1C is to halve, between 1990 and 2015, the proportion of people who suffer from hunger.

If Target 1A is achieved by 2015, poverty would not be eradicated but there would be a considerably smaller proportion of people who could not meet their daily basic needs. These targets are obviously linked together because poverty leads to hunger and malnutrition. If people have employment, they have an income and so they are less poor and can afford more and better quality food.

More opportunities for work will improve the lives of billions of people but providing full employment for its citizens is a major challenge to any government. Discrimination against women is also a serious problem in many parts of the world. If women are not empowered (MDG 3) and children do not receive an education (MDG 2), boys and girls will not acquire the skills needed for different roles in a growing economy. Employment will be difficult to find and people will remain poor (MDG 1).

Progress that has been made

Developing regions as a whole look set to achieve Target 1A of MDG 1. Table 1.3 shows progress that has been made in some regions. Eastern Asia has shown the largest decrease in the proportion of people living below the poverty line and its target for 2015 had easily been met by 2005. In Sub-Saharan Africa, progress is much slower and it is very unlikely that this region will meet its target.

India and China have already made significant contributions to the large reduction in global poverty. There will, however, still be several hundred million people around the world living below the poverty line in 2015. As populations continue to increase in many countries, it becomes more difficult for them to meet targets for poverty reduction.

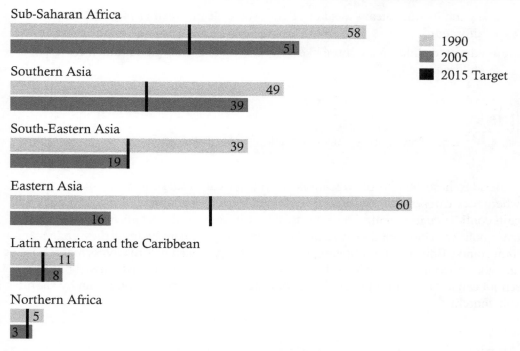

Figure 1.4 Percentage of people living on <US$1.25 per day in selected regions

Source: http://www.un.org/millenniumgoals/pdf/MDG%20Report%202010%20En%20r15%20

1. Which regions shown in Figure 1.4 have already reached their Target 1A for MDG 1?
2. Do you think Southern Asia is likely to reach its target?
3. Do you think Latin America & Caribbean is likely to reach its target?
4. Explain why a region may reduce the proportion of its people living below the poverty line but yet have more people living on less than US$1.25 per day.

Education

In some of the most poverty stricken settlements, after providing food and water for their children parents save towards their children's schooling. They recognise that the best way to reduce poverty and improve living standards is to gain an education. This is because:

- educated children are literate and numerate and are more likely to get jobs with a good income
- education teaches the importance of a balanced diet, hygienic living conditions and disease prevention and so leads to better health

- a good income means a balanced diet and a clean, weather-proof home can be afforded
- educated children are more likely to have careers, marry later and have fewer children.

task D Draw flow charts to illustrate the four bullet points above.

Besides these benefits of education, schools provide a safe environment for children where they can seek advice, make friends and learn a vast range of life skills. They will gain confidence in making decisions, take part in community affairs and maybe even enter politics. They will take care of the natural environment better if they understand its importance. Education is a lifelong process that begins well before any formal schooling and goes on long after leaving school or university. Adults who have missed out on school can attend adult literacy classes or other education centres often run by charities and churches.

task E
1. What other life skills may be learnt at school?
2. What sort of things might you learn after you have left school?

Traditional education

Traditionally, education took place in informal groups at village meeting places which may have been under a tree as shown in Figure 1.5. Skills in traditional crafts were passed down from older members of the community. Fathers taught sons and mothers taught daughters. Children learnt about their culture so they had a sense of belonging to a society whose ways they were expected to continue. Traditional education has an important role to play, for heritage is important to preserve. Ancient languages, art, ceremonies, music, dances and other customs can easily be lost if they are not passed on to the next generations.

Definition

Culture: the customs of a particular group of people

task F Discuss some of the moral values that may be taught in a traditional teaching situation. List the main features of your culture and find out what traditional forms of education exist in your society today. Interview an older member of the community to find out how they were taught.

Formal education

Traditional or informal education does not usually give children the modern skills they need to work in a rapidly changing world. Modern or formal education enables children to get jobs in industries and services as a country develops. In developed countries this education may be compulsory up until the age of 16 whereas in developing countries children may only attend school for a few years.

Definition

Literacy: the ability to read and write a simple statement, with understanding

Numeracy: the ability to understand arithmetic

Formal education takes place in classrooms in buildings designed for the purpose. Literacy and numeracy are key subjects at primary level. If children cannot read and write it is difficult for them to continue their education.

task G Make a list of everyday tasks where being able to read is important.

Table 1.3 Youth (15–24) literacy rates (2009)

Country	Per cent
Bangladesh	75
Botswana	95
Chad	46
China	99
The Gambia	65
Lesotho	92
Mauritius	97
Mexico	99
Nepal	82

Source: http://data.worldbank.org/indicator/SE.ADT.1524.LT.ZS

Table 1.3 shows that literacy rates vary quite considerably in the countries shown. In Chad, less than half the young adults can read and write but in Lesotho, another country in Africa, over 90 per cent of young adults are literate. In some countries such as China, nearly all the young adults are literate.

task H
1. Draw a horizontal bar chart to represent the data in Table 1.3. Use a scale of 1 mm to represent 1 per cent.
2. Describe the main features of the chart.

At secondary level subjects such as science, languages, geography and history are taught in greater depth in classrooms by trained teachers. The use of computers and other forms of modern technology have enabled students to access a vast range of information as shown in Figure 1.5. Examinations are taken and as a result students may gain certificates that enable them to find good employment or further their education at college or university.

Figure 1.5 Traditional and formal education

At the tertiary level, students specialise and learn the theory and skills they will need to become engineers, teachers, health workers etc. Trained people enable the country's economy to grow through increased production of goods and services. As countries develop, the governments acquire the money to fund the building and equipping of more schools.

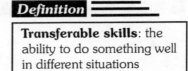

Definition

Transferable skills: the ability to do something well in different situations

In today's rapidly changing world, transferable skills are needed as well as the ability to solve problems and adapt to changing technologies. Some students now travel abroad to complete their education. Distance learning has become much easier if there is access to the internet and with rapid improvements in mobile phone technology, this will become more widespread even to very remote areas.

task I

Make a table of the difference between traditional and formal education under the following headings: Place, Subjects, Teachers, Equipment.

MDG 2 Achieve universal primary education

Target 2A is to ensure that all children in the world, boys and girls, complete a full course of basic schooling. It is understood that if boys and girls have equal access to education, it will make all the other MDGs that much easier to achieve.

Many countries have made excellent progress towards achieving this goal but some countries in Southern Asia and in Sub-Saharan Africa still have many children who do not go to school. It is unlikely that the goal of universal primary education will be met by 2015. One of the indicators for monitoring progress is the enrolment in primary education, 100 per cent being the target by 2015. Figure 1.6 shows the progress certain countries are making in terms of reaching this target.

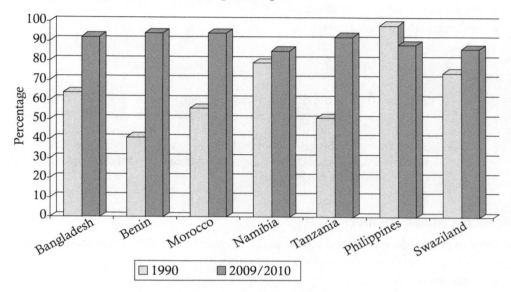

Figure 1.6   Primary school enrolment for selected countries

Source: http://data.worldbank.org/indicator/SE.PRM.NENR

task
J

Describe the progress that is being made towards achieving full enrolment in primary education in the countries shown in Figure 1.6.

Another indicator for monitoring progress towards MDG 2 is the proportion of pupils starting Grade 1 who reach the last grade of primary school. 100 per cent enrolment at Grade 1 will not ensure the goal is met if children drop out of school and fail to reach the final grade.

Some of the reasons why children do not attend school or drop out early are:

- cost of fees, uniform etc. for families, especially those living in poverty
- children are weak from hunger and disease and cannot walk to school or concentrate
- there are not enough schools and teachers especially in remote rural areas
- schools are too far away for families with no transport in rural areas

- children are needed to do domestic work, work on the farm or bring in income
- cultural beliefs that a girl's place is in the home
- some ethnic minorities are excluded from schools
- children often act as carers for sick relatives
- parents are ignorant of the value of schooling
- pregnancy and early marriage
- civil wars/natural disasters.

task K

1. What are some of the domestic chores undertaken by children?
2. How could civil wars and natural disasters prevent children from attending school?
3. Reasons why children do not attend school may be economic, political, environmental or social. Use these four headings and list the above bullet points under the correct reason.

Measures to help to meet MDG 2

In order to get children to attend school and keep them there through at least the primary grades, governments can take the following actions:

- abolition of school fees
- provision of enough schools, classrooms, teaching materials, teachers
- provision of free school meals (World Food Programme)
- mobile schools such as 'tent schools' in Mongolia
- laws to make basic education compulsory
- laws that put an end to child marriages and child labour
- rewards for families who allow girls to complete primary education.

Top-down and bottom-up decision making

Projects may be government-led or be inspired by community action. Government-led projects are sometimes referred to as 'top-down' as it is the highest authority in the land which makes the decisions and promotes the change. For example, communities cannot make laws to make education compulsory but governments can do this. Bottom-up decisions are often referred to as 'grass root' decision making as the idea comes from the community itself and the community takes a major role in making it happen.

Non-governmental Organisations (NGOs) and voluntary workers have a very important part to play as well. The community may be willing to build a school using their own skills and local materials but may not have the expertise or funding to provide the teachers and books needed for study.

With everyone – governments, charities, volunteers and communities – working together, progress towards getting all children to undertake a course of basic schooling can be made.

An example of a government-led project

In 2002, India began its Elementary Education Project. Its aim was to enrol all 6–14 year olds in school and avoid drop-outs. Primary school facilities were to be made available within 1km of all settlements and the programme not only supported teacher training but also helped produce teaching materials. The programme was launched by the Indian Government but additional funding and other support has been provided by The United Nations Children's Education Fund (UNICEF), The United Nations Educational, Scientific and Cultural Organisation (UNESCO), The World Bank, The European Commission and the United Kingdom's (UK) Department for International Development. In other words, a global partnership for development was put in place to help the Indian Government achieve its aim.

UNICEF runs global campaigns to raise awareness of the importance of schooling for all children. It helps governments to find out why children are not going to school so the right action can be taken to get them there and funding can be provided to help achieve this. It can suggest ideas that have been successful in other parts of the world. As well as text books, UNICEF helps to provide clean water and latrines at schools. Private latrines make a huge difference, especially to girls, and are crucial if they are to remain in school during adolescence. The main results of this project are:

- communities where no-one ever went to school, now have children enrolled in primary education
- many states are approaching MDG 2
- gender discrimination is disappearing as more girls go to school
- more children now progress from primary school to the next level
- drop-out rates have fallen.

An example of a community project

The Maria-Helena Foundation is a Canadian organisation that focuses on reducing poverty through education and health care in Pakistan, in partnerships with local NGOs.

The Foundation funds equipment and the construction of co-educational facilities that provide quality education at low cost to poor children. The local communities often provide the land and local donations help to cover operating costs. The fees are low and some scholarships are offered to very poor students. The teachers are usually women. An example is the Lieba Helena Primary School that was established in 2011 in Jhelum village in the Punjab with 210 students. The partner in Pakistan is the Tameer-e-Millat Foundation which supervises the construction and management of the school.

The Maria-Helena Foundation also helps to set up temporary primary home-schools for the poorest children, such as those from homeless families and for those who work on the streets and elsewhere.

Classes are often held at the teacher's home whose salary is paid for by the Foundation. Students do not pay any fees and books are provided with mats or benches to sit on.

Figure 1.7 Permanent Primary School
Source: http://mariahelenafoundation.org /media.html

Figure 1.8 Children in a class
Source: http://mariahelenafoundation.org /media.html

The Maria-Helena Foundation has helped reconstruct a school demolished by the 2005 earthquake and replaced one washed away during the 2010 floods. This ensures children can continue their education even after a natural disaster has struck.

The following quote is from the Foundation's website:

'Poverty and ignorance are at the root of many of Pakistan's problems. It is known that primary education and primary healthcare are essential foundations in reducing poverty.'

Source: http://mariahelenafoundation.org/profile.html

Summary

- A large number of people in the world cannot satisfy their basic needs
- Many people are unable to break out of the vicious circle of poverty without help
- Money from economic growth allows governments to invest in education
- The MDGs hope to improve the lives of those living in poverty
- Education plays a key role in raising living standards
- There are many reasons why children do not attend school
- Global partnerships result in progress towards the goal of universal primary education.

Poverty and health

🌐 Poverty and ill health

People who live in poverty cannot meet their basic needs and are more likely to suffer from ill health as they are unable to afford clean water, a proper diet, adequate shelter and health care. If people are constantly ill, their quality of life is affected and often one illness can lead to another.

Following are the implications of ill health:

- children miss schooling due to either being ill themselves or having to look after family members who are ill
- parents cannot look after their family properly or work efficiently on the farm and they may lose their job
- economic production is affected as the workforce is weak or absent.

A country's development will be slowed down if people miss work as a result of ill health. Many of the diseases suffered in developing countries can be prevented but health services have to compete for government funding with the many other demands on a country's budget such as road construction, schools and defence.

task A

Construct a vicious circle of poverty to show:
- how poverty leads to ill health and disease
- leading to weakness which means work is impossible
- so there is no income and this leads to more poverty.

Factors leading to good health

It is well known that good health depends on a number of factors such as:

- safe water, good sanitation and hygienic living conditions
- an adequate amount of food and a varied diet
- a spacious, weather-proof shelter and clean air
- a lifestyle that lacks stress and includes exercise
- knowledge of disease prevention and access to medical care.

Definition

Stress: a state of constant worry that can make people ill

The causes of stress are many but people who live in poverty may suffer from it because they worry all the time about how they will feed their children and how they will find the money for school fees. This stress often leads to depression and mental health problems, alcoholism and drug abuse, family tensions and breakdown.

task B

State other worries that people who live in poverty may have.

Measurement of health

There are many ways of measuring the health of a population. Two of the most common are Life Expectancy (LE) and Infant Mortality Rate (IMR). Figure 2.1 and 2.2 show the relationship between GNI per person for selected countries and the two indicators.

Definition

Life expectancy: an estimate of the number of years likely to be lived at birth

Infant mortality rate: the total number of infants dying before reaching their first birthday per 1000 live births in a given year

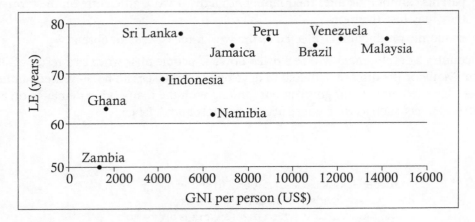

Figure 2.1 The relationship between GNI per person and LE

Source: http://data.worldbank.org/indicator/

The scatter graph in Figure 2.1 shows that, generally, as GNI per person increases, so the LE increases. The reason for this is because wealthier countries have more money to spend on health care and also on education into disease prevention. With a greater income, families can afford to access treatment and people are therefore more likely to live longer. If data increases proportionally, this is known as a positive correlation. Figure 2.2 shows that, generally, as GNI per person increases, so the IMR decreases. This is known as a negative correlation.

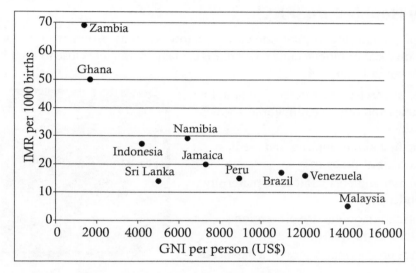

Figure 2.2 The relationship between GNI per person and IMR

Source: http://data.worldbank.org/indicator/

task C Explain why the IMR decreases as the GNI per person increases.

Prevention or cure

It is always better to prevent an illness rather than to try to cure it. Health workers give advice on disease prevention as less money is spent on treatment. People's quality of life is improved as diseases do not spread so much. Vaccinations, along with prevention, are also a major way of preventing disease. Figure 2.3 shows a nurse giving advice and vaccinations at a clinic.

Figure 2.3 Nurse giving advice and vaccinations

In the past, traditional medicine was used to try to cure illnesses and was based largely upon plants or animal parts collected from the wild. Knowledge was passed down from generation to generation and witch doctors were powerful members of a community. They may sometimes have done more harm than good although there is great interest in herbal remedies and more research is needed. It is vital that plants are conserved as they may contain cures for diseases that as yet we know nothing about.

Primary Health Care (PHC)

In developing countries hospitals are usually in towns. Many people who live in rural areas rely on local or mobile clinics where PHC may be available close to their homes such as shown in Figure 2.4.

A range of services are offered free or at low cost by nurses and other health workers which may include:

Figure 2.4 PHC clinic
Source: Wendy Taylor

- basic first aid for injuries and medical treatment of illnesses
- pre-natal and post-natal care, maternity facilities
- information on disease prevention such as hygiene in the home
- advice on the importance of a balanced diet
- vaccinations
- provision of vitamin and mineral supplements, rehydration solutions etc.
- family planning
- mental health care
- HIV/AIDS counselling
- home based care arrangements or referrals to specialist help in hospitals.

task D

How can parents be made aware of the importance of taking their children for vaccinations?

Figure 2.5 shows a flow chart of the benefits to a community of a village clinic. A clinic can improve people's standard of living in many ways and can help governments to meet the MDGs. The numbers in boxes refer to the MDGs listed in Table 1.2 (Chapter 1).

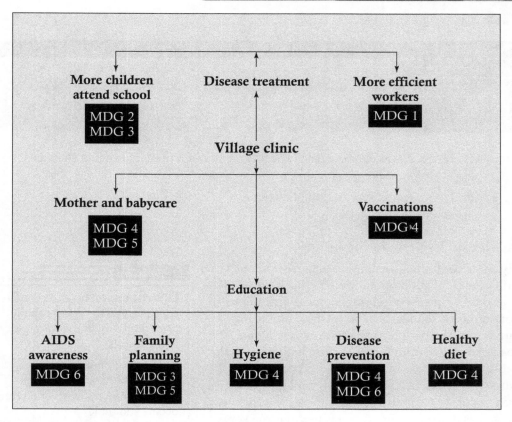

Figure 2.5   The benefits of a village clinic

 task **E**   Explain how a village clinic helps to improve people's standard of living.

Advice on the importance of a balanced diet

The body needs different types of food to grow and remain healthy and if it does not get a varied diet containing different nutrients it becomes malnourished. The main parts of a balanced diet are shown in Table 2.1. If people are malnourished they become weak and easily catch other diseases. So if malnutrition can be prevented, people will generally have better health. People who live in poverty cannot usually afford a balanced diet. Their meals may consist of one food such as rice which is called a staple diet.

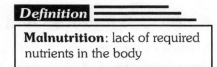

Definition

Malnutrition: lack of required nutrients in the body

Table 2.1 A balanced diet

Food Type	Use by Body	Food
Carbohydrates	Source of energy	Rice, maize, beans, millet etc.
Fats	Source of stored energy	Meat, fish, nuts, dairy products etc.
Protein	Growth and repair of tissues	Meat, fish, cheese, rice, peas etc.
Vitamins & Minerals	General good health, bones, vision	Fruit, vegetables etc.

Many different diseases can be caused if certain parts of a diet are missing such as:

- kwashiorkor – protein deficiency
- rickets – vitamin D or calcium deficiency
- scurvy – vitamin C deficiency.

Advice on hygiene in the home

Hygienic conditions are hard to achieve without safe water and good sanitation and this is why PHC is also often involved in bringing these facilities to communities. Hands must be washed after using latrines and before preparing food as germs can easily be spread from faeces to food which is a major cause of diarrhoea. In over-crowded conditions where water can become infected, cholera epidemics may occur where many people suffer severe sickness as well as diarrhoea. Food and water must be kept covered to keep it clean and stop flies from landing on it after they may have been on rubbish or faeces. Bodies and clothes need to be washed regularly with soap, if it is available, as soap contains antibacterial ingredients.

> **Definition**
>
> **Diarrhoea:** an upset stomach causes fluids to be lost rapidly from the body in the form of liquid faeces
>
> **Epidemic:** an infectious disease that is widespread amongst a population and often occurs suddenly
>
> **Antibacterial:** active against certain organisms that cause disease

task F

Design a poster to put on a wall in the waiting room of a clinic to show either how to eat a balanced diet or how to keep hygienic conditions in the home.

🌐 MDG 4 Reduce child mortality

MDG 4 focuses on reducing child mortality rates and fighting diseases which claim the lives of millions of children in developing countries each year. Target 4A is to reduce by two-thirds, the under-five mortality rate between 1990 and 2015. Figure 2.6 shows that five diseases account for over one-third of the deaths in children.

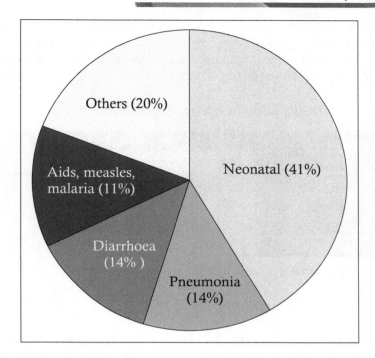

Figure 2.6 Causes of death in children under 5 (2008)
Source: http://www.un.org/millenniumgoals/reports.shtml (Report 2010)

Many children who live in poverty suffer from more than one disease at a time. For example, they may have to drink unclean water and so they often get diarrhoea. They become malnourished as they constantly lose the nutrients that they do manage to eat. They become weak and easily catch flu, whooping cough or measles, all of which can lead to pneumonia which is a serious infection of the lungs. Without treatment for this with antibiotics, it is difficult for children to recover if they are already weak. Sadly, many children cannot be given this treatment as either the family cannot afford it or they cannot get to a clinic in time. Being able to get rehydration solutions and vitamin and mineral supplements for the treatment of diarrhoea can save lives.

Definition

Neonatal: linked to new-born children

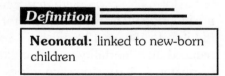 Draw a flow chart to show how a child who drinks dirty water may die.

Figure 2.6 also shows that the health of babies depends very much on the health of the mother during her pregnancy. If she suffers from malnutrition then the baby will be born weak and underweight.

Mothers can be encouraged to take their babies for regular check-ups to make sure they are growing properly. Mothers can be given advice on the importance of breast feeding infants, especially in areas where the water needed to mix with powdered milk is dirty. Table 2.2 shows the progress that certain regions are making to reach target 4A.

Table 2.2 Child mortality rates for selected regions (per 1000 live births)

Region	1990	2008	Target 2015
Sub-Saharan Africa	184	144	61
Northern Africa	80	29	
Southern Asia	121	74	
South-Eastern Asia	73	38	
Latin America & Caribbean	52	23	

Source: http://www.un.org/millenniumgoals/reports.shtml (Report 2010)

task H

Calculate the targets for the regions shown in Table 2.2 for 2015 and suggest which region is most likely to reach its target based on the progress made from 1990 to 2008. The first one has been done for you (two-thirds of 184=123. 184 – 123=61).

Child deaths are falling. In 2008, 10 000 fewer children died each day than in 1990. Some of the world's poorest countries have made considerable progress in reducing their child mortality rate but improvements are unlikely to be sufficient to reach MDG 4 globally by 2015 (*Source: http://www.un.org/millenniumgoals/reports.shtml Report 2010*).

Figure 2.7 shows the mortality rate for children under five for the countries in Africa in the form of a choropleth map which gives a general picture as the data is put into broad groups. The mortality rate for children under five varies from 17 per 1000 births in Libya to 180 per 1000 births in Somalia for the year 2010. All countries in Africa have reduced their mortality rate for children under five since 1990 but rates are still very high compared with developed countries. The child mortality rate for the United States (US) is 8 and for the UK it is 5.

task I

Approximately what proportion of African countries have a child mortality rate of over 100 per 1000 live births?

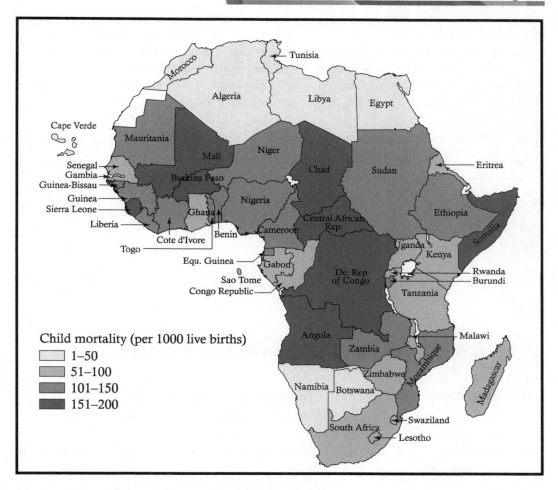

Figure 2.7 Child mortality rate for Africa (2010)
Source: www.worldbank.org/indicator/

Measles – a disease caused by a virus

One of the indicators for monitoring progress towards achieving MDG 4 is the proportion of one year old children immunised against measles. If a child is able to access this vaccine, then they are likely to be able to access other health services. A safe and cheap vaccine is available for less than US$1. Some other diseases for which there is a vaccine are TB, diphtheria, whooping cough, polio and tetanus. As a result of vaccination campaigns, infant mortality from measles has fallen as described in The Millennium Development Report.

Definition

Vaccine: a substance that provides immunity against a disease

Universal access: available for everyone

Between 1990 and 2007, 81% of countries reduced their under-five mortality rate and at the same time increased the percentage of one year olds immunised against measles..... In 1990/92, only 13 out of 126 developing countries had at least 90% of one-year-old children immunised against measles. In 2007, 63 countries recorded at least 90% coverage. In addition, 18 countries achieved universal access to immunisation.....
Bill & Melinda Gates Foundation and UN Millennium Campaign

Source: http://www.odi.org.uk/resources/docs/6172.pd

task J

Explain how each of the following helps to achieve progress towards MDG 4:
- affordable vaccines
- more clinics
- education of mothers.

🌐 MDG 6 Combat HIV/AIDS, malaria and other diseases

MDG 6 has three targets as mentioned here.
1. **Target 6A:** Have halted by 2015 and begun to reverse the spread of HIV/AIDS
2. **Target 6B:** Achieve, by 2010, universal access to treatment for HIV/AIDS for all those who need it
3. **Target 6C:** Have halted by 2015 and begun to reverse the incidence of malaria and other diseases.

HIV/AIDS – a disease spread by a virus

If someone is Human Immunodeficiency Virus (HIV) positive it means their body has produced antibodies to combat HIV which infects their immune system and stops it from working properly. A person may show no outward sign of being HIV positive for 10–15 years but eventually they suffer from a range of infections and diseases such as TB and cancer that the body cannot fight off as HIV has attacked its natural defence system. Then the person is said to be suffering from Acquired Immune Deficiency Syndrome (AIDS).

Antiretroviral drugs (ART) prevent the virus from multiplying and so delay the onset of AIDS in HIV positive people.

Ways HIV is transmitted

HIV may be transmitted by unprotected sex with an infected partner and from mother to child during pregnancy, birth and breast feeding. Sharing of contaminated needles in drug abuse and tattoos as well as infected blood transfusions can also spread the disease.

Methods of preventing the spread of HIV

- HIV prevention advice in schools, health centres
- free/cheap supply of condoms
- media advertising such as shown in Figure 2.8
- ART – this is particularly important for expectant mothers
- improved diet and hygiene to keep the body as strong and as free from disease as possible
- free testing service.

Figure 2.8 Advertisement against unprotected sex
Source: Wendy Taylor

A free testing service allows people to find out if they are HIV positive. The benefits of knowing this are:

- treatment with ART can be obtained
- precaution can be taken so the disease is not spread to others.

By 2009, over 5 million people had access to ART in developing countries. This was more than ten times the number treated in 2003 but in spite of this progress it is unlikely that Target 6B was met in 2010 (*Source: http://www.un.org/millenniumgoals/reports.shtml Reports 2010, 2011*). Target 6B is to achieve, by 2010, universal access to treatment for HIV/AIDS for all those who need it.

The World Health Organisation (WHO) and private organisations such as the Bill and Melinda Gates Foundation help countries to deliver programmes which reduce the spread of this disease which kills 2 million people each year and leaves many orphans to fend for themselves. Many countries have made considerable efforts to educate their young people about HIV/AIDS and numbers of newly infected people are falling as shown in Table 2.3, although numbers are still high. The effect of so many people being ill from AIDS has a major impact on their ability to work and therefore on the economic production in the country.

Table 2.3 People newly infected with HIV in selected regions.

Region	2001	2009
Sub-Saharan Africa	2.2m	1.8m
South & South-East Asia	380 000	270 000
Central & South America	99 000	92 000

Source: http://www.unaids.org/documents/20101123_globalreport_slides_chapter2_em.pdf

task K

Suggest **four** reasons for the reduction in the number of new HIV infections from 2001 to 2009 shown in Table 2.3.

Malaria – an example of a disease spread by insects

The following are some facts about malaria:

- malaria is caused by parasites that are spread through bites from infected mosquitoes
- mosquitoes breed in still water in puddles and ponds or in water collected in rubbish such as cans and plastic bags
- workers can be absent from work for several weeks
- malaria can be prevented and cured but the cost is huge
- most deaths are in children as adults have acquired some immunity
- many hospital admissions are related to malaria
- malaria has been successfully eliminated from some countries.

Definition

Immunity: ability to resist a particular infection

Methods of prevention

Mosquito nets can be treated with insecticide as the Anopheles mosquito usually bites at night. Rooms can be sprayed with insecticide. Although this treatment lasts for months, mosquitoes may become resistant to it and it then has no effect on them. Drugs to prevent and treat malaria have been developed but they are expensive. People can be educated to ensure water does not collect in areas close to where they live but where thousands of people live in poor housing conditions, close to each other, it is difficult to get everyone to co-operate.

The WHO is responsible for 'Roll Back Malaria'. This is a global partnership of 500 countries and organisations determined to fight this disease and eventually eradicate it.

Definition

Resistant: not being affected by something

task
L

Find out the name of a disease in your country that is transmitted by insects or animals, how it is spread and what is being done to control it.

🌐 Clean water and good sanitation

Clean water and good sanitation are essential for good health. Water is vital for life itself and without it, crops cannot be grown or livestock watered and many industrial processes would not be able to work.

In many developing countries clean water and good sanitation are not available. Hand dug pits that are also used by animals provide an often irregular and muddy water supply. Water may be collected from polluted streams as shown in Figure 2.9 or fetched from a lake several kilometres away.

If water is dirty it can cause diarrhoea and skin irritations as well as taste unpleasant. Clean water is a basic need used for drinking, washing and cooking. Pipes containing water that has been purified may reach individual homes in urban areas, but in rural areas clean water is usually from a single village standpipe or from a deep well. Water from far under the ground is usually uncontaminated. In towns, clean water can be bought in bottles but it is expensive and families in poverty cannot afford to buy it.

Figure 2.9 Drinking polluted water

Source: baker1674.wordpress. com/2011/06/01/womens-struggle-for-water

People wander out into the bush to pass urine and excrete faeces where privacy is hard to find and there is always the threat of sexual harassment and other dangers such as snakes. Pit latrines may be dug but these are usually shared by many families and soon overflow as there is nowhere to dispose of the waste safely. The overwhelming smell and flies are a constant problem. Hanging latrines may offer some privacy but are often suspended over a river which is used by the next community downstream for washing and other domestic uses.

task M

Make a list of some of the problems that may be caused by having to spend several hours every day walking large distances to collect water in heavy buckets.

task N

Read the following account and draw a simple illustration of the people in the story. In a 'speech bubble' write one sentence for each person to show how their life has been changed by the construction of a deep well like the one shown in Figure 2.10.

"My name is Sharna and I want to tell you about a wonderful thing that has happened to my family. We can now fetch clean water from a very deep well that has been dug for us in the middle of the village….and we have proper toilets at school. They have made such a difference to us all!

My younger brother used to miss school a lot as he was often ill with diarrhoea. Sometimes he was so weak by the time we had walked to school that he was too tired to learn anything and we had to carry him home. Now he has put on some weight and hasn't missed a day for several months."

"My older brother makes sure we all have clean hands before we sit down to eat together… and he even cleans the baby's hands for her like he has been taught at school.

Figure 2.10   A community well

My sister didn't like going to school as she hated having to go out and squat in the bush. She always went with a friend so they could watch out for wild animals or anyone coming as one of their classmates had been attacked. Now there are toilets and they have doors….and proper paper….and a basin with some soap!

In the past I had to go and collect the water from the river. It took me two hours and then I had to go and collect some firewood so we could boil the water. By the time I got home there wasn't time to walk to school. Now I can go everyday and so I don't miss any lessons.

We had to collect the water for Gran as it is too heavy for her to carry a long way. She is so happy now that she can collect her own water again and does not have to rely on us to help her. She is a very independent lady.

My Mother now has time and energy to make more baskets to earn money so we can keep going to school. She has also started growing vegetables so we can have different things to eat. She sleeps better now and is not so stressed from worrying about the water she has to find each day.

My Mother's friend is on the water committee. She feels important for the first time in her life and enjoys being allowed to make decisions. She enjoys talking to the other women at the well which has become a meeting place.

My Father is happy because he doesn't have to spend so much money on medicine for us. When we have used the water for washing, he can use it for his crops."

task

Make a table with the title – Benefits of Clean Water and Good Sanitation. Draw three columns headed 'social', 'economic' and 'environmental' and list the benefits in the correct column from the story above.

Add any other advantages that you can think of that are relevant.

task
P

If you have access to the Internet, research data on access to clean water and improved sanitation for your own country to be found on www.worldbank.org.
1. Draw pie charts to illustrate the situation in both urban and rural areas.
2. Describe the main features of the charts.

Practical Research Investigation

The value of a clinic to a community

Objectives
1. To investigate what services are provided by the nearest PHC centre
2. To investigate the distance to and accessibility of the nearest hospital
3. To investigate where people come from, their means of transport to the local clinic and how long it takes them
4. To find out the treatment available locally for certain diseases and the advice given to prevent them
5. To consider whether these diseases have been reduced
6. To identify areas that lack facilities and public transport where a mobile clinic may be of great value.

Methods
- a sketch map of facilities using local knowledge
- identification of frequency and route of bus services
- interviews with health care workers
- questionnaire for people attending the clinic to find out where they live, how they travelled and how long it took them
- group letter to the Minister for Health

Source: Adapted from Appendix to 'Scheme of work, Cambridge IGCSE Development Studies 0453'

- A country's development will be slowed down if the population suffers from ill health
- Prevention of diseases is better than cure and access to PHC is essential for good health
- Child mortality rates are falling but not fast enough to meet MDG 4
- Programmes to reduce the spread of AIDS are improving people's lives
- Clean water and good sanitation are essential for good health.

Summary

Poverty and gender equality

3

Learning Objectives

- ➤ To understand the general meaning of gender equality and inequality
- ➤ To consider the roles of women in society and the inequalities that exist
- ➤ To consider the ways that gender equality can be achieved
- ➤ To realise the importance of gender equality to development
- ➤ To associate gender equality with achieving several targets of MDGs.

 Gender equality and the MDGs

MDG 3 is to promote gender equality and empower women. Gender equality means treating boys and girls the same. There would be no discrimination and both would have equal opportunities in all things such as education, work and politics. It is generally accepted that if gender equality can be achieved, then it is more likely that the targets for the other MDGs will be met.

Women have so many roles in their societies that if they are given the right opportunities and influence they can make a big difference to their families' quality of life. The Beijing Platform for Action resulted from the UN Fourth World Conference on Women and is an agenda for women's empowerment. The UN produces a document every 5 years called 'The World's Women'. It assesses the progress that is being made to promote gender equality around the world and explains what more needs to be done to close the gender gap. Traditionally, men and women have had different roles as shown in Table 3.1.

Definition
Empower: give strength, authority and confidence
Gender gap: economic, cultural and social differences between men and women

Table 3.1 Traditional roles in a society

Men	Women
Hunters	Gatherers
Income earners	Domestic workers
Decision makers	Family carers
Land owners	Community workers

These customs that are passed down through generations are difficult to change. Today, even though many women are more empowered, they still perform many of their traditional roles as well as their new ones. Many men, the world over, regard a woman's place as being in the home as wife and mother and this tradition is hard to break even in the most developed of countries.

Men do not want their wives to be independent and so women are still suppressed in some societies and denied their human rights in the following ways:

- denied opportunities in education and employment
- instructed how to dress and how to behave
- given no freedom of movement or speech
- required to give any earnings to husbands
- not allowed to vote or enter politics
- subjected to harmful traditional practices and human trafficking.

task

A

Make a list of the sort of work men and women do in your society and decide to what extent there is gender equality.

Women and land

In many communities women do much of the farm work, especially if the men have migrated to find work elsewhere. Even so, they are not allowed to own land in their own right. Therefore, they cannot get loans in order to make improvements to their farm as they have nothing to give as security. In many societies, inheritance laws state that if a husband dies the land is transferred to a male heir. This could leave the woman with no-where to live and grow food. In areas of conflict where many men are fighting, this situation often arises.

In societies where women own land they are given more respect in their community. They are more likely to manage it in a sustainable way by preventing soil erosion and maintaining fertility and so produce good quality crops. Women are usually small scale farmers working independently and they often find it

> **Definition**
>
> **Security:** something pledged as a guarantee of repayment of a loan

difficult to grow enough food as well as look after their family. In many places they have formed self-help groups where women combine their efforts to produce more crops and support each other in a variety of ways such as childcare.

MDG 1 is to eradicate extreme poverty and hunger. It is estimated that there are over 900 million malnourished people in the world. Women need to be able to purchase fertilisers and good seeds and receive advice from agricultural experts in the form of new technologies in order to increase production.

Then they would get higher yields from their land which would reduce poverty and hunger. Women work just as efficiently as men but they lack the resources that are available to men farmers because of which they produce less. There is, therefore, a gender gap that a government can reduce by the following actions.

- Change the inheritance laws to prevent eviction of women by male relations
- Allow women to register land in their own name and so access loans
- Make agricultural services available to women as well as men
- Allow women to take places on Rural Development Boards.

Farmer Field and Life Schools (FFLS)

MDG 8 is to develop a global partnership for development. Many UN organisations work together with governments, NGOs and communities around the world to initiate projects that will help improve living standards in poorer countries. The FFLS is an example of this global partnership. These are run by the Food and Agriculture Organisation of the United Nations (FAO) together with the United Nations Development Fund for Women (UNIFEM) and the United Nations Population Fund (UNFPA) with funds from the government of Norway. These schools

Figure 3.1 A FFLS member in her field
Source: http://www.fao.org/gender/

provide life skills and knowledge in agricultural production and nutrition to both men and women whose lives have been affected by the civil war in Uganda. Figure 3.1 shows a female FFLS member growing okra plants in her field. In Northern Uganda, nearly two thirds of the population are unable to meet their basic food needs. The men often turn to drug or alcohol abuse which may result in domestic violence. Studies have shown that gender-based violence rises when there are food shortages.

At FFLS groups of men and women learn a variety of traditional and modern agricultural practices as well as processing methods, storage and conservation of resources. Discussions take place on healthy nutrition and HIV prevention, as well as issues of gender inequality and violence. Problems of unequal access to resources are discussed to promote positive changes in attitude. FFLS members, both men and women, are also able to obtain loans to help pay for children's education. By working together as equals and restoring income generating activities, cases of gender violence have decreased.

task B

Explain the social and economic benefits that would result from women increasing production on their land.

🌐 Women and work at home

Traditionally, it has been women who look after the family and home in terms of domestic work such as cleaning and cooking as well as caring for the older and younger members. Besides these tasks, in many rural areas, women and girls are responsible for collecting water and firewood for household use.

This affects them in many ways:

- there is less time for education and income-earning activities, rest and community affairs
- they are too tired to concentrate at school or work in the fields
- heavy buckets cause injuries and stress to weak bodies
- they are fearful of being attacked.

As populations increase, local fuel supplies get used up and so they have to travel further, which may double the time they have to spend collecting wood. These are time consuming daily chores. If electricity could be supplied to homes the impact on women's lives would be huge.

It would mean there would be:

- pumps to access clean, underground water nearby
- power for cooking, heating and lighting
- power for craft making and other income-earning activities to pay for the supply
- less smoke and fumes in the dwelling and so less respiratory problems
- radios and the internet for information and learning.

Women rarely take part in decisions on these matters which are of major concern to them but not seen as important by men. According to WHO, 'smoke rising from stoves and fires inside homes is associated with around 1.6 million deaths per year in developing countries – that's one life lost every 20 seconds to the killer in the kitchen'. Figure 3.2 shows a cooking fire made from dung and wood in a poorly ventilated home. By 2020, a UN project plans to put 100 million clean cooking stoves into homes in developing countries.

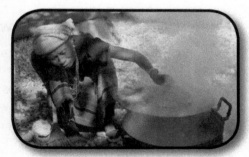

Figure 3.2   The killer in the kitchen

task C

1. Explain why 'the killer in the kitchen' affects women and children more than men.
2. How could providing electricity in the home help to empower women?

🌐 Women and work outside the home

Women approach problems in a different way from men. Women see things from another viewpoint and will offer alternative solutions to problems. Given equal opportunities they could make up to 50 per cent of the workforce and bring a range of skills and ideas to the economy.

task D

Identify a problem within your school or community. Divide the class into boys and girls and each group draws up a set of solutions to the problem. Compare the different approaches and decide whether the boys' or girls' ideas are the best or a mix of them both.

MDG 1 Target 1B is to achieve full and productive employment and decent work for all, including women and young people. The Beijing Declaration promotes the need for equal opportunities in education as well as the need for men to take a greater share of household duties. Between 1990 and 2010, only half of women were employed globally whereas for men the figure was just over 75 per cent.

Even if women take full-time employment they are still expected to undertake most of the duties of running the household that women have traditionally done. All across the world, women work longer hours than men and their 'double-day' can be both physically and mentally exhausting.

Problems for women in the workplace

Discrimination in the workplace is common even in the most developed countries. It can take many forms, some of which are more obvious than others:

- often women do not apply for promotion because they know the company or organisation is run by men who want to keep it that way
- wages are often lower for the same work done but women are reluctant to complain for fear of losing their job
- poorer working conditions and employment rights
- sexual harassment.

The 'glass ceiling'

Many women find it more difficult to gain promotion than men even if they have the same skills and experience. There seems to be some form of barrier that prevents movement up the career ladder, but it cannot actually be seen, hence the 'glass ceiling'. Different and lower expectations and attainments at school may have a major influence on the work women do and how far up the promotion ladder they can climb.

Juniors and managers are often mixed gender but senior managers and directors are still predominantly men in many large and small companies. Very few of the largest Multinational Companies (MNCs) have a woman as their Chief Executive Officer (CEO).

task E

1. Make a list of the sort of jobs within your own country that are dominated by men and women.
2. Consider the top positions in your school and other local organisations and state what proportion are women and explain why this may be the case.
3. Choose ten large companies with global brands such as Coca-Cola. Use the internet to find out how many of them have a woman as their CEO.

Ways to make the lives of working mothers easier

Mothers who go out to work do face different challenges from men if they are still the main person responsible for looking after the family.

If there are no women in positions of authority to bring about the changes needed to make their lives easier, the following measures are unlikely to be put in place:

- Job sharing
- Part-time working and flexi-time
- Mobile technology and video conferencing to enable home-working
- Affordable and reliable child care, crèches at work and care for the elderly
- Maternity benefits where a proportion of wages are paid for a number of weeks while on leave
- Networking groups for support
- Laws to prohibit gender discrimination in the workplace.

task F

1. Describe how a woman who manages a company that employs large numbers of women might influence their conditions of work.
2. What are the advantages and disadvantages for families of the mother going out to work?
3. What are the advantages and disadvantages for women of working from home?

🌍 Women and education

Figure 3.3 shows the youth literacy rate for men and women in selected regions between 1985 and 2009.

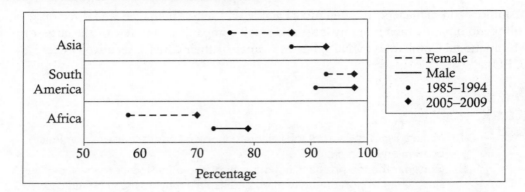

Figure 3.3   Youth (15–24) literacy rates (%)

Source: http://stats.uis.unesco.org/unesco/TableViewer/tableView.aspx?ReportId=201

1. Describe three main features of the graph in Figure 3.3.
2. Explain the many problems for women who cannot read and write.

Poverty and tradition are the main causes of low educational achievements for girls. In poor households girls are often married at an early age so the family obtains her dowry and has one less mouth to feed. This tradition is hard to break and in many countries of Sub-Saharan Africa large numbers of girls marry much older men when they are less than 15 years old. Marrying early, they often have more than 5 children and maternal mortality rates are high. Their role in the household leaves little time for learning even if they were allowed to study.

Without education, girls will not be empowered and will be unable to fulfil their potential and ambitions outside the home. Parents value the work a girl child can do at home more than the benefits of schooling. If money is short, families will educate their boys. Other reasons girls do not attend school include a lack of safe transport to get there and inadequate private sanitation facilities.

Target 3A of MDG 3 is to eliminate gender disparity in primary and secondary education, preferably by 2005, and in all levels of education no later than 2015. This target was set for ten years earlier than the other MDGs as it is recognised that equal access to education will make the other goals easier to achieve.

Table 3.2 shows the enrolment of girls in relation to boys for all levels of education in selected regions. The target to eliminate gender disparity in education is between 97 and 103. Differences in enrolment in education occur not only from region to region, but also within countries where situations in rural areas may be different from those in urban areas. The figures for the regions are therefore averages that may hide large differences between areas. If gender equality is achieved in all levels of education, women are more likely to gain employment and so contribute to the growth of the economy.

Table 3.2 Girls per 100 boys in education

Region	Primary 1999	Primary 2008	Secondary 1999	Secondary 2008	Tertiary 1999	Tertiary 2008
Sub-Saharan Africa	85	91	83	79	71	67
Northern Africa	90	94	93	98	74	95
Southern Asia	84	96	75	87	65	76
South-Eastern Asia	96	97	95	103	95	107
Latin America & the Caribbean	97	97	107	108	115	125

Source: http://www.un.org/millenniumgoals/pdf/MDG%20Report%202010%20En%20r15%20-low%20res%2020100615%20-.pdf

1. Describe the main features of the table in Table 3.2.
2. To what extent has gender equality been achieved in primary and secondary education in the regions shown?
3. Do you think it is likely that gender equality will be achieved in the different levels of education by 2015?
4. Explain why more boys attend school than girls.

Figure 3.4 shows the benefits for both the economy and society if women are educated.

Educating girls MDGs 2 and 3:
- reduces poverty and hunger MDG 1
- increases the chances of their children being educated MDG 2
- increases confidence to influence decisions made in the home MDG 3
- improves basic knowledge of disease prevention MDG 4
- reduces chance of early marriage and increases knowledge of family planning MDG 5
- combats spread of HIV/AIDS and other diseases MDG 6
- encourages sustainable development MDG 7.

Figure 3.4 Educating girls and the MDGs

Explain the many ways that the economy and society benefit if girls are educated.

The role of government

The government firstly has to ensure girls go to school and secondly that they move on from primary to secondary education and possibly even to college and university. The provision of free or cheap schooling may be easier than changing cultural attitudes to a woman's role in society.

Children are often directed in schools to study certain subjects such as the humanities for girls and science for boys. The government can make sure the curriculum is relevant to girls' needs and that girls are allowed to take the subjects originally reserved for boys. Girls need to be encouraged to become doctors and lawyers and so provide role models for future learners. If a few women have careers in scientific research then the research will likely focus on issues of interest to women. If more female teachers take positions in schools, more families will send their girls there and it will be clear to these girl children that it is possible to have a worthwhile occupation outside the home.

task J

1. Compare the subjects taken and career plans for students in your class.
2. How important do you think role models are in your life?

🌐 Women and health

MDG 5 is to improve maternal health. This has not shown as much progress as the other MDGs and over half a million women still die each year from complications of pregnancy or childbirth. In poor families caring for the mother's health is not a priority and mothers die for a number of reasons:

- lack of knowledge of care required during pregnancy such as adequate diet
- childbirth in unhygienic conditions with no midwife
- lack of transport to maternity facility
- lack of emergency facilities to deal with complications
- early pregnancy due to child marriages
- lack of family planning means body has little time to recover between pregnancies
- men do not allow their wives to attend clinics
- violence from men if unable to do domestic duties during pregnancy
- extra stress on a weak body already malnourished or suffering from HIV/AIDS.

If the health of women can be improved, then the health of the whole family generally improves. If mothers are ignorant of the health needs of their children then these children may die. Educated and healthy women take their infants for vaccinations, they understand the importance of disease prevention and ways to achieve this and they feed their children a balanced diet. One of the indicators for monitoring progress towards MDG 5 is the proportion of births attended by skilled health personnel.

Table 3.3 shows the progress that has been made in certain regions.

Table 3.3 Proportion of deliveries attended by skilled health personnel (per cent)

Region	1990	2008
Sub-Saharan Africa	41	46
Northern Africa	46	80
Southern Asia	30	45
South-Eastern Asia	46	75
Latin America & the Caribbean	72	86

Source: http://www.un.org/millenniumgoals/pdf/MDG%20Report%202010%20En%20r15%20
-low%20res%2020100615%20-.pdf

task K Draw a chart to represent the data in Table 3.3 and describe its main features.

The role of government

Governments need to provide pre and post natal care as well as family planning advice in local clinics that can easily be accessed by all women. Counselling on methods of HIV/ AIDS and other disease prevention should also be readily available. Preventing problems arising in the first place would save many women from dying from pregnancy, childbirth and preventable diseases.

Laws to stop violence against women are essential and these are drawn up by governments. Laws to increase the age at which children are allowed to marry makes significant difference as girls are much more likely to die in childbirth than older women.

task L Describe the violence against women that is likely to happen in your society and explain what the government is doing to prevent it.

🌐 Women and politics

As in the field of work, women have different ideas and views from men. To make sure women's issues are properly considered, women need to be able to influence decisions. This means women need to take their place in community councils as well as in national governments.

Before this can happen, the first stage is to make sure that all women are allowed to vote. Since 1995 when the Beijing Platform for Action was adopted, many countries have shown an improvement in getting women elected to parliament but there is still nowhere near equal representation.

In 2010, the figure was 19 per cent. One of the indicators for monitoring progress towards MDG 3 is the proportion of seats held by women in national parliaments and Table 3.4 shows the countries that are leading the way towards this target. In 2008, Rwanda became the first country to achieve a gender balance in its national parliament (*Source: http://www.un.org/millenniumgoals/pdf/MDG_FS_3_EN.pdf*).

Table 3.4 Countries with the largest proportion of women in parliament (2010)

Country	% Seats held by women
Rwanda	56
South Africa	45
Sweden	45
Cuba	43
Iceland	43
Netherlands	41
Norway	40
Finland	40

Source: http://data.worldbank.org/indicator/SG.GEN.PARL.ZS

Sometimes what is called affirmative action is needed. This means that measures are taken to make sure women have a much better chance to be elected. This can happen in various ways.

- Some seats in elected assemblies are actually reserved for women
- A certain percentage or quota of a list of candidates for election has to be women
- All women shortlists in selected constituencies.

Quotas and reserved seats may be used as a temporary measure just to get some women into parliament which will make it more acceptable and therefore more likely in subsequent elections. In 2008, 18 of the 22 countries that have over 30 per cent women in their national assemblies had some form of quota system. If these women do a good job, they could easily be re-elected without the need for a quota (*Source: www.unifem.org*).

task M

Consider as groups of boys and girls:
1. Whether or not affirmative action is likely to promote equal opportunities for all.
2. Why women tend not to go into politics.

Ghana has a Ministry of Women and Children's Affairs which helps to ensure that gender issues are considered at the highest level of decision making. Globally, women hold only 16 per cent of ministerial posts and so are rarely fully represented in the executive part of governments (*Source: http://www.un.org/millenniumgoals/pdf/MDG_FS_3_EN.pdf*).

task N

Find out how many Heads of Government in your continent are women, make a list of their names and countries and work out the percentage that are women.

It is often local authorities that provide the services that can make such a difference to women's lives. Women are only just starting to become involved in local politics in many communities but women will feel more able to express concerns about something if a local councillor is a woman. Women need to be involved in assessing the need for services in their community as well as designing and implementing any projects.

Services that can make a difference are:

1. Lighting – for safer streets, extension of working hours.
2. Water pumps – reduces time and energy collecting water.
3. Transportation – increases access to markets, health care as well as education and social activities, carries heavy loads.
4. Media technologies – allows information sharing, raises awareness.

Some success stories

Figure 3.5 gives some case studies of programmes and projects around the world that have increased empowerment of girls through a variety of means.

> The Female Secondary School Stipend programme in Bangladesh has provided money directly to girls and their families to cover tuition and other costs, on the condition that they enrol in secondary school and remain unmarried until the age of 18. By 2005, girls accounted for 56 per cent of secondary school enrolment in the areas covered by the programme, compared with 33 per cent in 1991.

> UNDP installed hundreds of diesel-run generators, known as multi-functional platforms, in rural areas across Burkina Faso, Mali and Senegal to help ease some of the most time-consuming chores for women, such as fetching water, grinding and milling. The scheme freed up a daily average of two to four hours for women in Burkina Faso and contributed to increasing the owners' annual income by an average of US$55 in 2009, producing net profits of US$248 per unit.

In Ethiopia, the UN Population Fund (UNFPA) supports a programme called 'Berhane Hewan' which advocates putting an end to child marriages and keeping girls in school. To encourage families to let the girls complete schooling, girls receive a female sheep upon completing the programme.

Egypt's Girls' Education Initiative and Food-for-Education (FFE) programme encourage girls to attend school by providing free education and by constructing and promoting 'girl-friendly schools'. In conjunction the FFE programme provides school meals to 84,000 children in poor and vulnerable communities.

In Cambodia, an initiative run by the UN Development Fund for Women (UNIFEM), in partnership with seven NGOs, provided training in political campaigning and governing to 919 women candidates. The initiative helped increase the number of women running for office from 16 per cent in 2002 to 21 per cent in 2007, and the number of women elected rose from 8.5 per cent to 15 per cent.

Figure 3.5 Success stories

Source: http://www.un.org/millenniumgoals/pdf/MDG_FS_3_EN.pdf

task O

Explain how empowering women will help countries to achieve MDG targets.

task P

Decision making exercise

Consider the following four ways of improving gender equality:

1. Invest in measures to ensure all girls attend school up to the age of 16
2. Increase access to cheap, clean energy supplies
3. Provide clinics with maternity facilities in all areas
4. Pass laws to prohibit violence and discrimination against women.

Place these methods in order of priority for a government to ensure gender equality. Explain why you have ranked the methods in the way you have and explain how each method helps to promote the empowerment of women.

- Achieving gender equality will help meet all the other MDGs
- Gender equality is a vital part of development
- Some progress has been made to promote gender equality especially in the fields of education and employment
- Much more needs to be done in terms of improving maternal health and women influencing decisions at all levels
- Simple measures can make the lives of women considerably better.

Summary

Poverty and politics

4

Learning Objectives

→ To understand the importance of political decisions in development
→ To appreciate that governments have different priorities
→ To understand the importance of peace, law and order and legitimate authority
→ To understand the difference between a dictatorship and a democracy
→ To understand the roles of the different institutions of government.

🌐 The role of governments

Politics is concerned with making decisions about all sorts of issues and can range in scale from small community matters to international agreements. A national government will decide:

- how the country's natural and human resources are used
- how the country's money is spent
- the laws by which the people are governed
- how the country's environment is protected
- whether or not development will be sustainable.

> **Definition** ═══════
>
> **Sustainable**: capable of being continued without permanent damage to the environment

There are three main political systems in which the state has different approaches to the distribution of the country's resources and exerts different levels of power and control.

1. **Capitalist** – a system based on private ownership that relies on market forces rather than state control.
2. **Socialist** – a system based on public ownership and government control over the allocation of resources.
3. **Communist** – an economy that is managed and often highly planned by the state and based on common ownership.

Government income and expenditure

A government gets its income from taxes, loans, foreign aid and from the users of services provided by the government. Taxes may be in the form of income tax from workers, business tax from industries, sales tax from when people buy goods and taxes on imports.

Some economic activities generate more income than others. For example, mineral rich countries will benefit from exports when prices are high as companies earn more money and pay more tax and individuals pay more tax as their wages rise. The money needs to be invested wisely in roads, schools and ports which can continue to generate income for the government. By spending money on transport networks and an educated population, governments hope to attract industries which will generate taxes in the longer term and create a more sustainable development when the minerals run out.

Different governments have different priorities in terms of drawing up its spending plans. Some countries spend very little on health and education services but large amounts on defence whilst others spend more on a range of social services. Citizens will not always agree with how the government spends their money.

Governments and conflicts

The main priority for any government is the security of its citizens. For development to happen it is vital for countries to be at peace. Threats from foreign powers and from conflicts within a country will result in more money being spent on weapons, training of the army and in intelligence gathering. This will mean less money for development projects. Schools, hospitals, ports, roads and factories which contribute to improved living standards can be destroyed by bombs in moments and the billions of dollars that have been spent are completely wasted. Other effects of conflicts on development can be very severe as described in Figure 4.1.

People, including civilians, are dying in hundreds from blast injuries and bullet wounds. Doctors are treating people on the pavement or in any building they can find as the hospitals have been bombed. We have no blood for transfusions or bandages and we are unlikely to get new supplies as the airport has been damaged and planes cannot land. People who are not injured are hungry as they are afraid to go out to find food due to snipers on the rooftops. In the rural areas, soldiers have stolen the livestock and crops so children in particular are becoming malnourished and falling ill with diseases. Many are trying to flee to the cities as they think they will be safer there but many have died on the journey through exhaustion or from drowning while crossing rivers where the bridges have been demolished. There is danger everywhere and most roads are blocked with burnt out vehicles so we cannot get to help these people. Our organisation is probably going to pack up and leave this country where we have operated for years as the situation for us all is just too dangerous.

Figure 4.1 An aid worker's report from a conflict zone

task
A

Write a newspaper article from the point of view of a worker in a factory whose workplace has been destroyed by bombs.

'The real reason for many conflicts is the struggle for the access to and control of the limited resources of our planet. A good number of African leaders have recognised the need for good governance in Africa. This is because, despite all the resources in Africa, development continues to lag behind due to lack of peace and sustainable management of resources. Corruption and mismanagement of resources frustrate development and exacerbate poverty.'

Wangari Maathai – Nobel Peace Prize Winner 2004 – Green Belt Movement

If a country can live in peace then a government can concentrate its efforts into reducing poverty and improving people's standards of living providing it is not corrupt and providing it maintains law and order. If the government's laws in an area are ignored then the resources can be taken illegally and a few people get very rich from money that should have been used for the benefit of the country. Sales from timber and gold should pay for many new schools and hospitals.

task B

Explain why it is important that a government maintains law and order in a country.

🌍 Forms of authority

Authority may be acceptable or not depending on how it has been gained. Some people may resent the ruler if they feel their authority is not deserved, either because it has been inherited or it has been taken by force. The authority must be accepted by the majority of people if a country is to be governed successfully.

Definition

Authority: the power to make decisions and give orders

Monarchs and chiefs

Traditionally, monarchs and tribal chiefs ruled over groups of people and were very powerful making all decisions relating to their area. They may have used advisers to help them make important decisions.

Some were very fair, but others took advantage of their power. They passed their authority to their eldest son on their death so people did not choose their leader. These children were brought up knowing their destiny was to lead and they were expected to be good warriors and wise in the ways of the culture of their society. They usually worked hard to earn the respect they needed from their people.

Colonialism

The age of exploration saw foreign European powers taking control of less developed countries all over the world as they wanted access to their rich resources of raw materials. A foreign government was imposed upon the indigenous people who were not allowed to influence any decision making. Figure 4.2 shows how the 'scramble for Africa' resulted in nearly all the continent coming under the influence of European powers.

Definition

Indigenous: native, a person born in a particular place

Colonialism: the occupation of another country in order to exploit it economically

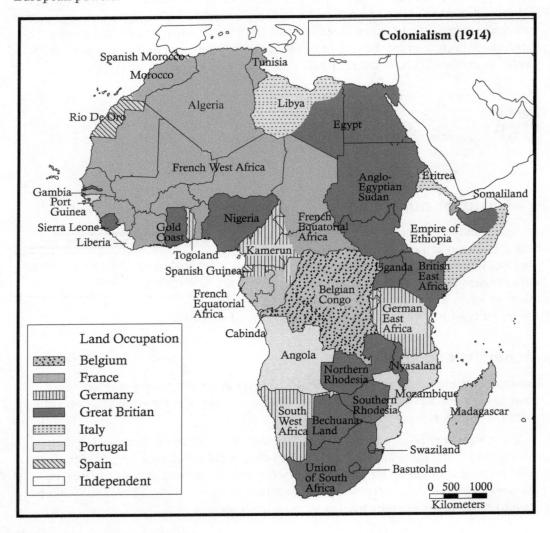

Figure 4.2 Africa in 1914

Source: http://exploringafrica.matrix.msu.edu/students/curriculum/m9/activity4.php

The colonial powers got richer as they exploited the country's natural wealth and took over land to farm in order to export minerals and crops to supply the growing industries and populations of the home nation. Native people were forced to pay taxes and worked for low wages in the mines and fields. However, roads, railways and schools were built to serve the colonists and these are still used today in many countries.

The indigenous population did not consider the colonial government to be a legitimate authority but any opposition was soon crushed by soldiers. Resentment and opposition grew and became organised into groups who wanted to run their country's affairs themselves. This movement grew after World War II and the desire for independence became widespread. Sometimes independence was achieved peacefully but elsewhere armed conflicts took place when the colonial power did not want to give up control. By 2000, Africa was a very different place as shown in Figure 4.3.

Definition

Legitimate: comply with rules, acceptable

Independence: being free from outside control

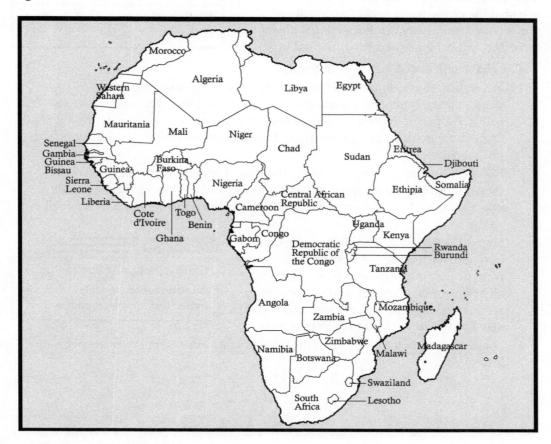

Figure 4.3 Africa in 2000
Source: http//rainforests.mongabay/com/20afrotropical.htm

task C

1. Select a country in which you are interested and find out which raw materials attracted the European power to colonise it.
2. Research its journey to independence.

Dictatorships

In many countries, the main group opposed to colonialism was often the party which won the first and only election. The leader became a dictator and no further opposition parties were allowed. As can be seen from Figure 4.3 political boundaries are sometimes straight lines and in many areas had no regard for tribal groupings which were sometimes split between countries. Within one country there were many different ethnic groups which often resented the ruling party. To keep control and prevent civil war, many dictators exerted power by force and had complete control of the military.

> **Definition**
>
> **Civil war**: a war between citizens of the same country

The characteristics of a dictatorship are:

1. No regular elections are held but in order to look legitimate to the rest of the world, dictators may hold scam elections where voting is not held as a secret ballot. People are bullied to vote for the dictator's party under threat of violence. Opposition political parties are banned but their name may be on the voting slip just for show.

2. Dictators and their advisers draw up the laws. They are above the law, which means it does not apply to them and so they can do as they please. Fair trials are uncommon and people imprisoned without charge. The military use force to keep control.

3. Human rights are lacking and people do not have the freedom to live their life as they want to. There is no freedom of speech as all newspapers, television and radio stations are controlled by the government and reports usually state how wonderful everything is.

> **Definition**
>
> **Ballot**: process of voting
> **Accountable**: required to prove that actions are reasonable

4. Dictators are not accountable to the people. They exert power over the people by force.

task D

1. To what extent are there basic freedoms in your country to live life as you want?
2. Do any particular groups lack human rights?

Corruption

Dictatorships are often corrupt as dictators need friends around them who they can trust to keep them in power. Cash to buy fine cars, food and houses usually keeps people loyal as they become used to a life of luxury. But this is the country's money which should be used for the benefit of all the people such as by supplying clean water to all areas. Palaces instead of schools are a sign of a corrupt regime and corrupt practices as shown in Figure 4.4.

Figure 4.4 Corrupt exchange of money

The quest for freedoms and accountability for government

In dictatorships, people do not choose who they want to represent their views in government and the authority of the regime is therefore not regarded as legitimate. There are no political debates as to how the country should be run. If people express an opinion that goes against the wishes of the dictator, they are likely to be gunned down in the streets or disappear.

> **Definition**
>
> **Corruption**: willingness to act dishonestly for personal gain

So change is very difficult to bring about but the struggle for freedom continues. This time it is not freedom from a colonial power but freedom from an autocratic regime.

> **Definition**
>
> **Autocratic**: a system of government with one person having complete power

In 2011, there were many uprisings in Africa and the Middle East as people in countries such as Tunisia, Egypt and Libya wanted the freedoms that they saw that citizens had in other countries. They wanted to have a say in how the country's resources were used and its wealth distributed. In other words, they wanted to become a democracy.

Tunisia

People took to the streets in December 2010 to show their concern over poor living conditions, high levels of unemployment and lack of human rights. Demonstrators risked the army opening fire on them to quell the uprising against their leader. An Ancient Greek historian said 'The secret of happiness is freedom. The secret of freedom is courage.' This show of opposition to the government by the Tunisian people was broadcast over the internet to all parts of the world. Pressure from world leaders persuaded President Ben Ali to leave before the people had to resort to violence to achieve their aim. The transition to democracy was relatively peaceful.

Libya

In some countries, the dictator will fight his own people to stay in power. Protests against Colonel Gaddafi's regime in Libya in 2011 led to a civil war which lasted five months.

The government controlled the military which fought the 'rebels' who had joined together as a fighting force, even though they were unorganised, from different cultures and religions and ill-equipped with weapons. Fierce fighting together with international pressure on the government led, eventually, to the dictator being captured and killed, and the country liberated.

A council was set up to oversee the transition of the country from dictatorship to democracy and nine months later the first elections were held for seats in the General National Assembly. This was the first free election in the country for 60 years.

task E

What are some of the problems that a new government, such as the one in Libya, might have to solve?

Democracies

'Neither peace nor development can thrive without democracy and respect for human rights.' United Nations (UN) Secretary-General, Ban Ki-moon – 2009

Democracy is one of the core principles of the UN. It is based on:

- government by the will of the people through elections
- the rule of law
- the exercise of human rights and fundamental freedoms.

The word 'democracy' comes from the Greek 'demos' meaning 'the people' and 'kratos' meaning 'authority'. The opening words of the UN Charter are 'We the Peoples…'. In other words, the will of the people is the legitimate authority of nations and the UN as a whole. Authority is accepted if people choose those in authority.

Characteristics of a democracy

1. Elections are held with all adults over a certain age having a vote in a secret ballot. Anyone can form a political party and stand for election and the more parties there are, the greater the choice people have. There is no threat of violence to anyone to vote in a particular way or inaccurate counting of votes.

2. Everyone is equal before the law including members of the government. All citizens have the right to a fair trial and an independent judiciary ensures this happens.

3. Human rights and fundamental freedoms include:
   - freedom of speech for all people and the media

Definition

Independent judiciary: judges and trials are not influenced by the government

Trade union: workers who form a group to negotiate better conditions and pay

- freedom of association – people have a right to set up and join any non-criminal group such as political, trade union and religious groups
- the right to hold a peaceful demonstration
- freedom of movement
- minority groups have the same freedoms as everyone else.

4. If the people are unhappy with the actions of the government, they can vote for another one at the next election which is usually within 5 years. This gives a government enough time to put its policies into practice but stops it from becoming too powerful or taking decisions that are disapproved by the majority of the citizens.

task
F

Why is it important to have:
1. A ballot that is secret?
2. Regular elections?
3. An independent judiciary?
4. Human rights?

Measurement of human rights

These essential elements of democracy are almost impossible to measure unlike other aspects of development as defined by the MDGs. The right to a fair trial, for example, would depend upon being able to define the term 'fair' – which could vary from country to country.

The different religious or political groups that are active within a country could easily be determined in a democracy, but this number could not be compared with similar groups in a dictatorship. This is because under a dictator these groups are often not allowed and so if they do exist, they exist in secret.

Political parties

These are formed to represent people with similar beliefs and outlook and may be based upon social class, ethnic groups or different ideas on the role of the state in people's lives. Before an election, each party draws up a manifesto which gives details of what it will do if it is elected to form a government. People then vote for the party that represents their views the best.

In the United Kingdom, the two main parties are the Conservative and Labour Party. At the 2010 election, the voting was such that no party had an overall majority as other political groups also managed to win some seats in Parliament. This can be seen in Figure 4.5.

Although the Conservative Party won the most seats, if all the other parties joined together to vote against their policies, they would lose and so they would not be able to implement their policies and govern. So the Conservative Party formed a coalition with the Liberal Democrats and each party had to make compromises to reach agreement on policies.

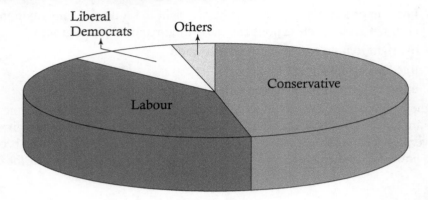

Figure 4.5 UK Election Results 2010
Source: http://news.bbc.co.uk/1/shared/election2010/results/

The party that forms a government sets up an Executive which consists of Ministers who run the different government departments, such as health, education, trade and industry. The leader of the government is the Prime Minister and the Ministers meet as a Cabinet. All elected Members of Parliament debate matters and form the Legislature, the law making body of the land.

Head of State

Democracies may have a monarch as Head of State such as the Queen of England who has no real power and authority but represents the nation abroad and is involved with ceremonial duties and she makes sure the constitution is followed. If the Head of State is a president, as in the United States, the democracy is then known as a Republic.

> **Definition**
>
> **Constitution**: a document that defines the function and administration of an organisation and the rules which its members must follow

task G

Draw up a constitution for a newly formed group set up to improve the environment of the school and its grounds. Decide who can join the group, what the roles of officials will be and how these people will be elected. Decide how funding will be acquired and what projects will be undertaken. Decide other rules of the group and how disagreements will be settled.

Lesotho is an example of a constitutional monarchy the main features of which are as following.

1. The Head of State is the King whose succession is approved by the College of Chiefs. His role is largely ceremonial.

2. The legislature consists of:
   - the National Assembly which is elected for 5 years. 12 parties are represented here with the Lesotho Congress for Democracy having a majority
   - a non-elected Senate composed of 22 principal chiefs and 11 members appointed by the King on the advice of the Prime Minister. The Prime Minister is the head of the government and is appointed by the King.
3. There is an independent judiciary.
4. Ministers for each government department form the executive or cabinet.

task
H Find out the main features of your own national assembly and government.

National plans and MDGs

A National Plan may include:
- encouragement for companies to set up factories
- laws to limit logging in the tropical forest
- supply of clean water to all areas
- quotas for women in parliament.

National Plans for development will include projects that address some of the MDGs. For example, by attracting new industries workers will receive an income so they will be able to afford to send their children to school and governments will get taxes which they can use to build more schools and train teachers. Progress towards achieving MDG 2 will therefore be made.

task
I Explain how bullet points 2, 3 and 4 of the National Plan shown above enable a government to make progress towards achieving all the other MDGs.

Large scale projects that benefit the nation as a whole, such as a main road linking the capital with the main port, can only be top-down projects as they will cut across many local authorities and need a level of funding that only the government can supply. However, the route taken may not suit a local community and a local group may set itself up to oppose the road.

Definition

Consultation: a process of seeking approval and information

However, governments have been elected to put the policies in their manifestos into practice and cannot allow communities to block major development projects that are vital, in this example, for increasing trade. An increase in trade will benefit all the country's citizens.

Major issues usually go out to public consultation and it is then that local people can make comments which are taken into consideration when decisions are made. Consultations cost money and take a long time but often it may be possible to reach a compromise where everyone is satisfied. In the example above, the local community may suggest a slightly different route for the road which is acceptable to everyone.

Local governments

Local or regional councils and assemblies make decisions on local planning issues and implement government policies at a local level. They draw up a Local Plan to form a framework for development and work with community groups to improve living standards. Councils are also usually responsible for providing local services such as waste collection.

People need to take an active interest in local politics. Local councillors are accountable to the people and they may not be re-elected if the public are not satisfied with what their councillor is doing for the community. Conflicts may arise between groups but it is the job of the councillors to try to reconcile these different opinions.

Local consultation is important because:

- local people need to make decisions that will affect them
- local people are familiar with local situations and understand local difficulties
- local people work hard to make a project a success if they are involved.

task J

Decision making exercise

Choose a relevant local issue such as soil erosion, street crime or the spread of malaria from stagnant water and divide the class into two groups (a) the government department and (b) the local committee.

Each group decides the best way to tackle the problem and then presents their method to the class. The class then weighs up the advantages and disadvantages of the proposals and decides which course of action would be the best to pursue.

Summary

- Political decisions restrict or promote development
- Countries are more likely to develop if they are at peace
- Different political systems operate in different countries
- Forms of authority must be acceptable to the people
- Many people in the world are still denied basic human rights
- Corruption often prevents general rises in people's standard of living.

Global patterns of development

5

Learning Objectives

- ✑ To appreciate that developed countries have similar characteristics
- ✑ To understand how development may be measured
- ✑ To understand the importance of the Human Development Index as an indicator of development
- ✑ To consider other indicators of development
- ✑ To consider the global challenges to development and the role of the UN
- ✑ To understand the importance of the earth's natural resources and the need for sustainable development.

🌍 Main features of development

Terms that are often used to describe low income countries are poor or Less Economically Developed Countries (LEDC). Terms used to describe developed countries are high income, rich, industrialised and More Economically Developed Countries (MEDC).

As countries develop changes take place politically, economically and socially. More developed countries tend to have:

- a more industrialised economy with exports of manufactured goods
- a mainly urban population
- a move towards a democratic government
- a population growing slowly or decreasing
- advanced infrastructure
- higher quality housing with clean water and good sanitation
- a larger variety of foodstuffs
- higher energy consumption
- adequate social security payments and pensions
- greater gender equality
- greater human rights and fairer treatment of minority groups
- better access to new technology
- a higher Life Expectancy (LE) and lower Infant Mortality Rate (IMR)
- a larger proportion of students in secondary and tertiary education.

Global patterns of development change with time as some countries become more developed and new nations are formed. Ways development can be measured are also changing.

In the 1970s, Chancellor Brandt of Germany proposed that a line could be drawn on a map of the world dividing the rich, developed countries from the developing ones. This became known as the Brandt Line and was quite a crude division based on a country's wealth. As most of the developed countries were in the Northern hemisphere, with exceptions such as Australia, these became known as the 'North' and the developing countries became known as the 'South'.

> **Definition**
>
> **Crude**: only approximately accurate

Now, in the twenty-first century, this line appears to be out-dated for three main reasons.

1. Progress within many nations has meant that they have become part of the developed 'North' even though their geographical location is in the Southern hemisphere. These economies are called Newly Industrialised Countries (NICs). They are ranked somewhere between developing and developed nations and are characterised by rapid industrial growth.

2. Other more recently formed nations such as those that were originally part of the former Soviet Bloc in the 'North' are not as developed as the former larger nation.

3. A more recent view of development looks at measures that include aspects of people's well-being in addition to income.

Brazil, Russia, India and China are the fastest growing economies and are sometimes referred to as the BRIC countries. They account for almost half the total world population and so have a huge domestic market. In 2001 and 2011, the US was the largest economy in the world in terms of its GDP. By the middle of this century, all the BRIC countries may have overtaken it.

🌐 The Human Development Index (HDI)

In the past, in order to assess the level of development of a country, GDP per person or GNP per person was the statistic most commonly used. In 1990, the United Nations published the Human Development Report which began with the words 'People are the real wealth of a nation'. In other words, development should not be measured in terms of monetary wealth alone but also by whether people can lead a healthy life with access to education. A new measure of development, the HDI, was devised.

In the HDI, literacy rates, school enrolment and life expectancy are combined along with GNP per person to make a broader index. The Report stressed the importance to people's well-being of having political freedoms and human rights and also being able to fulfil their life plans, but measurement of these is very difficult. Countries are ranked in terms of their HDI (which is a value with a maximum of 1.0) and are divided into four groups.

1. Very High Human Development: rank 1–47
2. High Human Development: rank 48–94
3. Medium Human Development: rank 95–141
4. Low Human Development: rank 142–187

These groups are shown on the world map in Figure 5.1.

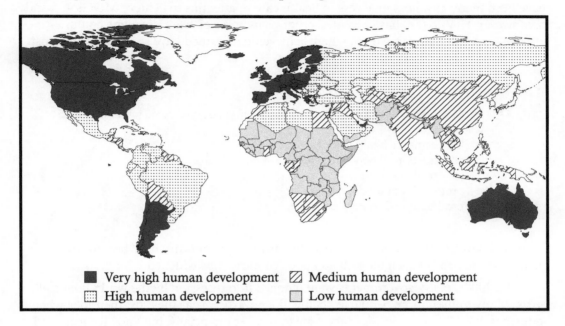

Figure 5.1 Global HDI (2011)
Source: http://hdr.undp.org/en/statistics

task
A

With reference to continents, describe the main features of the map in Figure 5.1.

The marked difference between the continents of South America and Africa are likely to be due to a large number of reasons. However, it is worth perhaps noting that South America was dominated by the Portuguese and Spanish colonists, while Africa was occupied mainly by the British, French and Germans. Exploitation of resources and the timing of independence and moves towards democracy may have been very different.

Also, African society suffered a great deal as a result of the Slave Trade with many millions of their strongest men and women shipped to work in the sugar and coffee plantations, mines and cotton fields of the Americas and West Indies.

Changes in the HDI 1990–2010

The Human Development Report 2010 states that in the past twenty years there has been substantial progress in many aspects of human development. Figure 5.2 shows how the HDI has changed in some countries. Great efforts have been made towards achieving MDG 2 with increased school enrolment for both boys and girls. Also there have been many advances in access to health care in attempts to achieve MDGs 4, 5 and 6. However, HIV/AIDS has prevented progress in terms of health in some countries, especially in Sub-Saharan Africa, where achievements gained have sometimes been lost.

task B

Explain how a large proportion of people in a country living with HIV/AIDS will affect:

- the country's health service
- construction of new infrastructure such as roads
- school attendance
- production of food
- production of goods for export.

Income levels still show a great inequality as the rich countries have become even richer and the gap between the rich and poor countries has widened.

In the 2000s, many governments were plunged into recession by the world financial crisis. Many million more people fell below the poverty line as they lost their jobs when industries closed. Countries may take time to recover financially, but knowledge gained about health and disease prevention is not easily lost.

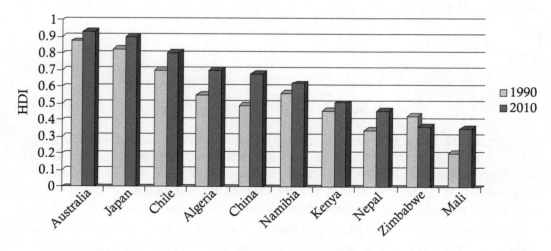

Figure 5.2 HDI for selected countries 1990–2010
Source: http://data.un.org/DocumentData.aspx?q=HDI&id=269

task C

Describe the pattern of change shown in Figure 5.2. Identify the anomaly and give a possible reason for this.

Progress has depended upon a number of factors:

- starting point – progress is easier from small beginnings
- government policies and will – accountable governments do more for people
- existing infrastructure – it is easier to build clinics if roads already exist
- history – colonialism and the amount of exploitation of resources
- willingness to introduce new, cheap technologies – mobile phones compared with landlines
- access to aid – countries are unwilling to give aid to corrupt dictators
- communication of ideas between nations – restricted by some dictatorships
- public access to information – knowledge is strength to make governments act.

As countries make improvements to people's quality of life, changes take place within the country. Some of the positive changes are:

- people are healthier and live longer
- more people are educated and incomes rise
- access to goods and services is greater
- people have greater power to select the government of their choice
- concerns of citizens are addressed and human rights improved
- minority groups are considered.

There are also some negative changes such as increased inequality as the wealth gap widens between the rich and the poor.

task D

Consider some of the problems caused by inequality in terms of wealth within a country.

New data

It is very difficult to measure people's freedoms and the level of inequalities, but these issues are very important. In 2010, new indices were introduced into the HDI which included a Multi-dimensional Poverty Index (MPI) which gives a more comprehensive picture of people living in poverty. The MPI has three dimensions, health, education and living standards. Within these there are ten indicators of deprivations.

These are lack of adequate nutrition, children not attending school, death of a child in the family, as well as a lack of electricity, clean water close to home, improved sanitation, and items such as a radio and bicycle. Most of the indicators relate to MDG targets. The index shows how many features of a good standard of living are missing at the same time. Other dimensions can be added in future, such as gender equality and employment when relevant data becomes available in more countries.

Definition

Deprivation: suffering a lack of important requirements for a reasonable standard of living

Utilities: useful services such as piped water, electricity

Welfare: a system that helps to meet the needs of poor people

Multi-dimensional: having many aspects

Other indicators of development

There is now a vast amount of data available that measures many aspects of development besides the more common ones such as literacy rates. There is data available on The World Bank website for over 2000 indicators. Some of these are shown in Table 5.1.

Table 5.1 Development indicators for selected countries (2009/2010)

Country	HDI Rank	Internet users per 100 people	Mobile cellular subscriptions per 100 people	Mammal species threatened	Electric power consumption (kWh per person)	CO_2 emissions (tonnes per person)
US	4	74	106	37	12,914	18.0
Sweden	9	90	116	1	14,142	5.3
Japan	11	78	97	28	7819	9.5
Mexico	56	31	81	99	1943	4.3
Russia	65	43	166	32	6133	12.0
Brazil	73	41	104	80	2206	2.1
China	89	34	64	74	2631	5.3
S. Africa	110	18	101	24	4532	8.9
Indonesia	108	11	88	183	590	1.7
India	119	8	61	94	571	1.5
Ethiopia	157	1	8	32	46	0.1

Source: http://data.worldbank.org/indicator

task E

1. Draw a scatter graph, similar to Figure 2.1, to show the relationship between HDI rank and internet users. Describe and explain the relationship shown on the graph and identify any anomaly.

task F

2. Looking at the data, do you think there is a relationship between HDI rank and mobile phone subscriptions and also between HDI rank and the number of mammal species threatened? Try to give a reasoned explanation.
3. Rank the countries from high to low in terms of electric power consumption per person. How does the list compare with the list of countries ranked by their HDI? What is the relationships between the two sets of data?

The internet and mobile phones have meant that people now have vast amounts of information available to them, about almost everything. Technology has changed so quickly that some countries have missed out a stage. In the case of telephones, countries that did not have a system of landlines in many rural areas have not installed these but have gone straight to mobile phone telecommunications and installed masts instead. Some of these can be seen in Figure 13.1 (Chapter 13).

Definition

Anomaly: something that does not fit the general pattern

task G

1. Explain how the internet results in progress in people's education and health care.
2. Make a list of some of the things that a mobile communication system can do now and summarise its advantages and any disadvantages.
3. Consider what it must be like for people in countries where government restricts access to information.

🌐 International challenges to development

The human development reports have shown that development can be achieved by various means and what may work in one area, may not necessarily work in another as each country's history and geography are different.

Definition

Sustainable: capable of being continued without permanent damage to the environment

No single strategy works well everywhere although lessons can be learned from other places. What is so important, however, is that progress today must be sustainable so it can also be achieved by future generations. Many challenges that face the world are beyond the ability of nations to meet on their own as they cross political boundaries. Actions in one country have reactions in others around the world.

Some of these challenges are:

- international migration
- climate change

- water supplies
- soil degradation
- loss of habitats and biodiversity
- human trafficking
- HIV/AIDS
- financial instability
- terrorism and war
- natural disasters.

task H Select three challenges that might apply in your country and explain how each one may restrict development.

All these challenges will have a major impact on development and may require adjustments to government plans. The poorer countries will find it the hardest to adapt to changes. It is difficult for so many countries at varying levels of development and with different outlooks to come to any worthwhile agreement. Putting any agreement then into practice is even more difficult and usually very slow. Policing whether or not countries are actually doing what they said they would do is harder still. What is vital is that global institutions and conferences include all countries and are not dominated by the more developed ones. Global problems need global solutions, but no country will want conditions being put upon it unless it has taken part in the negotiations.

The role of the UN

The UN has a large number of agencies such as the United Nations Children's Fund (UNICEF) that concentrate on different global development issues. A summary of the origins and work of the UN is given in Figure 5.3.

> The United Nations is an international organization founded in 1945 after the Second World War by 51 countries committed to maintaining international peace and security, developing friendly relations among nations and promoting social progress, better living standards and human rights.
>
> Due to its unique international character, and the powers vested in its founding Charter, the Organization can take action on a wide range of issues, and provide a forum for its 193 Member States to express their views, through the General Assembly, the Security Council, the Economic and Social Council and other bodies and committees.

Figure 5.3 The United Nations
Source: http://www.un.org/en/aboutun/index.shtml

The work of the United Nations reaches every corner of the globe. Although best known for peacekeeping, peace building, conflict prevention and humanitarian assistance, there are many other ways the United Nations and its system (specialized agencies, funds and programmes) affect our lives and make the world a better place. The Organization works on a broad range of fundamental issues, from sustainable development, environment and refugees protection, disaster relief, counter terrorism, disarmament and non-proliferation, to promoting democracy, human rights, gender equality and the advancement of women, governance, economic and social development and international health, clearing land mines, expanding food production, and more, in order to achieve its goals and coordinate efforts for a safer world for this and future generations.

Figure 5.3 The United Nations (Contd.)
Source: http://www.un.org/en/aboutun/index.shtml

The earth's natural resources

All human activity depends fundamentally on the resources provided by the planet on which we all live. The food we eat comes directly (fruit, vegetables) or indirectly (cattle, hens) from the plants that grow in the soil of the earth. Much of the pollination of crops depends on bees and other insects. Our houses and roads are built from wood from forests or from materials dug out from the rocks. All the products used in everyday lives come from the earth – plastic from oil, glass from sand, steel from iron ore, paper from trees, textiles from plants, animals and minerals. Trees provide oxygen for all living things to breathe and water from rainfall comes from the oceans and seas that cover much of the planet. The earth and all its natural products within its crust and atmosphere can exist without humans, but humans cannot exist without using these resources. The main natural resources are shown in Table 5.2.

Definition

Natural resources: products of the earth that are used by man

Table 5.2 Human use of earth's major natural resources

Resource	Some human uses
Air	breathing, disposal of fumes, transport
Water	drinking, irrigation of crops, cooling processes, power supply, hygiene, transport
Rocks	gravel, clay, hard core, soil, metal ores, coal, oil, natural gas, gemstones
Soil	growing crops, rearing livestock
Plants	trees, food crops, biofuels, fibres, medicines
Animals	hunting, livestock, fish, bees, work

Development in terms of economic growth and improved living standards puts demands on the resources provided by the earth.

These demands are becoming greater for two main reasons:

1. The world's population is growing dramatically and by the year 2050 it is predicted to be over 9 billion. This is shown in Figure 5.4.

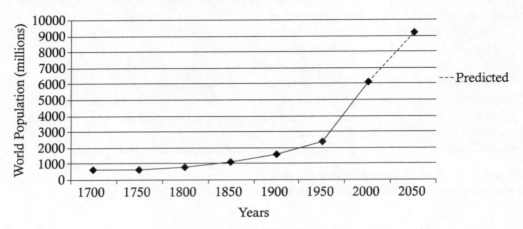

Figure 5.4 World Population Growth
Source: http://www.census.gov/

2. As people rise above the poverty line they demand more goods and services to support their increased standard of living. 'Wants' become 'must haves' as can be seen in Figure 5.5.

Figure 5.5 'Wants' become 'must haves'

Economic activity relies upon the earth's natural resources. In extracting and using these resources, the natural environment can be damaged. Soil can become eroded, fish stocks depleted and minerals exhausted. Air and water can be polluted, forests destroyed and biodiversity lost.

The economic growth of the last century by developed countries took place with few people stopping to consider the impact it was having on the earth itself. Resources were consumed as if they were going to last indefinitely.

However, many resources upon which industry depends, such as metals and oil, are finite resources and will eventually run out. They are called non-renewable resources and need to be conserved and used responsibly.

> ### Definition
>
> **Finite resources**: a limited supply of materials that will eventually run out

task

1   Make a list of non-renewable resources and then make a list of renewable resources such as solar power which will not run out.

Sustainable development

The natural environment has to be looked after if economic activity is going to be able to continue to provide a better quality of life for people in the next generation...and the next...as shown in Figure 5.6. This is what is meant by sustainable development.

Sustainable development enables people throughout the world to satisfy their basic needs now but makes sure future generations can also look forward to a similar standard of living. It enables economic growth to take place without causing permanent damage

Figure 5.6   Family of several generations

to the natural resources of the planet upon which all life on earth depends. To achieve this is one of the most important challenges facing all the nations of the world. Figure 5.7 shows a simple diagram of sustainable and unsustainable development.

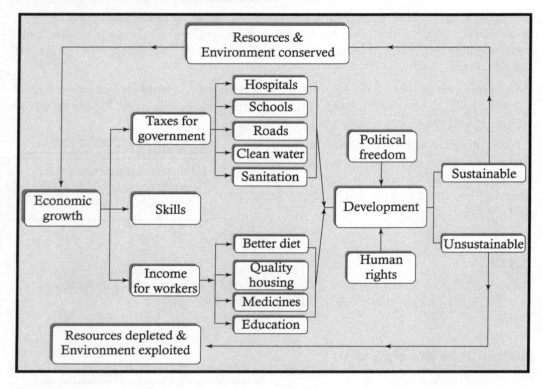

Figure 5.7 Sustainable and unsustainable development

Governments have begun to understand that decisions made today have to balance the needs of society with economic growth and protection of the environment. However, political decisions are often made with immediate results in mind. Concern for the welfare of the planet in the long term is difficult for governments in many developing countries when many of their people are starving. Due to the huge debts that many developed countries have built up, economic growth is needed to help to pay these back or standards of living will fall as governments find money in other ways by reducing services.

Governments in many developed countries now try to give the impression that they are 'green' but focus still tends to be on industrial growth and even more consumption of goods.

Figure 5.8 Only one earth

Definition

Green: support protection of the environment

There are major efforts to reduce waste, to recycle, and to reduce energy consumption but a totally sustainable approach is very remote and probably unachievable. The future of human life of the planet may depend on the decisions made in the next decades.

The natural world must be able to sustain future generations in a quality of life that is acceptable…and there is only one earth as shown in a view from space in Figure 5.8.

Practical Research Investigation

Relationship between different indicators of development

This is described in detail in Appendix I.

Summary

- Countries at similar levels of development have similar characteristics
- Global patterns of development change over time
- Changes in the HDI show people's lives are improving in many countries
- Global challenges can restrict development
- Demands on the earth's natural resources increase as populations and economies grow
- Sustainable development is essential to meet the needs of future generations.

Questions

Question 1

1. Study Figure 1A which shows the percentage of children in primary school in five countries in 1991 and 2005.

	Bangladesh	Ghana	Morocco	Turkey	Venezuela
1991	78	54	56	69	87
2005	85	64	88	91	91

Figure 1A

(a) Millennium Development Goal 2 is to achieve universal primary education.

    (i) Explain the phrase *universal primary education.* [1]

    (ii) Which country had the lowest percentage of children in primary education in 1991? [1]

    (iii) Which country achieved the largest increase in the percentage of children in primary education between 1991 and 2005? [1]

(b) Millennium Development Goal 3 is to promote gender equality and empower women. The target was to eliminate gender differences in education by 2005.

Study Figure 1B

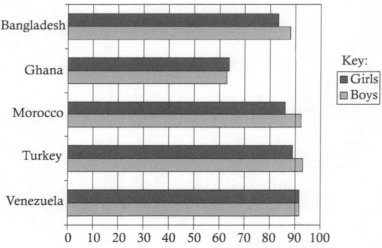

Figure 1B   % of children in primary school in 2005

(i) What is meant by *gender equality*? [1]

(ii) Which country in Figure 1B has the greatest gender equality? [1]

(iii) Did the countries in Figures 1A and 1B reach the target for Goals 2 and 3 by 2005? Explain your answer using examples. [3]

(c) Study Figure 2 which shows what some girls said about their life and their education.

- 'My parents think I am their property, to use how they want.' *Girl aged 14, Bangladesh*
- 'When my brother and I both passed our school exams, my father couldn't pay for us both to stay at school, so I had to stay and help at home.' *Girl aged 12, Ghana*
- 'My father says there is no point in educating girls because they only leave home and get married.' *Girl aged 10, Morocco*
- 'In rural areas the elders think that girls are born to give birth and for cleaning the house. They don't send them to school.' *Girl aged 15, Turkey*
- 'I want to work and study. I don't want to be like a girl I know who is only a year older than me and is getting married.' *Girl aged 13, Venezuela*

Figure 2

(i) Give **two** reasons why more girls than boys drop out of education. [2]

(ii) Suggest **four** reasons why it is important for families that both the mother and the father are educated. [4]

(d) Describe in detail how government policies could encourage gender equality and empower women. [6]

Cambridge 0453 P1 Q2 Oct/Nov 2010

Question 2

(a) Study Figure 3 which shows the Human Development Index (HDI) for 2006. HDI measures the development in a country by using a combination of indicators of life expectancy, literacy, education and standard of living.

(i) Name a country with:
- a high HDI
- a medium HDI
- a low HDI. [3]

(ii) Put the following continents in rank order according to their HDI. Your rank order list should begin with the continent with the highest HDI.

Africa   *North America*   *South America* [1]

(b) Study Figure 4 which shows indicators of levels of poverty and development for selected countries in Africa.

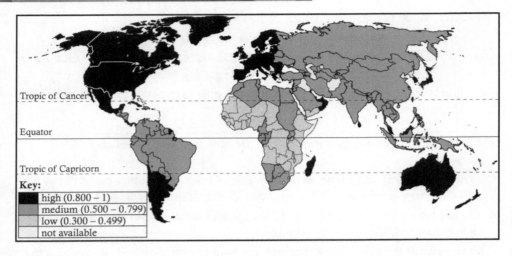

Figure 3

Country	GDP per person (US$)	Energy use per person (kg oil equivalent)	Number of doctors (per 100 000 people)	Adult literacy (percentage)
South Africa	3489	2587	69	87
Egypt	1220	785	212	58
Angola	975	606	8	67
Kenya	450	494	13	85
Tanzania	287	465	2	78
Uganda	249	776	5	70
Ethiopia	97	299	3	43

Figure 4

(i) For each of the following, name **one** country which is likely to:

    A – have the lowest percentage of people who can read and write

    B – have the easiest access to a doctor

    C – use most resources per person to provide fuel and power. [3]

(ii) Explain what is meant by GDP. [2]

(iii) To what extent is there a relationship between GDP per person and energy use per person? [2]

(iv) Give three disadvantages of using GDP per person as an indicator of development. [3]

(c) (i) Give two examples of aspects of development which are difficult or impossible to measure. [2]

(ii) Human rights have an impact on the development of a country. Suggest ways by which human rights can be measured. [4]

Cambridge 0453 P2 Q1 a,b, c Oct/Nov 2009

Question 3

Study Figure 5 which is about a survey carried out in Burkina Faso (a country in West Africa).

Location of Survey – Rural Burkina Faso

Aim – to find out if having a village library is likely to encourage reading and improve literacy levels. (Literacy is the ability to read and write).

Method of Data Collection – Questionnaires of students in village schools.

Villages Chosen – the 8 closest villages with schools along the tarred road in South Western Burkina Faso. Two of the eight villages have libraries, six do not.

Samples of Students Chosen – All students in one class aged 14 to 16 years, in each of the 8 village schools.

Total Number of Responses – 496 students (67% boys and 33% girls).

Pilot study – Carried out in a local school.

Figure 5

(a) (i) Suggest **one** reason why a pilot study was carried out. [1]

(ii) Give **one** other method which could have been used to choose the eight villages in Burkina Faso for the survey. [1]

(iii) Describe **one** advantage and **one** disadvantage of the sampling method used to select students to complete questionnaires. [2]

(b) Study Figures 6A and 6B, which show selected results of the survey.

Type of village in which student lives	Average number of books read in last 30 days	Average number of books read in last year
Without a village library	1.5	6.9
With a village library	2.2	12.6

Figure 6A Average number of books read by students from villages with and without libraries

Type of village in which student lives	Students who use a village library regularly (%)	Student who use their school library regularly (%)	Student who read library books regularly (%)
Without a village library	16	47	49
With a village library	88	33	92

Figure 6B Students interviewed who use libraries and read regularly

(i) Using graph paper present the data shown in Figure 6A using a suitable method. [3]

(ii) What conclusion can you draw from Figures 6A and 6B about the impact of village libraries on literacy levels? Refer to statistics to support your conclusion. [4]

(c) Study Figure 7, which shows three students who are planning research enquiries on literacy in their local communities.

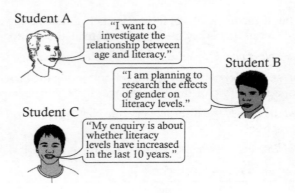

Student A
"I want to investigate the relationship between age and literacy."

Student B
"I am planning to research the effects of gender on literacy levels."

Student C
"My enquiry is about whether literacy levels have increased in the last 10 years."

Figure 7

(i) The sequence of enquiry shown below is a useful way to organise research. Choose one of students A, B or C from Figure 7 and write down the letter of that student. Describe how the research enquiry could be carried out. Use the ideas in the sequence of enquiry to organise your answer. [8]

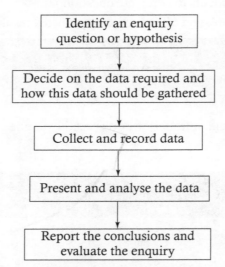

Identify an enquiry question or hypothesis

Decide on the data required and how this data should be gathered

Collect and record data

Present and analyse the data

Report the conclusions and evaluate the enquiry

(ii) Describe and explain any difficulties which you think the student you have chosen might have in carrying out this enquiry. [6]

Cambridge 0453 P2 Q3 Oct/Nov 2009

World trade

Learning Objectives

- To understand the reasons for trade and be able to define trade terms
- To appreciate the importance of a country's balance of trade
- To study ways to reduce a trade deficit
- To appreciate that trade and trading partners change over time
- To consider trends in the trading of goods and services
- To understand the value of free trade zones and world trade agreements
- To understand the importance of Fairtrade to farmers.

The importance of trade

People have always traded goods and services. From very early times, surplus goods and services have been exchanged or bartered. Some eggs are swopped for some beans or a lift to market may be given in exchange for help to mend a broken tool. With bartering no money changes hands but it is a simple form of trade between two people.

If the person with surplus eggs wants some beans but the person with the surplus beans does not want the eggs but wants some maize, more people get involved and a more complicated trade takes place. This is when money starts to change hands in order for people to get what they want. Countries cannot produce everything they need because either they do not have the necessary natural resources or they do not have the skills and technology.

A country exports whatever it can produce in order to get foreign exchange which it then uses to pay for the import of the goods and services its people want. With trade, consumers have a wider choice of price and quality of goods due to competition between suppliers. Producers have a bigger market in which to sell more goods.

Definition

Natural resource: a product provided by the earth

Import: bring goods and services into a country from another country

Export: send goods and services to another country for sale

Foreign Exchange: the currency of other countries used for trade

Commodities: raw materials such as fuels and other minerals as well as agricultural products

Trade is usually divided into:

- Goods or merchandise which includes commodities, semi-processed goods and manufactured goods.
- Services which includes financial services, construction work, tourism etc.

task A

1. Make a list of some of the natural resources your country has and a list of some that your country lacks.
2. Name three very important natural resources and explain why they are important.
3. Would you say your country was rich in important natural resources?

It is generally assumed that in order to develop, countries need to trade. Table 7.1 gives the HDI rank of nine countries and their trade per capita (US$).

Table 7.1   HDI rank and trade per capita

HDI rank	Trade per capita (US$)	HDI rank	Trade per capita (US$)
1	63 300	100	2 100
20	18 500	120	3 700
40	16 000	140	500
60	4 800	160	400
80	4 900		

Source: http://stat.wto.org/CountryProfile/WSDBCountryPFTechNotes.aspx?Language=E; http://hdr.undp.org/en/media/PR3-HDR10-HD1-E-rev4.pdf

task B

Draw a scatter graph to show the data. To what extent is trade a good indicator of levels of development?

Balance of trade

The difference between the value of a country's imports and exports is a major factor influencing its wealth and therefore development. If the value of a country's imports is greater than the value of its exports, it has a negative balance of trade or a trade deficit.

If the value of its imports is less than the value of its exports, then it has a positive balance of trade or a trade surplus. To overcome a trade deficit, it is necessary to reduce imports or increase exports or both. This can be done in various ways:

- develop industries to supply the domestic market to reduce imports of goods such as clothing – this is called an import substitution strategy
- encourage the growth of industries that will export high value goods, either processed food products or manufactured items – this is called an export orientated strategy

> **Definition**
>
> **Devaluation:** when a country's currency is reduced in value compared with other currencies

- increase exploitation of mineral wealth for export
- increase the production of crops for export
- develop other industries such as tourism
- devalue the currency.

Devaluation helps reduce a trade deficit by making exports cheaper and imports more expensive. Suppose 100 Peruvian Nuevo (N) will buy 75 Brazilian Real (R) then R1 costs N1.33. If the Real is devalued so that N100 will buy R85, then R1 costs N1.18, so the Real is cheaper for the Peruvians to buy which is why it is called devaluation. An item worth R75 being imported into Peru will originally cost N100. The same item after devaluation will only cost N88.50. It is then cheaper for the Peruvians to buy Brazilian goods and so the Brazilians can export more to Peru. As the N is now more expensive for Brazilians, they now need to find R85 to buy an item worth N100, instead of R75, so they are likely to import less from Peru.

task C

Use your own currency and that of a trading partner to illustrate on a diagram or sketch how devaluation could benefit your country.

Colonial trade and neo-colonialism

European countries wanted raw materials from their colonies so the colonies exported these goods at low prices and the European countries imported them. The Europeans processed the raw materials and used them to manufacture goods which they then exported overseas. As they had added value to the raw product, they received a higher price for their exports. Much of this trade was between the rich countries of Europe and the poorer countries in the southern continents.

As colonies gained independence, these developing countries still relied on the export of low value primary products to developed countries, initially to their former colonial power. They developed a negative balance of trade as they imported expensive manufactured goods that the country needed from the developed countries.

> **Definition**
>
> **Neo-colonialism:** new form of dependence of a developing country on another country

This economic dependence after independence is known as neo-colonialism. Developed countries continue to exert an influence over the politics, society and environment of former colonies as well as over their economy.

The EU, for example, negotiated contracts with the governments of several West African countries to allow fleets from EU countries to fish these rich waters. Huge ships removed so many fish that the local economy that depended on fishing has collapsed and local fishermen, who have fished these seas sustainably for generations, have had to migrate to search for jobs elsewhere.

Chad's changing trade and trading partners since independence

Since independence in 1960, Chad's trade with its former colonial power, France, was typical of that of many countries as can be seen in Table 7.2 and Figure 7.1. Chad suffered from decades of civil war and its development was also limited by its landlocked position and droughts. Trade with its neighbours, Nigeria and Cameroon, was small in volume as they produced similar goods.

Chad's trade deficit grew as the manufactured goods cost more to import than the money it received from exporting the primary products of cattle and cotton. Chad encouraged foreign investment from the US and China to develop its oil industry.

Table 7.2 Chad's changing trade and trading partners

	Imports		Exports	
	Origin	Products	Destination	Products
1960s	Mainly from France in decade after independence	Manufactured Goods	Mainly to France	Cotton Cattle
1970s	Nearly 50% from France	Manufactured Goods	Nearly 75% to France	Cotton Cattle
1980s	France still main supplier, followed by the US	Manufactured Goods Food Products	Diversified to include other European countries, Cameroon and Nigeria	Cotton Cattle
2000s	China 17% France 16%, Cameroon 12% US 7%	Machinery Vehicles Food Textiles	United States became the major export market (89% in 2009) France now less than 5%	Oil Cattle Cotton
2000 (estimate)	US$223 million		US$172 million	
2010 (estimate)	US$2.9 billion		US$3.2 billion	

Source: https://www.cia.gov/library/publications/the-world-factbook/geos/cd.html; http://lcweb2.loc.gov/cgi-bin/query/r?frd/cstdy:@field(DOCID+td0089);

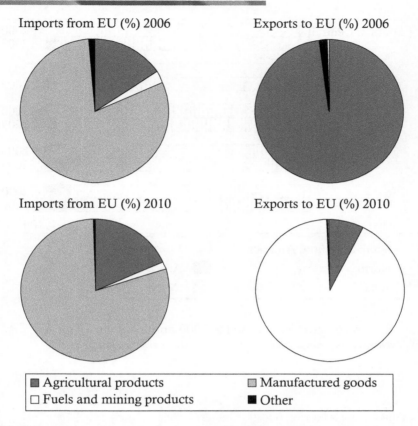

Imports from EU (%) 2006

Exports to EU (%) 2006

Imports from EU (%) 2010

Exports to EU (%) 2010

■ Agricultural products   □ Manufactured goods
□ Fuels and mining products   ■ Other

Figure 7.1   Chad's merchandise trade with the EU (2006 and 2010)
Source: http://trade.ec.europa.eu/doclib/docs/2006/september/tradoc_113365.pdf

task D

1. Describe the main changes that took place in Chad's trading partners and products over the last fifty years.
2. What has happened to Chad's balance of trade between 2000 and 2010? Suggest a reason for this.
3. Describe Chad's trade with the EU between 2006 and 2010.

🌐 Trends in world trading partners

As the trade between the former colonies and the colonial powers declined as in the case study of Chad, countries found new trading partners. However, in the year 2000, Africa still exported half of its goods to Europe as shown in Figure 7.2.

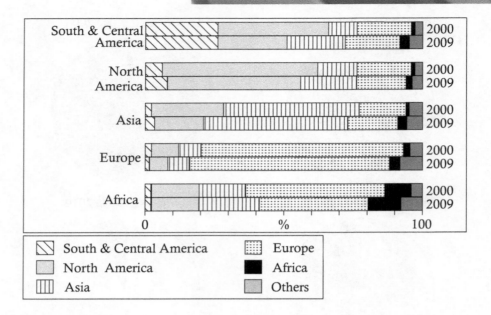

Figure 7.2 Exports by continents (%) for 2000 and 2009

Source: http://www.wto.org/english/res_e/statis_e/world_region_export_09_e.pdf

task E

Answer the following questions after studying Figure 7.2:
1. Which three continents trade amongst themselves more than with other continents?
2. What proportion of Europe's trade is within Europe itself?
3. What are the two main changes in the trade partners of South and Central America between 2000 and 2009?
4. What are the three main changes to Africa's trading partners between 2000 and 2009?

Trends in the trading of goods and services

Food exports to India, China and Russia are increasing as populations continue to grow and increasing living standards mean a greater demand for a variety of produce. Demand for manufactured goods grows faster than people's demand for food so trade in these is growing at a very rapid rate.

'Needs' have become 'wants' and are now 'must haves' as the latest fashion in clothing or electronic gadgets gets worldwide advertising on social networking sites and televisions. NICs such as Brazil produce large numbers of manufactured goods as well as agricultural products.

Sudden export booms of fuels or minerals usually indicate:

- reserves have just been exploited as investment became available
- new technology has required new materials such as coltan which is a rare mineral in demand now for mobile phones.

Figure 7.3 shows the merchandise and services exported from five mentioned countries in 2009.

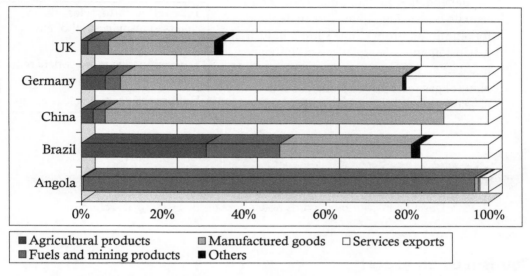

Figure 7.3 Exports of selected countries in 2009

Source: http://stat.wto.org/CountryProfile/WSDBCountryPFView.aspx?Language=E&Country=AO, CN,BR,DE,GB,NE

Study Figure 7.3 and then copy the following paragraph adding the name of the correct country in the spaces.

Agricultural products still account for a large proportion of the value of _____ 's exports. Countries such as _____ have developed their mineral and oil reserves which now account for almost all of the country's exports. _____ now manufactures goods on a huge scale and these account for over 80 per cent of its exports. _____ continues to be a major exporter of manufactured goods. _____ has focused on services to the extent that 65 per cent of its exports are based on the tertiary sector of the economy.

Angola's need to diversify

An over-reliance on two non-renewable resources – oil and diamonds – has meant there is a need to diversify Angola's economy. Extractive industries provide few new jobs as when one area becomes exhausted, the workers all just move on to the next.

The government is diversifying the economy in the following ways.

1. A Special Economic Zone in the capital, Luanda, has been created for import substitution industries. Goods normally imported for the domestic market are now made in the capital itself and include agricultural products, clothing, plastics and electrical equipment. These can also be exported.

2. Other products are being mined to reduce the dependence on diamonds. Demand for bauxite is growing rapidly due to demand for aluminium from China's rapid industrial expansion and as a replacement for copper in cables.

3. Natural gas reserves are being used to develop petrochemical industries.

> **Definition**
>
> **Extractive industries**: those that take resources out of the ground
>
> **Diversify**: give more variety to a range of products
>
> **Exhausted**: completely used up

task G

1. Explain why the Angolan government might be concerned about the large percentage of its exports being fuels and mining products.
2. Describe in your own words how Angola is diversifying its economy.

Tourism as an export

The growth of the tourism industry continues to be an important export earner for developing countries. The Seychelles now has a tourist industry that contributes to over 30 per cent of its GDP. Over half of Africa's export of services is now tourism which means many tourists go on holiday to African countries and spend money there. Low cost airlines now do long haul flights meaning more people can afford to travel longer distances. After the EU and the US, China has the biggest earnings from tourists.

task H

Choose any country which has a growing tourist industry. Describe the features of the country that attract people to visit it and state the sort of things on which tourists might spend their money.

Finance and insurance exports

The EU is the largest exporter of commercial services and over half of this takes place within the EU itself. London is a major financial centre and exports financial and insurance services worldwide. As its manufacturing exports have reduced, the growth in the export of services has been vital to the UK economy as shown in Figure 7.3.

The US is ranked second but India and the Russian Federation are rapidly increasing their export of commercial services.

Computer and Information Technology (IT)

This has been the fastest growing service export since 2000. India's computer services exports were worth US$15.8 billion in 2005. China is rapidly growing its IT services and Malaysia now outsources (see Chapter 9) for well over 1000 international companies. Computer and IT services have therefore become an important export of Asia. Brazil and Costa Rica now do the outsourcing of IT services for North America and the Russian Federation does the same for the EU.

Communication and construction

Telecommunications is a rapidly growing sector and the export of mobile phone services is a large source of revenue for some countries such as Kuwait. China is building roads and railways across the globe such as the railway from Malange to the Angolan coast. Angola gets a cheap loan and infrastructure in return for China getting the construction contracts and access to oil reserves. Angola sells the oil at market rates – a global partnership with both sides gaining benefits.

Colombia's and Brazil's changing view of the world

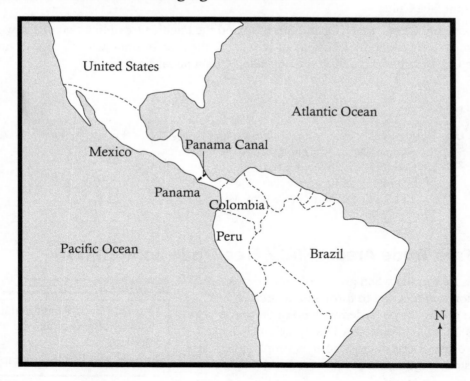

Figure 7.4 Colombia's important trading position

Colombia holds a very important position between the Atlantic and Pacific Oceans (see Figure 7.4) which link its two main trading partners of the twenty-first century – the US and China. Since 2000, South American exports to China of oil, copper and soya beans in particular, have doubled. Already trade with Asia has overtaken that to Europe as shown in Figure 7.2.

Five per cent of world trade currently goes through the Panama Canal. The Colombian's are considering a rail link between the two oceans and the Chinese are investing in the project as it can be used to transport Colombian coal to the Pacific ports for export to China and China will get another access to the eastern coast of the US. Colombia wants to grow its economy by increasing its fuel and mineral exports but investment is needed to do this and the Chinese seem to be willing and able partners.

task I

Why do you think the Chinese are interested in the Colombian railway when there is the Panama Canal between the two oceans?

The Trans-Amazonian Highway was planned in the 1970s as a way of opening up Brazil's rainforest. This road has since been continued across Peru to link the Atlantic Ocean with the Pacific. Brazil now has all year round access on paved roads to ports in Peru that face China.

Brazil and China are NICs and this road and the Pacific Ocean link two of the world's fastest growing economies. Instead of looking to the east for trade with Europe or north to the US, Brazil now looks west to Asia and China in particular.

task J

Draw a sketch map of the area shown in Figure 7.4 and mark on it with arrows the trade routes mentioned above. Label them:
1. Early trade with former colonies and rest of Europe
2. Twentieth century trade with the US
3. Twenty-first century trade with Asia.

🌐 Free Trade Areas (FTA) / Free Trade Zones (FTZ)

These are formed when groups of countries within a region join together to form a trade area within which goods can be traded with no quotas or import tariffs imposed at customs. Free trade zones make the process of trade across borders simpler and faster as customs regulations are removed and therefore there is less paperwork.

Definition
Quota: physical limit to the quantity of goods allowed to be imported **Import tariff:** a tax on imports

A FTA is protected from competition from outside it by two methods.

1. Foreign countries are only allowed to send a certain amount of goods into the zone (a quota) which prevents a flood of foreign goods from entering an area.
2. Foreign countries have to pay a tax to send goods into the zone (a tariff), which makes their product more expensive than those made within the zone and so protects domestic industries.

Often there is a move towards a single currency to make the process of trade even more simple as exchange rates do not need to be calculated.

> **Definition**
>
> **Exchange rates:** the value of a currency for the purpose of converting it to another

Southern Africa Development Community (SADC)

This is a group of 15 states shown shaded on Figure 7.5 with a huge potential domestic market of over 250 million people. Six of these countries are landlocked and so they rely on their neighbours with seaports to trade outside the region. South Africa is the only member of the G20 – a group of the major and emerging world economies.

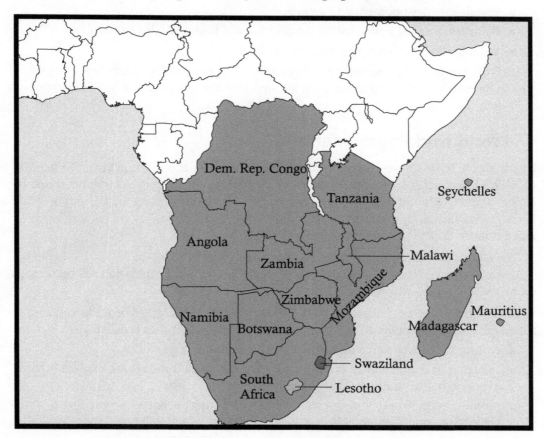

Figure 7.5 Members of SADC

task K

State the countries in Southern Africa which are landlocked and which countries they will probably send their goods through for export to (a) North & South America and (b) Asia .

Many of these countries are developing rapidly with GDP growth rates of over 5 per cent and as economies grow and more people have jobs, they have more income to spend on goods. If these can be obtained from within the region, it benefits the region rather than more developed countries in other continents.

SADC promotes intra-zone trade by organising the removal of import tariffs and 85 per cent of all trade within SADC was free of these in 2008. It also helps to make the process of going through customs easier, cheaper and quicker. SADC also supports:

- co-operation and investment between member countries
- peace and stability within the region
- sustainable development and growth
- democracy as the path to reducing poverty and improving living standards
- the eventual formation of a single currency.

SADC represents the smaller states in international negotiations and plays a bigger part in discussions of global issues than the smaller nations could ever hope to achieve on their own.

World trade agreements

International trade for developing countries is essential for economic growth. Target 8B of MDG 8 is concerned with the need for the least developed countries to have access to export markets without tariffs or quotas. Large trading blocs such as the EU put up trade barriers to countries outside their group. They want to sell goods to other countries but make it more difficult for other countries to sell goods to them.

The EU also gives subsidies to farmers for managing their land in a way that benefits the natural environment. This is an extra payment and so EU farmers can sell their crops more cheaply on the world market.

The World Trade Organisation (WTO) deals with the global rules of trade and tries to get international co-operation to make sure trade flows as freely as possible by:

- cutting tariffs and reducing subsidies on agricultural goods
- reducing or completely removing tariffs on non-agricultural goods, especially those exported by the least developed countries
- promoting trade in environmental technologies such as renewable energy generation, pollution control and waste treatment which will enable developing countries to obtain new technologies quickly at lower costs.

The trade in oil

Oil is a commodity in great demand in all countries for industries and transport. Its value as an export is therefore high. The main oil producing countries joined together to form The Organisation of the Petroleum Exporting Countries (OPEC). The aim of OPEC is to prevent prices fluctuating on the world market so there is a regular supply of oil to consumers, a steady supply of export income to producing countries and a reasonable return for the oil companies such as BP and Exxon Mobil.

The countries that are now members are: Iran, Iraq, Kuwait, Saudi Arabia, Venezuela, Qatar, Indonesia, Libya, The United Arab Emirates, Algeria, Nigeria, Ecuador, Gabon and Angola.

task L

On a map of the world, shade the OPEC countries and name them. Show their level of development according to their HDI in an appropriate way on the map using the data in Figure 5.1. Are all the OPEC countries those of very high or high human development? Attempt to explain your answer.

It is relatively easy to create an organisation like this when there are only a few countries worldwide that have oil reserves and only a few very large oil companies who do the exploration and extraction. With agricultural crops it is more difficult to control supplies and incomes as there may be hundreds of small producers in over a hundred countries.

Trade in agricultural products

Prices of agricultural products vary tremendously on the world market for a number of reasons:

- changes in supply – due to weather conditions, political instability, farmer's decisions
- changes in demand – due to health scares, fashion, seasons, alternative products.

task M

Explain how the causes listed above might lead to changes in supply and demand of food crops. Use examples of crops to illustrate your ideas.

If there is high demand and supply is low then prices are high. If demand is low and supply is high, then prices are low. This fluctuation in price of agricultural products makes it very difficult for farmers.

They decide to plant a certain crop but before it is ready to be harvested the demand for it may fall and they may have to sell it at a low price. They have to judge the market often several months ahead.

Producers (farmers) only get a very small fraction of the price consumers pay in the shops for food products and the further a product has to travel, the greater the costs involved. The prices may be so low that they are less than the cost of production. This makes it very hard for farmers to budget or to consider investing in new techniques that would increase their output.

The producer is always the base of the supply chain, which goes like this.

Most of the money is made after the product leaves the farm. So if a bar of chocolate sells in the US for US$1, the cocoa farmer may only get 6 per cent of that price – or 6 cents. Farm costs of fuel and fertiliser continue to rise but an increased price in the shops gets split between everyone else in the supply chain. If farmers can process their product then they will get a bigger share of the price of the final product but taking the risk of investing in processing works is a big decision.

Trade in products like cocoa and coffee are run by monopolies. These huge companies keep prices low to attract customers and the farmers have little choice but to sell their crops to these big businesses.

Definition

Monopoly: a single company controls the supply of or trade in a particular product

Fairtrade

Fairtrade enables farmers and workers in developing countries to get a fair price for their crop.

Farmers and workers receive a minimum price as well as an additional Fairtrade premium which farmers can choose how to invest in their business and communities for a sustainable future. This may be in social, environmental or economic developmental projects. Fairtrade enables them to improve their position and have more control over their lives.

Fairtrade mark is an independent consumer label seen on a product that meets the international Fairtrade standards. It shows that the product has been certified to offer a better deal to the farmers and workers involved.

Figure 7.6 FAIRTRADE Mark
Source: http://www.fairtrade.org.uk/what_is_fairtrade/fairtrade_certification_and_the_fairtrade_mark/the_fairtrade_mark.aspx

task

Explain how receiving a guaranteed minimum price for a product as well as an additional premium makes it easier for farmers to manage their accounts.

- The export of high value goods will promote development
- Trade deficits can be overcome in a number of ways
- The products, countries and continents, trade and trading partners change over time
- Trade in fuels and mining products is becoming increasingly important to some countries
- Trade in services is growing very fast
- Free trade zones promote trade within regions
- Fairtrade helps those involved in trade in low value agricultural products.

Summary

Unit 2 — Industrial development, trade and globalisation

Processes of industrial production

Learning Objectives

» To appreciate how the importance of the different sectors of the economy changes as countries develop
» To understand the factors of industrial production
» To study the links between the different sectors of the economy
» To understand the meaning of production terms
» To understand the role of governments in production and the ways to achieve more sustainable development
» To appreciate the difference between the formal and informal economy.

Sectors of the economy

Production is the process by which something is made. People's needs and wants have to be satisfied in order for countries to develop. Work in the production of goods and services provides citizens with income which they use to improve their quality of life. The government receives tax revenues which it uses to construct infrastructure to promote further development and improve people's access to services which they can now afford.

The making or manufacture of goods usually requires links between different sectors of a country's economy with each part dependent upon the others. There are three main sectors of an economy.

1. **Primary sector** – activities that use land and sea to produce food and extract natural resources such as farming, fishing, forestry, mining and quarrying.
2. **Secondary sector** – industries that process raw materials and manufacture goods such as milling, spinning, pulping, moulding plastics, making soap and assembly of cars.
3. **Tertiary sector** – provision of services to the rest of the economy and the people of the country such as banks, shops, transport, education and entertainment.

Some examples of the different activities in each sector are shown in Figure 6.1.

task A

Make a list of 5 'needs' and 5 'wants' for individuals and state which sector of the economy provides them.

Flower farming   Car assembly   Bus service

Figure 6.1 Sectors of the economy

Changes in employment structure as countries develop

As countries develop, the proportion of people employed in the three sectors changes as each sector becomes more or less important. Figure 6.2 and the accompanying table shows the percentage of people employed in the different economic sectors in a developing country, a NIC and a developed country.

Country	Primary	Secondary	Tertiary
Developing	80	7	13
NIC	27	35	38
Developed	2	29	69

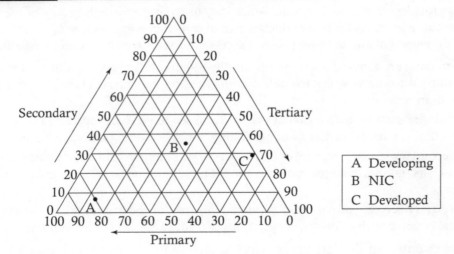

Figure 6.2 Employment structure for countries at different stages of development

task B

Represent the data in one other way and describe the main changes in employment structure that take place as countries develop.

The reasons for the changes may be summarised as follows:

- **Early stage of development** – most people live and work on the land in the primary sector. Crops and minerals are exported as raw materials due to lack of industrial production. Low prices for these mean there is little income to invest in secondary and tertiary industries.

- **Middle stage of development** – processing and manufacturing industries are set up to add value to raw materials and so a large workforce is needed in the secondary sector. Agriculture becomes mechanised, some resources become exhausted and the rural population migrates to the towns for better pay and conditions in the growing industries. Services such as transport and energy supply develop to support the growing economy and money from exports is available for education and health services.

- **Late stage of development** – automation of factory work and increased demand for services as quality of life improves mean people move from the secondary to the tertiary sector. Many large companies move the manufacturing part of the business to developing countries where labour costs are less. Governments have tax revenues to spend on more hospitals and construction projects which employ large numbers of workers.

Telecommunications and ICT services expand at a fast rate to keep up with changing technologies. These are often referred to as the quaternary sector of the economy but are usually classed as a service.

task C

Explain in your own words the reasons for the changes described in Task B.

Factors of production

All industries have the same general requirements. These are the inputs needed to produce something that will generate economic gain or provide a service. Industries use a combination of the following factors to produce outputs.

- **Land** – physical land and its natural resources
- **Labour** – human resources in the form of skilled or unskilled workers
- **Capital** – financial resources in the form of loans or personal investment and technology used in production such as machinery, computers (capital goods)
- **Enterprise** – ability to organise and manage these factors in a successful business.

These four factors of production are needed in industries that manufacture goods which can range from small cottage craft production to the construction of a large tanker. Industries rely on some factors more than others. For example, large car assembly works as shown in Figure 6.1 require large areas of land and high capital investment whereas small craft industries will rely more on the skill of their labour force.

Lesotho crafts

Figure 6.3 shows craft workers making hats on the streets of Maseru, the capital of Lesotho. The main features of this small craft industry are:

- simple technology in the form of scissors and needles
- labour intensive as the human hand does the work
- high level of skill
- process – design and weaving
- raw materials – grass, dye
- outputs – hats, bowls and mats
- waste products – grass clippings.

Figure 6.3   Hat making in the street
Source: Wendy Taylor

The hats and mats are consumer products or finished goods as they are ready for sale to the customers.

Karakul Carpets – a weaving industry in Namibia

To increase the scale of production, some technology is usually needed and premises from which to run a business. Karakul Carpets uses Namibian Karakul sheep wool to make carpets of mainly ethnic designs at a manual weaving mill. The main features of the small industry are:

> **Definition**
>
> **Labour intensive:** large amounts of labour are required
>
> **Simple technology:** basic tools such as hoes, chisels

- intermediate technology in the form of hand looms
- labour intensive as designers and hand weavers are needed
- process – spinning, washing and weaving
- raw material – pure wool, dye
- outputs – rugs, carpets and wall hangings
- waste products – bits of wool.

If waste products can be used, they are called by-products and in this case the waste wool may be a by-product if it is used for stuffing toys.

The hand looms are the most suitable or appropriate for the craft weaving industry and so are appropriate technology. If these industries invested in automated looms, there could be problems such as:

- people would become unemployed
- the rugs would all be identical and mass produced and the market of people who want something individually made would be lost
- they may not make enough profit to make the extra investment worthwhile and the business would close

- energy costs would rise
- they may not have the skills to maintain and repair the more complex machine
- spare parts may be difficult to obtain.

The benefits of automation are that the quality is always the same and the quantity also increases.

task D   Explain why the use of machines increases the quantity produced.

Fruit 'n' Go – a large soft drink company

Production takes place in a large factory and has the following features:

- complex technology in the form of fruit pressing, bottling and canning machines
- capital intensive as machines do much of the work
- unskilled repetitive factory work and skilled managers, sales and marketing team
- raw materials – oranges, sugar, water, preservative
- outputs – bottled or canned orange drink
- waste products – used water, unusable fruit.

> **Definition**
>
> **Capital intensive:** large amounts of capital are invested in the business
>
> **Complex technology:** advanced machinery and computers

This is a simplified account of this industry's features. It needs bottles and cans, energy to run the machines and it needs huge amounts of water to wash the fruit and to cool the machines. All of the items needed to produce a product are called inputs and these are shown in Table 6.1.

> **Definition**
>
> **Inputs:** the requirements for industrial production
>
> **Outputs:** all that is produced by an industrial process

Table 6.1   Inputs, processes and outputs of Fruit 'n' Go

Inputs	Processes	Outputs
Capital	washing	orange juice
Energy	pulping	waste fruit
Land	mixing	waste water
Water	bottling	
Sugar	canning	
Oranges		
Labour		
Enterprise		
Containers		

task E

Draw up a table similar to Table 6.1 for both Lesotho Hats and Karakul Carpets.

The bottles are most likely to be made elsewhere at a specialised plastic moulding works. Plastic is made from oil and so will have had quite a journey by the time it reaches a consumer.

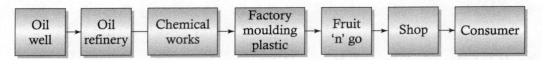

Oil well → Oil refinery → Chemical works → Factory moulding plastic → Fruit 'n' go → Shop → Consumer

The plastic sheets that are produced at the chemical works are semi-processed goods because they are of no use unless they are processed further such as being moulded into a bottle. They are producer goods as compared with consumer goods as they are of no use at this stage to the buying public. Producer goods are used for industrial use elsewhere, either as semi-processed goods or as parts for something else, such as a tyre for a car.

> **Definition**
>
> **Specialised**: concentrates on one particular product or activity

The cans have a similar journey.

Bauxite mine → Aluminium smelter → Sheet metal works → Can factory → Fruit 'n' go → Shop → Consumer

The chemical and sheet metal works are known as heavy industries as their raw materials are bulky and heavy and the machinery is often large. Industries making bowls and drinks are light industries.

Fruit 'n' Go is a secondary industry but it depends upon primary industries and other secondary industries to supply what is needed to make the product. It also depends on the tertiary sector to bring in the raw materials and bottles, provide the supplies of water, power and educated workers, market the product and distribute it to the retailers or docks. Table 6.2 shows how all the different sectors of the economy are linked together with the factors of production.

task F

Choose a secondary industry in your own country and draw up a table similar to that in Table 6.2 to show how it depends on the primary and tertiary sectors as well as other manufacturers in the secondary sector of the economy.

Table 6.2 Some requirements for Fruit 'n' Go production

Sector	Land	Labour	Capital
Primary	Farmland for orange trees, sugar beet/cane	Farm workers	Farm machinery and trucks, wages
	River catchment for water	Water purification workers	Reservoirs, pumping machinery, wages
	Mines, oil wells	Miners, drillers	Mining equipment, rigs, pipelines
Secondary	Fruit n Go factory site	Production workers, managers	Wages, loan repayment or rent, machinery, energy
	Sugar refineries, bottle and can factories	Production workers, managers	Wages, loan repayment or rent, machinery, energy
Tertiary	Sites for warehouses, shops	Shop and supply chain workers	Wages, rent, storage, shop furniture
	Roads, railways, lorry parks	Drivers	Wages, trucks, trains
	Banks	Finance workers	Wages, rent
	Schools	Teachers	Wages
	Energy distribution	Maintenance workers	Wages, maintenance

Location of industries

Manufacturing industries are often located close to the supply of their raw materials. A small craft industry such as Lesotho Hats will set up near where the special grass grows otherwise any small profit would disappear in transport costs especially if the price of fuel is high. A wool weaving business will reduce costs if it is located near sheep farms as fleeces are bulky to transport. Oranges are perishable, heavy and they do not pack easily together so it would make economic sense to locate the pulping works near the orange groves.

Industries such as oil refineries which process imported raw materials are often located at ports. Assembly works such as for cars need to be located where transport links are good as they consist of a range of components such as tyres, seats and wiring that are often made in different places. Some industries need large amounts of water so are to be found next to rivers. Industries that are more flexible in their location may be found on industrial parks that offer new purpose-built factories and government grants. These industries usually produce small, high value goods which rely on skilled labour. These sites are usually on the edge of towns where all modern services are provided.

Economies of scale

There are several ways companies can make savings by increasing the size of their operations. These can be grouped into four economies of scale.

Definition

Economies of scale: the average cost per unit produced is reduced as production increases

- Financial
- Managerial
- Marketing
- Purchasing.

A large company might be able to take on a larger loan at a lower interest rate than a smaller business. By employing more people, specialisation of labour is possible and this can also reduce costs. It is usually cheaper to buy and transport in bulk so companies who buy huge amounts of raw materials can make big savings. Companies who can reduce their costs this way can sell their product more cheaply and still make a good profit. By selling more cheaply, they are more likely to sell more products. This also applies to many consumer goods in markets and shops as shown in Figure 6.4.

Figure 6.4   Market trader

task G

Explain how a large company can make more savings in production costs than a smaller company.

Division of labour

Work in a factory is usually shared out so that different workers do different jobs in the production process that suit their level of ability and talent. This continues the tradition of division of labour that existed in early societies (Chapter 3). Some factory jobs are very repetitive and boring and doing the same small job every hour every day can become unpleasant. These types of job are usually unskilled and low paid. The advantage for the factory is that the workers know exactly what to do and can do the task quickly and efficiently. For factory managers, time is money in the production of goods.

In the Fruit 'n' Go factory, people are employed to do different jobs such as filling the pulping machines, accountants, quality controllers and cleaners. These people have different skills and are usually paid wages that depend on their qualifications and experience. People specialise in different jobs. It would be unusual to find an accountant cleaning windows or a human relations secretary in charge of a complex machine operation.

Skilled workers have been trained to do a particular task and have a special ability or expertise. Accountants would probably be able to clean windows but cleaners would not be able to do an accountant's work without some training. Skilled workers are produced by an education system that prepares students for the world of work.

task H

1. What are the advantages and disadvantages for companies and workers of people specialising in doing different jobs?
2. Make a list of the workers at your school and divide these into skilled and unskilled jobs.

task I

Decision making exercise

As the Managing Director of Fruit 'n' Go, you needed to decide which form of container to use for the orange drink. You need 5 million each year. The main features of each are shown in Table 6.3 with some factors ranked low to high (1–4). Decide which one you would choose and give reasons for your choice and why you have not chosen the others.

Table 6.3 Drink containers

Container	Features
Plastic bottle	Made from non-renewable oil Recyclable Cost per unit – US$0.34 Ease of transport – 2/4 Customer preference – 4/4 Reliability of supply – 2/4
Glass bottle	Made from non-renewable sand, soda ash and limestone Recyclable Cost per unit – US$0.32 Ease of transport – 1/4 Customer preference – 2/4 Reliability of supply – 3/4
Can	Made from non-renewable aluminium and tin Recyclable Cost per unit – US$0.32 Ease of transport –3/4 Customer preference – 3/4 Reliability of supply – 1/4
Carton	Made from renewable wood Recyclable Cost per unit – US$0.24 Ease of transport – 4/4 Customer preference – 1/4 Reliability of supply – 4/4

Sustainability in the production process

All industries have an impact on the environment whether it is in the form of extraction of natural resources or disposal of waste products. The Fruit 'n' Go factory uses oranges and sugar as a main ingredient and these are renewable as they grow each year. Water is a precious resource and it uses 1.5 litres of water to make 1 litre of drink. Some drink containers are made from non-renewable resources.

Companies are making efforts to reduce their impact on the environment in many ways. The three main ways to sustainable development are listed below.

1. Reduce the use of non-renewable natural resources because:
   - otherwise they will run out and will not be available to future generations
   - their extraction from the earth causes loss of biodiversity and destruction of ecosystems.
2. Increase the use of recycled materials because:
   - this reduces natural resource extraction
   - less waste will go to landfill sites and pollute water sources.
3. Use renewable resources wisely such as:
   - manage the land to keep it fertile and protect it from soil erosion
   - minimise water use and clean it before returning it to the environment.

The role of the political process in production

A government's role in production is to set the laws and regulations that determine how the industries operate. These may include laws on:

- working conditions in the factory
- the use of child labour and discrimination in the workplace
- pollution and waste disposal to help to protect the environment.

Governments also decide how the tax from the company's profits will be spent. It could be used to improve the country's infrastructure or it could be used to support a luxury lifestyle for politicians.

Private and state-run organisations – the formal economy

Private companies are owned by individuals or shareholders who make the decisions on how to run the company although they have to follow regulations set by the government. Competition results in high levels of efficiency and the production of high quality goods. Prices are set by supply and demand. Private companies pay taxes that the government can spend on running state owned companies.

Companies that are run by the state are often in key industries such as steel making or coal mining and service industries such as education and health. These are run for the benefit of a country's citizens rather than to make a large profit.

There is little choice for consumers and wages are not usually as high as in the private sector. The quality of products and service is often lower. Most countries have a mixed economy combining both private and state production and provision of services. People who work in private and public companies work in the formal economy.

task J

Make a list of ten different jobs people have in the formal economy.

task K

Choose a public service industry such as education, health or railways. Describe the factors of production and explain how the service industry is linked to the primary and secondary sectors of the economy.

The informal economy

In developing countries, there are not enough jobs in the formal sector for all those that need employment. In many countries, governments do not supply payments to those out of work. This is either because there would be so many people needing help that their budget could not cope, or their priorities may be on defence spending or improving schools. So in order to survive, people set up their own businesses often from home or on the streets.

No tax is paid but these people earn an income to buy food and other needs. In doing this they support other activities which help to improve other people's standard of living. For example, a young woman invests in some scissors and cuts people's hair in her room. She gets paid and may use this money to buy some soap and the soap seller gets money to buy something else. When this happens with thousands of different examples of money changing hands, an informal economy grows and sustains itself. Sometimes employment in the informal economy is greater than that in the formal economy. The informal economy of Kibera, Nairobi, is described in Chapter 11. Main features of the informal economy are:

- easy to enter as few skills needed
- self-employment with help from family members only
- income is low and unreliable
- working hours are long
- no regulations on working conditions but no legal protection either
- small scale and run from a home base
- no tax paid to government.

Figure 6.5 shows the sort of informal activities that go on in many cities around the world.

Out on the streets of Mumbai, informal activities can be seen and heard everywhere as over two thirds of the jobs here are informal ones. Children as young as five, polish a businessman's shoes. All sorts of goods are laid out along the streets – pots, soap, trainers, mobile phones as well as food and clothes of all sorts. If there is a market for something then someone, somewhere will have a stall or area of pavement selling it.

I stopped and spoke to a young woman and this was her story. 'When the factory closed my husband lost his job and so now I walk to the market twice a week to buy onions, peppers and chillies.

What I don't sell I have to carry home and bring back for the next day. Some days I earn almost nothing but I still have to pay the authorities to leave me in peace.'

Behind the doors of the dwellings of Dharavi, one of Mumbai's shanty towns, there is a hive of activity. Sewing machines make clothes and bags, pots mix up small bits of soap leftover from hotels, scissors cut hair and outside stoves make pancakes.

Some enterprising young men have got together and bought a big TV. They charge people to come and watch the football. Only drinks and snacks sold by them can be eaten watching the match.

Figure 6.5   The streets of Mumbai

task L

Make a list of the meaning of the different industrial terms used in this chapter.

Summary

- As countries develop the proportion of people employed in agriculture decreases
- Methods of production vary in scale and levels of technology
- Production depends upon links with other sectors of the economy
- Industrial production has impacts on a country's natural resources
- The informal economy provides an income for people who cannot find formal employment.

Debt and aid

Loans and debt

After independence, governments of developing countries needed to borrow money for a number of reasons. They needed money to allow them to construct the infrastructure that would attract industries to help the economy to grow and also to build schools and hospitals. If they had a trade deficit they needed to pay for essential imports. If there was conflict within their country or with other nations then they had to arm the military.

Infrastructure includes:

- roads, railways, ports, airports
- distribution of energy and water supplies
- sanitation and waste disposal
- schools and hospitals
- telecommunications and the internet.

task A

Rank the different forms of infrastructure shown above in terms of importance for an industry wishing to set up in a country.

The money countries need to borrow comes in the form of bi-lateral or multi-lateral loans. A bi-lateral loan may be given from one government to another government. The agreement by the German government to provide a low interest loan to the Namibian government to finance the expansion of the hydroelectric power plant at Ruacana was a bi-lateral loan.

The debt will only grow slowly if it is not paid off because it has been lent at a low interest rate (see below).

The main lenders of multi-lateral loans are the World Bank, the International Monetary Fund (IMF) and continental organisations such as the Asian Development Bank and the African Development Bank. Together with providing loans and grants for investment in infrastructure, the IMF also works to keep the global financial system as stable as possible. The Lesotho Highlands Water Project (see Chapter 19) was partly funded by loans from The African Development Bank, European Development Fund and the World Bank.

Definition

Bi-lateral loan: a two-sided loan such as money lent by one government to another

Multi-lateral loan: a many-sided loan such as money lent by international groups

Interest rates

Unlike a gift, a loan has to be paid back, usually within a given time limit. Loans usually have to be paid back with interest. Compound interest means that the interest for the first year is added to the original loan so that it too earns interest during the next year, and so on. If the loan is not paid off, it grows by more each year as shown in Table 8.1.

Definition

Interest: money charged to the loan as payment for the money lent

Table 8.1 Compound interest on a loan of $100 for 5 years

Interest rate	Year 0	Year 1	Year 2	Year 3	Year 4	Year 5
10% for 5 Years	100.00	110.00	121.00	133.10	146.41	161.05
10% then 20% after Year 2	100.00	110.00	121.00	145.20	174.24	209.09

If a country borrows $1 million at 10 per cent interest, after five years it will owe $1 611 000. If the country pays the loan back, the lender gets a profit of $611 000 which is the interest that was charged on the loan. However:

1. If the country fails to pay back the loan, in 8 years the country will owe over double what it originally borrowed.
2. If, after year 2 the interest rate rises to 20 per cent, payments build up very quickly and in just 5 years, the country owes over double the loan.

When a country borrows money, it is said to be in debt. Governments hope that the way they have invested the loan will generate money to pay it back. However, it usually takes many years to actually build infrastructure and get the benefits from it. In the meantime, the debt will grow due to the interest charged on it. If the government needs to borrow more money, the debt will grow even further. Sometimes a government needs to take out another loan to pay off the interest on the original loan so that it does not keep growing.

The debt can eventually become so large that the country has no hope of ever paying it back and the debt becomes unsustainable.

Unsustainable debt

Unsustainable debt may have built up for a number of reasons:

- large loans were offered by banks and taken out at low interest rates
- large loans were offered by foreign governments in return for the right to exploit minerals
- rise in interest rates
- low prices for agricultural exports
- rise in oil prices – this increases costs worldwide for industries and transport so cost of imports of manufactured goods rises
- new loans taken out to pay interest on the old ones
- corrupt rulers borrowed large sums to build palaces
- global financial crisis reduces exports as countries cut back on what they buy.

Debt and development

Table 8.2 shows the size of the debt of certain countries compared with their GDP.

Table 8.2   Debt and GDP for selected countries 2010

Country	GDP (US$billion)	Debt (US$billion)	GDP growth (%)
Philippines	200	72	7.6
Pakistan	177	57	4.1
Mexico	1036	200	5.5
Guinea Bissau	0.8	1	3.5
Brazil	2143	347	7.5
Mauritania	4	2	5.2
Burkina Faso	9	2	7.9

GDP growth rates show the rate at which production of goods and services in a country is increasing. The larger the per cent increase, the more money is available to pay off debt or improve standards of living.

task B

Answer the following questions:
1. Which country has a debt greater than its GDP?
2. Which country has the fastest growing GDP?
3. What proportion of its GDP is the debt of Mauritania?
4. By how much is Brazil's GDP growing each year?
5. How do you describe the debt of Brazil in relation to its GDP?

Huge debts restrict development and increase poverty. Instead of developing new industries to export goods and building new schools or providing clean water supplies, money is used to pay off the debt. Some countries pay several times more in debt payments than they spend on education and health.

task C

Explain how development will be affected if less money is spent on education and health care.

If a country gets into serious debt, it has a number of options, but there are problems associated with all of these choices as shown in Table 8.3.

Table 8.3 Methods of debt reduction

Option	Problem
Reduce imports	Imports are often needed to produce exports
Produce manufactured goods for domestic market that are otherwise imported	Requires finance to set these up and MNCs usually do this
Increase exports	May lead to exploitation of resources by MNCs
Reduce spending on healthcare, education etc.	Affects the poorest people the most
Increase production of cash crops	Reduces land for growing food and needs imports of fertilisers
Devalue the currency	Makes imports more expensive
Change loan conditions so longer payback time	The debt will continue to grow
Take on another loan to pay off the original one	The country's debt gets bigger

Debt relief

As there is no simple solution, what usually happens is that the country seeks help from the IMF. The Heavily Indebted Poor Countries (HIPC) Initiative was launched in 1996 by the IMF and World Bank to help very poor countries manage their debt.

By 2011, 36 countries had received some reduction in the amount they were expected to repay.

To qualify for help, the country has to make certain changes to the way it is run. This may include a move towards a more democratic government as well as efforts to fight corruption. A Poverty Reduction Strategy (PRS) must include measures to make sure that the money saved on debt payments goes to reducing poverty. The IMF and the World Bank decided in 2010 to support debt relief for Guinea Bissau as the African country had controlled spending, increased political stability and achieved objectives in its PRS such as:

- introducing free primary education in public schools, and raising enrolment rates
- providing vaccination to more than 90 per cent of children
- raising awareness of HIV/AIDS.

task D

Explain why Guinea Bissau needed help from the IMF and why the IMF supported some debt relief for this country.

Benefits of debt relief

Debt relief reduces the debt that poor countries have to pay back. The many benefits of this to developing countries can be considerable.

1. **Political** – the government can concentrate on the economy and improving people's quality of life.
2. **Environmental** – developing countries have less need to exploit their natural resources to pay off the debt which will help to protect the environment.
3. **Social** – more money is available for schools, clinics.
4. **Economic** – infrastructure such as roads can be constructed to encourage economic growth.
5. **Humanitarian** – poverty is reduced.

Global campaigns to cancel the debt

Many people feel that some of the debt owed by countries must be written off for humanitarian reasons. People today are suffering from having to pay money back that should not have been lent in the first place, often decades ago. In 2000, the biggest ever petition with 24 million signatures from 166 countries called for the cancellation of the unjust debt of the poorest countries and the Jubilee Debt Campaign and others continue to work to achieve this. Unjust debt is from loans that were given:

- irresponsibly with no thought as to how they could be paid back
- for expensive projects that were of little use
- to corrupt dictators.

The most powerful countries in the world are referred to as the G8 – US, UK, Japan, Germany, France, Canada, Italy and Russia. These industrialised countries meet at summits to discuss global issues such as debt. Words do not always turn into actions at these summits inspite of many large public demonstrations such as the one in 2005 shown in Figure 8.1. These eight wealthy countries control and contribute large amounts of money to the IMF and World Bank and could make a real difference in meeting target 8D for MDG 8.

Target 8D is to deal with the debt problems of developing countries through national and international measures in order to make debt sustainable in the long term.

Making poor countries continue to pay debts for which the present people are often not responsible means that the rich countries continue to have power over the poorer ones and the flow of money between them continues to widen the wealth gap. Developing countries remain dependent on developed ones.

Figure 8.1 Make Poverty History rally, London 2005

Aid

It is a strange situation whereby developed countries and international banks receive debt payments in one hand and give out aid payments with the other to the same country. While developing countries continue to pay the debts they owe, most of them will need help in the form of aid.

1. To undertake measures to improve the living standards of their people.
2. To provide infrastructure to encourage industries whose exports will help to pay off debt and stimulate the economy.

Aid may be in the form of money, goods or technical aid. It is usually aid rather than investment by foreign companies that sets up schools, clinics and provides clean water supplies.

> **Definition**
>
> **Technical aid**: expertise and skills such as those used by engineers, doctors etc. and equipment such as mechanical diggers and hospital scanners

Aid effectiveness

Aid is help that is given to countries in need but it is not so much the amount of aid that is important but the way it is used. A huge amount of money donated to a cause is useless if most of it is either lost in administration or is stolen by corrupt officials.

To be effective, aid needs to be delivered by experienced organisations that know the area in which they will be working and have a good record in delivering results.

It is difficult for aid workers to be effective if they are working in areas of conflict where people are constantly moving to escape the fighting.

According to The World Bank, 'Aid effectiveness is the impact that aid has in reducing poverty and inequality, increasing growth, building capacity, and accelerating achievement of the Millennium Development Goals...'.

task E

Describe the many problems that aid workers face when working in war zones.

Reasons for aid being given

Humanitarian

In cases of an emergency such as in the event of a natural disaster, people and governments around the world give money to charities to help relieve suffering. If people give money and then find out that it has never reached the victims of the disaster, then next time there is a natural disaster they may be more reluctant to donate.

Humanitarian aid is also given when there are longer term problems such as those caused by drought. Giving has never been easier and can be done in various ways as shown in Figure 8.2.

Figure 8.2 Ways of giving to charities and disaster appeals

Economic

Countries depend on trade and a government might wish to protect its export market and its private companies abroad by giving aid to a country in need.

Political

Countries may feel an obligation towards their former colonies. In the past, tied aid was common but today some favour in return is implied rather than an agreement being clearly stated. Aid may have been given to build a dam but the donor was given the contract to do the work. By giving aid, a developed country may put pressure on developing countries to vote with them on international issues debated at the United Nations. Aid can be a way of one country exerting power over another.

Definition

Tied aid: aid that has conditions attached to it

The main donors

1. Foreign governments

Bi-lateral aid is often given from a colonial power to its former colony such as the UK still gives India a large amount of aid each year as described in Figure 8.3. Governments are keen to help poorer countries build infrastructure to help their economic growth and provide aid for social projects to improve people's standard of living.

The UK is set to give over £1 billion in aid to India over the next few years to help its 400 million poor people. However, UK taxpayers are concerned that they are now helping a country that can afford a space programme and has many very wealthy people. Many feel the Indian government could do more to help reduce poverty amongst its own people especially as it now gives out aid overseas itself. While the UK government wants to help the millions who still live under the poverty line, at the same time it sees that India's economy is growing rapidly and there is a huge market for UK goods.

Figure 8.3 UK aid to India

2. International agencies

Multi-lateral aid is from international bodies such as UNICEF. Funds for these groups come from individuals, private companies, foundations and governments. This aid is often used to fund social projects for which a developing country would otherwise have to take out a loan which would lead to more debt.

UNICEF and WHO, together with other partners including the Japanese government, have worked to eradicate polio in Angola by vaccination of nearly six million children.

task F

1. Identify projects within your own country that receive large multi-lateral aid donations.
2. State the groups providing the funds and describe the economic and social benefits of the project.
3. Consider whether or not there are any problems associated with the projects.

3. Charities

Charities are NGOs and range in scale from those that focus on helping a particular settlement to international organisations such as The Red Cross and Oxfam.

There are three main types of aid that charities give:

- emergency aid at times of natural disaster such as food, shelter, medicine and other essential products
- infrastructure developments to improve living conditions such as improved water supplies and school buildings
- solutions to problems over the longer term such as control of soil erosion.

Grass-root schemes work closely with local people. The charities provide the necessary funds and expert assistance to set up a project. These may be church groups or NGOs set up by individuals who care about a particular community or problem.

task G

1. Describe the short and long term aid given by a charity working in your country in terms of money, goods and expertise.
2. Explain the advantages and disadvantages of the aid.

The Send a Cow Scheme

Send a Cow is a charity that works with traditional African farmers to help them grow enough food to eat and produce enough to sell. It does this by firstly identifying the local needs and then training farmers in groups so they can help each other improve their traditional farming ways.

The training includes how to develop sustainable mixed farms with advice on crop growing and livestock care. Cows, chickens, fruit trees and seeds as well as tools are provided if necessary to get families started and help gain self-sufficiency as can be seen in Figure 8.4.

Figure 8.4 Send a Cow Scheme
Source: http://www.sendacow.org.uk/news-rwanda-remembers

The charity appreciates that other issues are also important to the success of development programmes so courses in subjects such as gender equality, health and hygiene and HIV/AIDS awareness are also given. The farmers are expected to pass on the benefits they have received to others in the community.

By giving and sharing, communities are strengthened and more people are helped. The following accounts show the wide range of benefits that can be gained from small schemes such as these.

This cow is transforming our family life. She is providing milk for our children, which we could not afford before. We have a surplus to sell, which covers school expenses and family healthcare. Her manure fertilises our garden, which yields enough vegetables to eat, share with neighbours, and sell. We are helping our neighbours set up their own vegetable gardens, which is deepening our friendships.

Margaret Mukabasinga, Rwanda

Source: http://www.sendacow.org.uk

I live on a hill, on very infertile land. Only half-a-hectare is suitable for growing crops. Before the project, I couldn't afford even kerosene or household utensils, and we ate mainly cabbage, potato and false banana. Since my training in soil and water conservation, I have covered the hillside with trees! That protects my land from erosion, and gives me saplings to sell. I have also set up a vegetable garden, using compost. Now I know how to use my local resources efficiently, I have not needed government food aid.

Kuste Gebela, Ethiopia

Source: http://www.sendacow.org.uk

task H

1. Draw a spider diagram to show all the benefits to a local community of the Send a Cow Scheme.
2. Identify on the diagram using MDG 1, MDG 2 etc. how the different benefits help the countries meet some of the MDGs.

Problems with aid

Many development projects, both large and small, depend on aid to set them up and keep them going. Communities all across the world rely on help from volunteers and money from many different sources to supply sometimes their basic needs. There are, however, problems with giving help and money in this way:

- funds can be used for the wrong purposes by corrupt officials and never reach the people for whom it was intended
- funds may be spent on large projects that only benefit a few people in a limited area
- large projects may cause social and environmental problems
- people may become lazy and rely on hand-outs
- governments depend on foreign countries to provide infrastructure instead of using public funds
- aid projects may include inappropriate technology which cannot be maintained
- aid may be used to purchase weapons.

Summary

- Countries borrow money for a number of reasons from many different sources
- Countries may become unable to repay their debt due to the interest charged on the loan
- Debt restricts the money a government has available to improve people's living standards
- Debt relief is essential if countries are to develop
- Aid takes many forms and is needed for different reasons
- Aid can make a huge difference to the quality of life in many communities.

Foreign direct investment and globalisation

9

 Foreign Direct Investment (FDI)

In order to develop, countries need to trade and the higher the value of the goods they export, the more likely it is they will have a positive balance of trade. Often there is a need to increase the capacity to trade, and loans are usually needed by developing countries to put basic infrastructure into place. When there are adequate ports, roads, energy and water supplies then industrial production can follow allowing countries to develop with the money generated from exports. This either takes the form of extracting fuel and minerals from the earth or processing and manufacturing goods.

In the early stages of development, countries rarely have their own industries to do this on a large scale so governments try to attract foreign investment. This is usually private sector companies which are Multinational Companies (MNCs) and the investment they bring is called Foreign Direct Investment (FDI). The economy is a capitalist one.

> **Definition**
>
> **Multinational:** operating in several countries
>
> **Capitalist:** an economy in which trade and industry are controlled by the private sector for profit

In order to start paying back the investment quickly a company can sell minerals from its mines and a factory can sell goods. These companies create jobs and wealth by increasing exports and reducing imports. MNCs are usually Public Limited Companies (PLCs) which means they are owned by people who have bought shares in the business. Most of the top companies in the world in terms of revenue invest in foreign countries.

Angola's huge oil reserves and diamonds attracted FDI and revenues from the export of these products are now being used by the government to fund health and education services. These services tend not to attract foreign investment as they do not generate money directly. There is nothing a foreign company can sell to make money. However, a skilled and healthy workforce will help the country's development in the longer term.

task A

Decision making exercise

A mining company wants to obtain a rare mineral essential for the growing electronics industry. There are four possible sites. The operating costs are the same for each country. Prepare a report explaining which site the company should choose and the disadvantages of the other sites.

1. Country A – Reserves are worth US$120bn. There is an excellent road network to ports and schools provide technical training. Mining would require the destruction of the last habitat of upland forest monkeys.
2. Country B – Reserves are worth US$130bn. Infrastructure is good and there is an educated workforce. Five communities would require re-settlement at an extra cost of US$10bn - US$30bn. Pollution of local water sources with toxic materials is likely.
3. Country C – Reserves are worth US$200bn. The country is landlocked and roads to the borders would need re-surfacing at an extra cost of US$10bn. Relations with governments of the surrounding countries are not always good and so access to their ports may be limited.
4. Country D – Reserves are worth US$600bn. The country is holding its first democratic election after a civil war that lasted 10 years. Much of the infrastructure has been destroyed and the country is one of the least developed in the world. Total extra costs are unknown.

The important role of governments

MNCs are more likely to be attracted to invest in a country if the country appears to be politically stable with little chance of civil war disrupting supplies. Governments decide which foreign companies can invest in the country. They grant licenses for exploration of minerals and so determine how the country's resources will be developed.

Some countries limit FDI in order to protect their own growing companies from competition but sometimes governments have little choice but to attract MNCs and they do this by offering:

- low tax rates or even tax 'holidays' for a number of years
- few laws to protect the environment
- relaxed labour laws and absence of trade unions
- free trade zones with no tariffs to reduce import costs.

task B

Describe the protection that should be given to the workers and the environment that may be lacking if governments want to attract FDI.

Advantages and disadvantages of MNCs

For the developing country, there are a number of benefits which may outweigh the disadvantages which are shown in Table 9.1.

Table 9.1 Advantages and disadvantages of MNCs

Advantages	Disadvantages
High employment for local people	Industry is usually capital intensive
Skills learnt	Many skilled workers are brought in from overseas
Export of goods will earn money to pay for imports	Profits go out of the country and many components have to be imported
People have money to spend on goods, education etc. which increases demand for services which provides further employment	Wages are very low for very long hours and poor working conditions cause bad health
Bigger choice of goods to buy	Goods are too expensive for local people
Taxes for government from the MNC's profits and workers' wages	Low taxes or tax free due to competition from other developing countries
Revenues for governments can be spent on improving infrastructure	Corrupt governments will not use the revenue to reduce poverty

If people have an income, are healthy and educated, they will buy products and use services. The domestic market will grow and foreign investors will benefit as they will be able to sell more goods. So it is in the interest of MNCs to help to improve people's quality of life. In remote mining regions, foreign investors may need to build a settlement for the workforce where children can go to school and health services are provided. Traders arrive and set up shops to serve the workers and in this way local businesses grow and the local economy benefits. This is called the 'multiplier' effect.

Definition

Multiplier effect: an investment leads to further spending and income and so has additional effects and benefits

task C

Make a list of all the possible benefits MNCs can bring to a developing country.

FTZs and MNCs

FTZs (described in Chapter 7) attract MNCs as there are no tariffs to pay on imports and MNCs usually have to import parts from around the world so this reduces costs. FTAs do not only have to be groups of countries such as SADC.

Lekki is a free trade zone based around a new port being built 50 km from Lagos in Nigeria. It is a partnership between the Lagos State government and Chinese businessmen. Nigeria hopes to attract MNCs who will manufacture goods that are in high demand on the world market such as electronics and clothing and so bring in foreign exchange. This should stimulate the local domestic economy which will create more jobs. It is doing this in a number of ways:

- making available Nigeria's vast wealth of natural resources including oil and timber
- providing an export location
- providing access to a huge market in Nigeria and other countries in Africa
- no import tariffs or quotas, no licences or taxes
- preferential tariffs and no quota on goods exported to the EU.

> **Definition**
>
> **Export orientated strategy**: production for the purpose of selling goods abroad

task D

1. Describe fully the export orientated strategy at Lekki.
2. Explain why the possibility of trade with the EU is such an attraction.
3. Explain how the local economy might be stimulated.

 Special Economic Zones (SEZ) and MNCs

If a country's infrastructure is generally poor then a special zone may be created where roads, energy and water supply etc. are all provided in the hope that it will attract MNCs. By providing jobs, the local economy can grow as people will have money to spend on more goods and services and industries may grow up to supply the larger MNCs with parts and services.

The Cavite Zone SEZ

The Philippine Economic Zone Authority supports the Philippine government in its efforts to create employment and generate more exports by attracting foreign investment into the country. It does this by means of a variety of incentives that are available in over 200 SEZs that have been set up, such as an income tax 'holiday' for up to 8 years, no import taxes and zero tax paid on utility bills.

> **Definition**
>
> **Hub**: the centre of activity
>
> **Strategic**: an essential part of a plan to achieve a long term aim

The Cavite Zone near Manila, is one of the largest SEZ in the Philippines where over 250 companies are now operating, employing over 70 000 people. It is close to what is fast becoming a major logistics and transhipment hub in SE Asia. It is in a strategic location in an area with a rapidly growing, huge domestic market with good access to China, Japan and the US. The balance of trade from the Cavite Zone has shown a trade surplus since 1995, shown in Figure 9.1, and so is achieving the main aim of SEZs.

Figure 9.1 Balance of trade of the Cavite Zone

Source: http://i-site.ph/philippineodatrail/wp-files/jbic/2004/Cavite_export_processing_zone_development_project_2004.pdf

task E

1. What was the value of exports from the Cavite Zone in 2002?
2. What was the value of imports to the Cavite Zone in 2002?
3. What was the trade balance in 2002?
4. Describe the main trends in the trade of the Cavite Zone shown in Figure 9.1.

Case Study of San Technology

San Technology is a high-tech Japanese company producing electronic components in the Cavite Zone. Like many MNCs, San Technology designs and researches the products in the home country and manufactures them abroad where costs are lower.

Definition

High-tech: advanced technology especially electronics

The reasons it chose Cavite are:

- labour costs are less than those in Japan and likely to remain low
- most people speak English and levels of education are relatively high
- the government promotes FDI and there is a relatively stable political situation
- it is a good location for trading
- rents are reasonable.

Nearly half of the products are sold to companies in other Special Economic Zones in the Philippines, such as Hitachi, who make the consumer goods. San Technology imports 90 per cent of the parts and materials it needs mainly from Japan.

If it increased the amount of materials it bought from local companies, this would reduce its costs as well as further benefit the local economy. Local industries could manufacture the packaging required using locally sourced renewable materials such as bamboo shown in Figure 9.2.

Figure 9.2 Bamboo
Source: Cynthia Tipper

task F

Suggest the environmental, economic and social benefits of using locally grown bamboo instead of plastic (refined from oil) for packaging.

Problems caused by MNCs

There are many MNCs which are making great efforts to reduce their impact on the environment and local communities where they operate. However, the main purpose of the MNC is to make a profit and the way to do this is by cutting costs. 'The bottom line' is a term taken from a sheet of accounts showing a company's profit on the bottom line. It has come to mean that profit is all that really counts and is the most important factor.

Many companies make out they care about the environment and communities but often it is merely a way of attracting more customers or investors rather than any real concern for the state of the planet.

The natural environment

Any industrial production has an impact on the natural environment whether it is in the form of extraction of raw materials or disposal of waste into the air and rivers. Resources may be exploited with no thought of sustainable development and of preserving some for future generations. Pollution prevention costs money and so would reduce 'the bottom line'.

The social environment

Farmers or even whole communities may need to be relocated as powerful businesses take over their land. Compensation for loss of property, farmland, fishing grounds and cultural sites is rarely given proper consideration. Local communities may have their water supplies polluted.

In the workplace, trade unions are often not allowed and requests for better pay or improved working conditions are met with dismissal. There is much temporary work and so little job security. Wages are low as there is always someone unemployed willing to work for less. Child labour, the cheapest of all, is often used.

After a ten hour shift with few breaks, six or even seven days a week, many workers do overtime due to the poor pay. Safety measures are often lacking and so working conditions may be dangerous. Dust and smoke cause poor health in workers. Higher wages and better working conditions cost money and so would also reduce 'the bottom line'.

Figure 9.3 indicates how unaware most people are of the social and environmental costs of production.

Figure 9.3   Behind the scenes

The problem for governments

Some MNCs have revenues that are greater than the GDP of some countries and so these companies are sometimes more powerful than a country's democratically elected government. This can be seen in Table 9.2.

Table 9.2   Selected MNCs' revenue and selected countries' GDP (US$billion)

MNC	Revenue (2011)	Country	GDP (2010)
Wal-Mart	419	Colombia	289
Royal Dutch Shell	378	Malaysia	238
Sinopec	273	Bangladesh	100
Toyota	222	Burkina Faso	9

Source: www.worldbank.org; http://money.cnn.com/magazines/fortune/global500/2011/index.html

If a country's government introduces laws to keep its air and rivers clean, and laws to stop the use of child labour, it will cost the MNC money. This will increase the price of its product in shops and so they may lose sales to another company which operates in a country where there are no such laws. The MNC can simply move and set up in a country that has fewer laws. So governments who try to protect their environment and the human rights of their people may have job losses and less tax revenue if the MNC moves elsewhere. There is no international law to control the activities of MNCs.

Regional groups such as SADC can make sure that wherever the MNC goes within the Group, the same legislation will apply but that will not stop the MNC from moving to a country outside the Group. International laws may be necessary to limit the power of MNCs but policing these on a global scale is difficult and powerful business lobby groups and corruption certainly do not help.

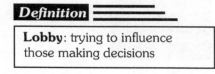

> **Definition**
>
> **Lobby**: trying to influence those making decisions

The EU became concerned about the huge number of low price shoes flooding their markets so it imposed import tariffs on shoes from China and Vietnam. The MNC concerned simply switched production to somewhere else showing that even the biggest trading bloc in the world, the EU, has little impact on MNCs' activities.

The role of shareholders

MNCs are owned by shareholders who elect people to run the company. Shareholders are people or organisations such as pension funds which invest money in a company to allow it to operate. The MNC's main objective is to produce a profit which

> **Definition**
>
> **Ethical**: relating to good and right principles

can be shared amongst its investors by way of a dividend. People buying shares could make a big difference by making ethical investments in companies who are trying to protect the environment and communities where their industries are situated. Some of the efforts at sustainability made by companies can be seen in Table 9.3.

Table 9.3 Efforts at sustainability by major producers

Industry	Efforts made
Computers	Bamboo packaging instead of plastic – renewable, biodegradable, locally grown
Oil	Employees work in conservation projects to understand importance of biodiversity
Heavy machinery	Tree planting and lake creation around the factory for new habitats
Cars	Cars totally recyclable at end-of-life to reduce waste going to landfill sites
Trainers	Working to eliminate the use of hazardous chemicals – water based adhesives rather than solvent based ones will improve workers' health
Textiles	Increased machine efficiency to reduce water and energy use

Table 9.3 Efforts at sustainability by major producers (Continued)

Industry	Efforts made
Soft drinks	Quality of waste water improved so that it is clean for community use
Packaging	New technology enables less material to be used such as thinner metal in cans Increased use of recycled materials
Mining	Training of local people in applying for contracts to bring jobs to local community
Textiles	Staff canteen sources locally produced food providing extra market for farmers
Banking	Business coaching for young entrepreneurs to bring skills to the community and independent businesses

The role of consumers worldwide

MNCs succeed or fail on the basis of sales. Mostly people buy what they like or what is the cheapest but when they spend money they make choices. MNCs supply what people want to buy. This is known as supply and demand.

People all over the world can influence the activities of MNCs if they choose carefully what they are buying. Fierce competition in the world market for shoes, clothes and electronic goods will always mean MNCs try to reduce costs.

The buying public needs to understand that in this global partnership for development (MDG 8), it may be necessary to pay more for the goods we buy so that workers and the environment can be protected around the world. People can buy products from companies who are trying to:

- reduce their use of non-renewable raw materials, water etc.
- reduce waste and packaging and use recycled materials
- reduce the use of harmful chemicals
- employ local people on decent wages and support local community projects
- protect the natural environment.

Then MNCs who try to protect the natural environment and care about local communities will survive and those who do not will fail.

task G Undertake a survey within your class to find out what are the main factors that influence which goods people buy.

The role of environmental activists

Environmental activists can use the internet to shame companies with famous brands who might be poisoning local water supplies or illegally destroying forest habitats.

Definition

Brand: a mark on a product that identifies a certain company

MNCs cannot escape the bad publicity by moving elsewhere as the internet is international in scope. If enough people stop buying these MNCs' products, then they might improve their operations.

task
H
1. List what you consider to be the top ten most famous brands in the world.
2. Compare your list with others.
3. Group the brands into the types of product they make.

The role of the United Nations

Companies need to make sure that it is not just their main assembly plant that has high social and environmental standards but also all producers of their components. The United Nations has a Global Compact which promotes corporate responsibility as an international problem which needs an international solution.

> *Definition*
>
> **Corporate**: relating to a large business

🌐 Outsourcing and globalisation

Figure 9.4 shows the different sections of a large company. In the past, the company would undertake all these operations on one site where the industry started. It may then have contracted out some of the work to local firms who could do the work as easily and often better on their own site. Many companies now outsource much of their business. Improvements in transportation and communication have meant that these outsourcing companies can be located anywhere in the world.

> *Definition*
>
> **Globalisation:** international influence on the development of business and trade links worldwide with the aid of telecommunications

There are some activities, however, that cannot be outsourced. Fitting and maintenance of appliances and construction work all have to be done on the local site, so some particular workers will always be needed everywhere. Some of these are shown in Figure 9.5.

> *Definition*
>
> **Outsourcing**: transferring part of the work of a company to another organisation somewhere else

Outsourcing of manufacturing

Labour is much cheaper in developing countries and many MNCs have moved the manufacturing section of their business overseas. All administration continues to take place in the developed country where the company originated including marketing and sales.

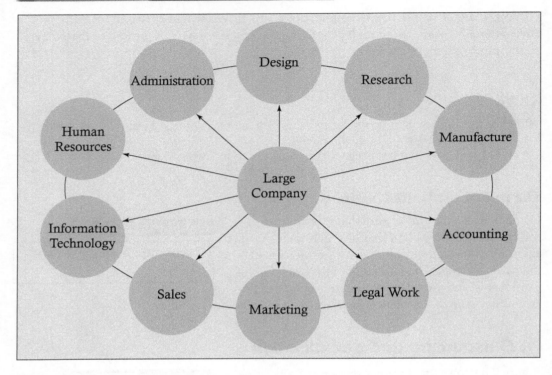

Figure 9.4 Parts of a large company

The research, design and development of ideas also usually remains in the home country as engineering expertise is harder to outsource and a complete loss of jobs to overseas would not be sensible.

James Dyson, the British inventor of the bagless vacuum cleaner manufactured the cleaners in the UK until 2002. Due to manufacturing costs being 30 per cent lower in Malaysia (a NIC), production moved there resulting in 800 jobs being lost in the UK. 1200 engineering jobs in research and development were kept in the UK as was much of the administration.

Figure 9.5 You cannot outsource me

task I

Describe the impact that losing their jobs can have on people.

Outsourcing of services

Someone in the UK who rings their local bank usually speaks to an operator in an Indian call centre many thousands of miles away. Modern communications means much can be done the other side of the world where labour costs are lower. Advice and transfer of money takes place remotely and so location is not important.

Definition

Remotely: far away but accessed immediately via telecommunications

task J

Explain how outsourcing work to developing countries stimulates the local economy.

Some IT services in the UK have outsourced work to both India and Brazil. This has two advantages.

1. The company can offer a 24 hour service to the public without people doing night shifts.
2. Work on a computer programme can continue non-stop.

task K

With the help of a world map explain how the companies are able to do this without having to employ people on night shifts.

🌐 The importance of transportation to globalisation

Outsourcing of goods and services depends on transportation by road, rail, sea and air and on telecommunications. Supply chains are now interconnected across the globe with the internet being used to trace the whereabouts of goods at any one time and to make transactions.

International trade now consists more and more of semi-processed goods and producer goods which move across the world before becoming a consumer good. A part may even travel between countries more than once. Two major improvements that have made the transport of goods easier are the following.

1. Containerisation

As goods are moved from lorry to train to ship to lorry, the process is much easier if all the goods are inside one standardised container which will fit on all the different methods of transport. Easier means quicker which means cheaper. Figure 9.6 shows some containers that have come straight off a ship at a port and now waiting to be loaded onto a train.

2. Electronic tracking and billing

At each stage of a journey, a barcode on the goods is electronically scanned and recorded so

Figure 9.6   Containers at port
Source: Stephen Taylor

shippers know where their goods are at any one time. People receiving goods can look on the internet to find out the expected delivery time or if the goods have been delayed.

task L

Paraguay, a landlocked country in South America, exports leather goods to an inland town in Italy. How many stages are there in the journey? Explain how containerisation and electronic tracking help the buyers and the sellers of the goods.

Ports

As the volume of goods moved between countries grows, the capacity of ports has to be increased to handle the extra trade. If there is little space along the coast, a distribution centre may be built inland such as the cold-storage container depot at Viana, inland from Angola's main port of Luanda. Port activities may have a negative effect on local communities as congestion leads to air pollution as lorries wait in queues.

Railways

Before the railways, ships and animals moved goods huge distances along ancient trade routes. The Benguela railway built by Britain to export copper from Central Africa was just one of the many rail routes along which trade later took place.

Today, regional projects such as the plan to connect Tanzania, Burundi and Rwanda and national projects such as the proposed link between Lagos and Kano in Nigeria show how trade still leads to changes in transport networks. South Africa is considering a high speed rail link between Johannesburg (the main centre of industry) and Durban (the main port). Besides providing jobs, these projects benefit trade within Africa and also with other continents.

Roads

Roads are vital in linking the areas of production to the rail stations or ports. Individual farms and industrial areas cannot possibly all have rail links but all-weather surfaced roads are the beginning of what may be a very long journey across the world to a consumer. New roads are being built to make trade easier, such as the continuation of the Trans Amazonian Highway to the Pacific Ocean. In India, the value of rural roads to trade for local communities is considered in Chapter 20.

task M Consider the advantages and disadvantages of road and of rail travel for the movement of goods.

Logistics

Logistics is the term used to describe how the movement of goods is managed from its point of origin until it reaches the consumer. It includes not only transportation, but storage, tracking and security. It co-ordinates different parts of a complicated system and the more efficient it is, the faster and more cheaply the goods are moved. As trade volumes have grown around the world, logistics operations have become more and more important to businesses in making sure goods arrive safely and on time.

- Developing countries often have to rely on FDI in the form of MNCs to extract resources and produce goods for export
- MNCs bring economic and social benefits to a country
- MNCs may cause problems for communities and the natural environment where they operate
- Globalisation and outsourcing of production and services promotes development
- Improvements in transportation and communication systems are essential for economic growth.

Summary

Questions

Question 1

Figure 1 shows the percentage of the male population in six countries employed in different sectors of the economy.

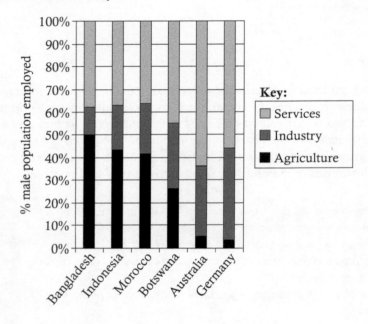

Figure 1

(a) (i) What percentage of the male population of Bangladesh is employed in agriculture? [1]

    (ii) Name **one** country in Figure 1 which is at an early stage of development. [1]

    (iii) Describe how the percentage of people employed in the different sectors of the economy changes as countries develop. [2]

    (iv) Explain why the percentage of people employed in the different sectors of the economy changes as countries develop. [3]

(b) Study Figure 2 which shows different types of services.

    (i) What is meant by services? [1]

    (ii) Choose any type of service and describe how it changes as a country develops. [3]

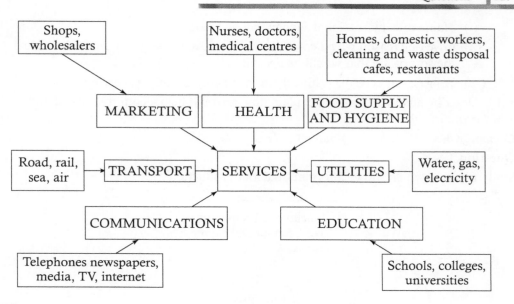

Figure 2

    (iii) What type of economy has some services in private ownership and some in public ownership? [1]

    (iv) Describe some of the advantages of **either** private ownership or public ownership. [2]

  (c) Choose an example of a manufacturing industry and describe how its production process and its output are linked to the other sectors of the economy and to global trade. [6]

Cambridge 0453 P1 Q3 Oct/Nov2010

Question 2

  (a) Study Figure 3 which shows different kinds of foreign aid.

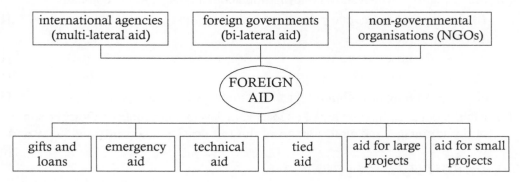

Figure 3 Aid Donors

(i) Name one international agency that gives aid. [1]

(ii) Give one reason why a country might be given emergency aid and describe the sort of aid that would be needed. [2]

(iii) Suggest one type of technical aid that a country might receive. [1]

(b) Describe an aid project and explain how it would help a country's social and economic development. [6]

Cambridge 0453 P1 Q4 b (i), (ii) and (iv) and c Oct/Nov 2010

Question 3

Study Figure 4 which shows information about production.

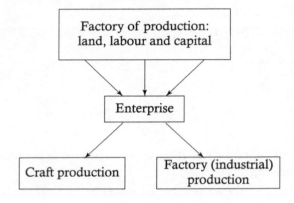

Figure 4

(a) (i) What is meant by *land as* a factor of production? [1]

(ii) Name **two** types of capital used in industry. [2]

(iii) What is the purpose of enterprise in the industrial process? [1]

(iv) How do labour and technology used in factory production differ from those used in craft production? [2]

(b) Study Figure 5 which shows information about a large clothing company.

(i) In what type of country does Gap have its shops? [1]

(ii) What is meant by:

   A *free trade zones* [1]

   B *specialised skills* [1]

(iii) Explain fully how Gap is typical of a multinational company. [5]

(c) Multinational companies are often located in developing countries. Describe some of the advantages and disadvantages of this to a developing country and its citizens. [6]

Cambridge 0453 P1 Q2 Oct/Nov 2008

Gap

Gap is a world leader in the clothing industry. The company has created on image of fashionable, affordable clothing. It has become one of the most profitable and fastest growing clothing retailers,with shops in the USA, UK, France, Germany, Canada, and Japan. At first the company sold clothing which was sewn in the USA from home-grown cotton. More recently it has become one of the world's leading clothing companies, buying products from suppliers in approximately 50 countries. Its brand names are Gap, Old Navy and Banana Republic.

Like other multinational (transnational) companies. Gap takes advantage of new opportunities in global manufacturing to make it more efficient. It saves money by having products made by companies in free trade zones in developing countries. It also uses the specialised skills of different regions, for example Asian people who are skilled at working silk. The management, research and development departments of Gap are in the USA and are continually adjusting its products as fashions change.

Figure 5

Unit 3 | Population and development

Population change and policies

10

🌎 Global population

In 1900, the world's population was 1.5 billion. In the year 2011, the world's population reached 7 billion and about 80 million people are added to the world each year. The world's population has grown at a fast rate over the last few decades and is predicted to grow even more by 2050 as shown in Figure 5.4. Population growth has implications for development as governments have to provide services to more people to ensure everyone has a reasonable standard of living. The rate of growth varies in different parts of the world and in some countries the population is actually decreasing. Figure 10.1 shows how the world's population is distributed across the different regions.

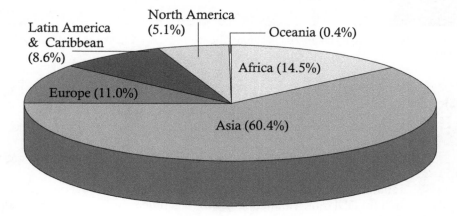

Figure 10.1   Regional distribution of world population (2007)
Source: http://www.un.org/esa/population/publications/wpp2006/WPP2006_Highlights_rev.pdf

task A

Describe the continental distribution of the world's population.

Population growth rates

Table 10.1 shows the population of selected countries from each continent, their natural population growth rate and their HDI rank. A growth rate of 2 per cent means that for every 100 people in a country, a further 2 are added each year. So for a country such as Angola with a population of 13.3m and a natural population growth rate of 2 per cent, this would mean that 266 000 more people would need food, housing and services each year.

Table 10.1 Population statistics for selected countries (2010/2011)

Country	Population (millions)	Natural Population Growth Rate (%)	HDI Rank
Angola	13.3	2.0	146
Kenya	41.1	2.5	128
Pakistan	187.3	1.6	125
Indonesia	245.6	1.1	108
UK	62.7	0.6	26
Germany	81.5	–0.3	10
Brazil	203.0	1.1	73
Mexico	113.7	1.1	56
USA	313.2	1.0	4
Australia	21.8	1.1	2

Source: https://www.cia.gov/library/publications/the-world-factbook/geos/as.html; http://hdr.undp.org/en/statistics/

task B

1. Calculate how many more people are added to Indonesia's population each year.
2. Calculate how many more people are added to Brazil's population each year.
3. Rank the countries from high to low in terms of (a) population growth rates and (b) HDI rank. Compare the two rank orders and state to what extent the lists are similar.

If more and more people are added to the country's population each year, the task of increasing the living standards of the people becomes much more difficult. More people each year require basic services and at the same time more people are seeking an improvement in their quality of life. To meet this increasing demand more pressure is put on the country's resources.

The growth of a population depends upon the following.

1. The Birth Rate (BR) – the number of people born.
2. The Death Rate (DR) – the number of people who die.
3. Immigration – the number of people who move into the country to live.
4. Emigration – the number of people who leave the country to live elsewhere.

The Natural Increase (NI) is the difference between the BR and the DR. If the DR is greater than the BR, the population will decrease naturally. Germany's BR is 8/1000 population and its DR is 11/1000. This means more people are dying than are being born which explains its negative growth rate in Table 10.1. If the BR is considerably larger than the DR, there is a 'population explosion' which has serious consequences for development.

Definition

Population explosion: the inhabitants suddenly increasing in number

Angola's growth rate

Angola's BR is 43/1000 population and its DR is 23/1000 population. In this case, the NI is 43 minus 23 which is equal to 20/1000 population. So the population of the country is growing naturally by 20/1000 people per year or by 2/100. This is a natural growth rate of 2 per cent.

The net migration into Angola is 0.82/1000 population which is 0.082/100. So the total population growth rate for the country is 2.08/100 people. This is usually given as a percentage figure, which in this case is 2.08 per cent. When net migration is taken into account as well as natural population growth, Angola's population grew by 276 640 in 2010, of which over 10 000 were migrants.

🌐 Population structure

It is important for governments to know how the population is growing and also how the population is made up in terms of the proportion of the population in each age group. Statistics for these are obtained from a census.

Definition

Census: an official count or survey of a population

Countries at different stages of development have different population structures and these can be shown on a population pyramid (age-sex pyramid). A population pyramid is divided into genders and age groups. Sometimes the figures for the different age groups are given as a percentage of the total population or the figures are given in millions (or thousands). The age groups are then grouped together to form the dependent and independent populations.

A country that is in the process of development is likely to move through different stages in terms of changes to its population structure. As countries tend to follow a similar pattern as they develop, it is possible for governments to forecast the changes that are likely to take place and plan their development projects accordingly. For example, if the population is ageing and fewer children are being born then there is no point in building a lot more schools.

task C

Suggest why the data collected in a census may not be reliable.

Countries in early stages of development

The population structure of Niger, a country ranked as one of low human development, is shown in Figure 10.2.

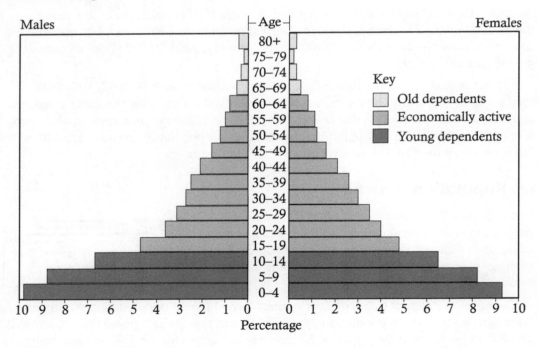

Figure 10.2 Population pyramid for Niger, Africa

Source: http://unstats.un.org/unsd/demographic/products/dyb/dyb2006/Table07.pdf

task D

From Figure 10.2 estimate the proportion of the population that is dependent on the working population.

The main features of the population structure of Niger are:

1. A large proportion of the population are children aged 0–14 which means a high BR.
2. A small proportion of the population are aged over 65 which means a high DR.
3. A very small proportion of the population are aged over 70 which means a low LE i.e., life expectancy.
4. A large proportion of children are under 15 which means a high dependency ratio.

Niger has a high BR of 51 births/1000 population and a high DR of 14/1000 population. The natural growth rate is therefore 3.7 per cent. 49 per cent of its population are aged 0–14 and as this large proportion of children move up into the years of child bearing the population will continue to increase.

Globally women tend to live longer than men, but risks from frequent childbirth tend to increase the chances of women dying early in the least developed countries. This helps explain why there are fewer females than males aged over 80.

Causes of a high birth rate

A high BR in the least developed countries is due to a number of reasons:

- little family planning and education in birth control
- contraceptives are unavailable, too costly or forbidden for religious reasons
- children are needed to work at home, on the land or earn money
- children are needed to look after the elderly in the absence of pensions
- lack of education and therefore careers for women
- traditional beliefs such as that girls are ready to marry at very young ages
- large families indicate male virility and enhance prestige in the community
- high IMR means families have many children in the hope that some survive.

Fertility rates

Fertility rates give the average number of children that women have and these rates for each continent can be seen in Figure 10.3.

task E

Describe the main features of the chart shown in Figure 10.3.

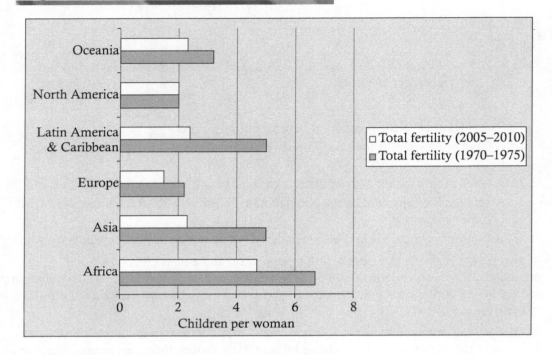

Figure 10.3 Changing fertility rates for continents

Source: http://www.un.org/esa/population/publications/wpp2006/WPP2006_Highlights_rev.pdf

Methods to reduce the birth rate

There is a need to bring about changes in the attitudes of men to the role of women in their society. Empowerment of women will allow them to be educated and have careers which mean they may marry later and have fewer children. A job will mean an income so they will not depend on their children going out to work or looking after them when they are old. Governments need to provide family planning services in all areas so women understand the importance of child spacing to protect their health and the health of their children. Contraceptives should be freely available or cheap.

Laws to raise the age at which girls are allowed to marry, to abolish child labour and make schooling compulsory for both boys and girls are also essential. Educated women understand methods of disease prevention and the importance of taking their children to clinics for check-ups and vaccinations. Improving health care and providing clean water and good sanitation to make sure more infants survive will reduce the need to have large numbers of children.

task F

From the paragraph above, describe how women can be empowered by government action to reduce the BR.

Figure 10.4 shows a vicious circle of poverty and how it can be broken by the education of girls and women in family planning issues.

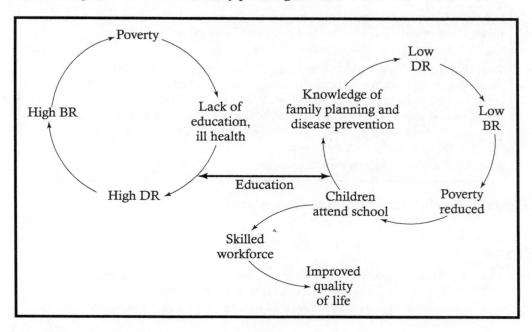

Figure 10.4   How to break a vicious circle of poverty

MDG 5 is to improve maternal health. Target 5B is to achieve, by 2015, universal access to reproductive health services. However, many husbands do not wish to consider family planning and women are often subjected to domestic violence if they raise the issue with their husbands. Many women in traditional patriarchal societies would be unlikely even to consider discussing the issue.

During the 1990s, use of contraceptives increased among women in almost every region, but since 2000 progress has slowed down and in some regions such as Sub-Saharan Africa use of contraceptives is still very low. If women who want to avoid pregnancy had contraception available to them the number of maternal deaths would be reduced as the timing and spacing of pregnancies would enable women to look after themselves. However, government policies and funding have not kept up with the demand for family planning.

Effects of a high birth rate

A high BR can mean that parents cannot afford to look after the whole family. It may mean that children do not go to school as they are needed to bring income into the household to help feed the growing family. Families may not be able to afford healthcare for all their children.

Figure 10.5 shows what is happening in rural Mozambique due to high fertility rates.

In Mozambique, for example, high fertility rates are a public health issue, particularly for mothers who do not have at least two years between pregnancies and who are therefore weakened and vulnerable to illness.

Women in rural Mozambique typically do all the farming, and if pregnancy or poor health prevents them from producing enough food for the family, the children risk going hungry or becoming malnourished. In one northern province, Cabo Delgado, where almost one in three girls is married before the age of 15 and where only 3 per cent of the female population uses modern contraception, about 59 per cent of children are chronically malnourished.

Source: Extract from http://www.unfpa.org/swp/

Figure 10.5   High fertility rates in Mozambique

task G

1. Explain how children in large families can become malnourished.
2. Explain how this can become costly for the government.
3. Explain how high BRs may lead to countries missing some targets for the MDGs.

Over 40 per cent of the world's population consists of young people under 25 years old. The youth want a good education and health care and also employment that will allow them to fulfil their potential. Global recessions mean unemployment levels are high but for developing countries to grow economically these young people need to be able to contribute their energy and skills. If they do not then this is a terrible waste of talent.

Causes of a high death rate

A high DR in the least developed countries is due to a number of reasons:

- lack of clean water supplies and good sanitation
- inadequate health facilities
- poor quantity of food and lack of a balanced diet
- lack of education into disease prevention and healthy living
- HIV/AIDS and other disease epidemics
- war and natural disasters such as drought.

task H

Describe the methods that could be used to reduce the DR.

Countries in middle stages of development

Figure 10.6 shows the population pyramid for Sri Lanka which is ranked as one of medium human development.

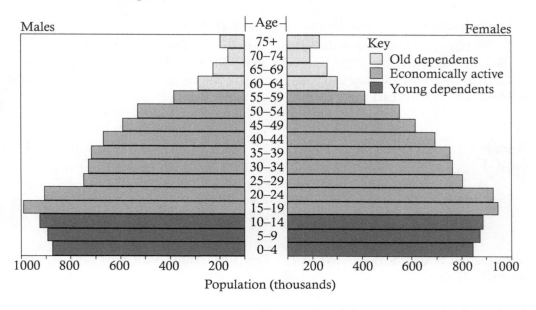

Figure 10.6 Population pyramid for Sri Lanka
Source: http://unstats.un.org/unsd/demographic/pro.ducts/dyb/dyb2006/Table07.pdf

The main features of the population structure of Sri Lanka are:

1. A small proportion of children in the lower age groups which means a falling BR.
2. A large proportion of people living into middle-age and beyond which means a rapidly falling DR.
3. A large proportion of people living over 75 which means a longer LE.
4. A large independent population which means a low dependency ratio.

task 1 Sri Lanka's BR is 17/1000 and its DR is 6/1000. Calculate its natural growth rate and from Figure 10.6 work out the percentage population aged 0–14. Compare these figures with those of Niger.

Causes of a falling birth rate

As countries develop, the BR starts to fall for a number of reasons:

- government policies to increase family planning education and knowledge of birth control

- availability of low cost contraception
- increased empowerment of women through education
- reduction in the IMR – there is less need to have many children to ensure some survive
- abolition of child labour/improved technology on farms.

In this stage of development, the BR has started to fall but has not fallen as rapidly as the DR. While health care has improved, many parents still want large numbers of children as traditions are hard to break. The large numbers of children in the age groups 0–14 will be of child bearing age themselves in a few years.

task J Consider the 6 bullet points in 'Causes of a high DR' on page 138. Draw a spider diagram with writing or sketches to show all the factors that could lead to a reduction in the DR. Develop the health and education points to give examples such as 'increased vaccination'.

As the DR is reduced people live longer. This is happening in all areas of the world as shown in Table 10.2.

Table 10.2 Life expectancy at birth (years)

Major Area	2005–2010		2045–2050 (estimate)	
	Male	Female	Male	Female
More developed regions	72.9	80.2	79.4	85.4
Less developed regions	63.7	67.2	72.1	76.5
Least developed countries	53.4	55.8	65.4	69.1

Source: http://www.un.org/esa/population/publications/wpp2006/WPP2006_Highlights_rev.pdf

task K Draw a bar chart to represent the data shown in Table 10.2 and describe the main features of the chart.

Countries in late stages of development

Countries that are the most developed have the highest HDI rankings. Countries in late stages of development are often characterised by populations that are growing naturally only slowly, or they may even be decreasing. Immigration, however, may be high and so reverse this trend. Figure 10.7 shows a population pyramid for Norway, ranked first in the world HDI rankings for 2011.

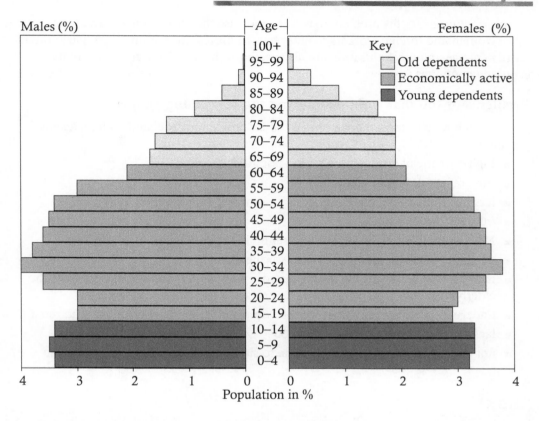

Figure 10.7 Population structure of Norway
Source: http://unstats.un.org/unsd/demographic/products/dyb/dyb2006/Table07.pdf

The main features of the population structure of Norway are:
1. A small proportion of children which means a low BR.
2. A large proportion of people are over 65 which means a low DR.
3. A fairly large proportion of people live to over 80 and some to over 100 which means a high LE.
4. A large proportion of the population are not in the working age group which means a high dependency ratio.

High dependency ratio

A falling BR and increased LE means that there is a high dependent population and a smaller independent population. There are growing numbers of old people and fewer people of working age. This is called a high dependency ratio and it means that each worker may have to support more of the dependent population.

In some cases, companies may find it difficult to employ enough workers. Economic growth will be difficult, exports may decline and trade deficits increase.

Some solutions to this problem may be to increase the retirement age and to encourage more women and foreign workers to enter the workforce. Retraining as people approach retirement age and mechanisation are also methods that can be used to ensure the economy continues to grow.

Problems of too many old people and too few young people

Besides a labour shortage, there are many other problems associated with an ageing population:

- higher financial burden on working population/raised taxes
- time off work for caring duties
- less innovative workforce/difficulty in adapting to new technology
- influx of foreign workers
- MNCs less likely to be attracted to set up in the country or may move out
- need for more care homes/services for the elderly
- increased waiting time for health care due to high demand on services from the elderly
- underuse/closure of facilities for the young – further travel for those who remain
- lack of young consumers to buy goods
- not enough workers in years to come to support growing number of elderly.

task
L

Using speech bubbles for different people, illustrate the social and economic effects of an increasingly elderly population on the workers of a country.

Services for the elderly

In 2011, there were less than 1 billion people over the age of 60 in the world. By 2050, this number will rise to 2.4 billion. Elderly people who cannot look after themselves are looked after either by the state or more usually by their families. In rural Mexico, the government pays people over 70 a small allowance so they can contribute to the household income so they are not seen as a burden.

In developed countries, the elderly are provided with many services by the government. Some of these are shown in Figure 10.8. In developing countries even the most basic of services may not be afforded and an increasingly ageing population is a real worry for these governments.

The economy will suffer if workers have to stay at home to look after their old parents. If children are the carers they will not go to school which will affect future economic growth and a government's ability to improve living standards. As more people live longer more people get diseases associated with old age. Alzheimer's disease and surgery such as hip replacements increase the strain on health services.

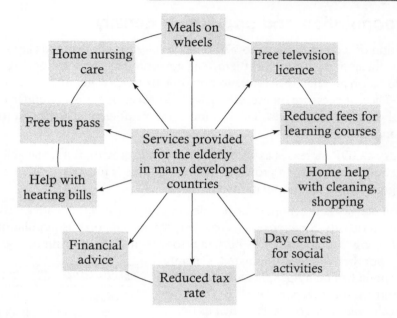

Figure 10.8 Services provided for the elderly

China's policy for its ageing population

'China is getting old before it is getting rich'. Government policy is to look after the elderly in their own homes rather than having to provide extra accommodation and services and this is generally the solution older people prefer anyway. However, the government is encouraging the private sector to build care homes and make available products that make older people's lives easier.

In Shaanxi province, extra allowances are given to older people i.e., 80–89 year olds get 50 yuan per month, 90–99 year olds get 100 yuan and those over 100 years get 200 yuan (over US$30). Committees have been set up to organise activities for older people and ensure their rights are protected. There is even a special college which teaches them computer skills, painting and other crafts. By 2015, the government will provide all elderly people in rural areas with state pensions to ensure equity with those in urban areas.

Definition ═══
Equity: fairness

task M

1. Explain how the elderly might be encouraged to play a more active role in your community.
2. List some of the products that would make older people's lives easier.
3. Explain how a large elderly population might affect the development of a country.

Overpopulation and population density

The population of a country may grow so rapidly that people's demands are greater than the ability of the country to support them. The governments cannot supply sufficient housing, education and health services to everyone or clean water and good sanitation to all areas. There is pressure on everything and the government is put under immense strain as it always has more to do. The resources are insufficient and the country is said to be overpopulated.

If a country's GDP increases as a result of economic growth, it may be able to provide the extra services required for a growing population. This is unlikely if there is a high population growth rate or a population explosion.

Population density is the number of people per unit area of land. Cities have a very high population density. Singapore is a crowded city but supports its population to high standards of living through use of its human resources in finance, insurance and trade services. It is not therefore overpopulated. Calcutta on the other hand has many people living in extreme poverty and is overpopulated. At the other end of the scale, vast areas of deserts such as the Sahara and other inhospitable regions of the world have low population densities.

Definition

Inhospitable: a difficult environment in which to live

Population Policies

Many people believe that some form of population control is necessary if the earth is going to be able to sustain the human population that is putting increasing demands upon its resources. Various governments have adopted a range of policies in attempts to control their population growth such as China's One Child Policy. As population structures change some governments have to adopt measures to try to increase their population growth, such as in Russia.

China's One Child Policy

In the 1970s the fertility rate in China was over 5. Today it is less than 2. This is largely due to China's One Child Policy which has been responsible for the fact that there are now 300 million less children in China today than there would otherwise have been. However, some feel the BR would have started to reduce anyway due to greater access to family planning and education of women in general.

The main features of this policy which vary from state to state are:
- couples are only allowed to have one child
- the age at which people could marry was raised
- priority is given in job applications and extra pension benefits
- preferential hospital treatment and schooling as well as housing benefits are given

- heavy fines are handed out on the birth of a second child which can be three times the annual income of the couple
- propaganda spreads the message
- communal pressure is put on women to ensure targets are met.

There are exceptions to the one child rule such as if a first baby is disabled and also in rural areas if the first child is a girl. Ethnic minorities are allowed more than one child as are parents now if both the mother and father are single children themselves. There are many issues resulting from the policy such as rich people could afford to pay the fines but many poorer women have been forced to abort second babies and be sterilised.

Some new-born girl babies were killed or abandoned at birth as couples wanted a male heir. In 2000, there were 21 million more young men and boys under the age of 20 than young women and girls. Table 10.3 shows how fertility rates are lower in China than in India and its population is likely to stop growing sooner.

Table 10.3   Population statistics for China and India

	China	India
Total population 2011	1.35b	1.24b
Increase 2001–2011	69.7m	170.1m
Fertility rate	1.6	2.5
Year population likely to stabilise	2025	2060

Source: http://www.unfpa.org/swp/

Russia's population policy

Russia's BR is 11/1000 population and its DR is 16/1000 population. The natural population growth rate is minus 0.5 per cent. It is estimated that Russia's population could shrink by over 40 million by 2050. Population decline is a serious problem. Russia is a huge country and as populations fall in remote areas, services decline which means people often move elsewhere leaving vast areas uninhabited. With a shrinking army the country becomes unable to defend its borders and threat of invasion by foreign forces becomes very real. Fewer economically active people mean less production and fewer taxes even though the numbers of elderly people may be rising and they require more services and pensions. The number of consumers of goods falls and this, together with the possible lack of workers does not encourage investors.

Russia has therefore had a policy to try to increase its population and it has done this in two main ways.

1. Increase the number of births. Since 2006, a financial incentive of US$10 000 has been given to families on their child's third birthday. Rewards were given to anyone who gave birth on June 12, Russia Day and propaganda posters showing patriotic women with three children have been widely displayed.

2. Encourage immigration, especially Russian speaking migrants.

Reducing the very high mortality rate for men of reproductive age through better health care and also developing pre-school education to help working mothers are other options to solve the problem.

task

N

1. Describe the problems there may be in China as a result of the gender imbalance in the population.
2. Describe the problems that may arise if large numbers of foreign workers immigrate into a country.

- Population growth depends on a number of factors
- Changes in BR and DR result from and have consequences for development
- An ageing population will be an issue for all countries at some stage
- Population policies can help to address population issues.

Summary

Urbanisation

11

Learning Objectives

- ꙮ To understand the difference between urbanisation and urban growth
- ꙮ To consider the reasons why people move from rural areas to towns
- ꙮ To understand people's perceptions of life in urban areas
- ꙮ To appreciate conditions in shanty settlements
- ꙮ To consider ways life in these settlements can be improved
- ꙮ To realise that urbanisation has impacts on rural areas.

Urbanisation and urban growth

Countries in the early stages of development have a large proportion of people living in rural areas. As countries develop, more people move from the rural areas to live in the urban areas. Urbanisation results from this movement. Urban growth occurs as a result of this migration as well as from natural population increase. Table 11.1 shows the percentage of people living in urban areas for selected countries. The countries are grouped largely by continent.

> **Definition** ═══════════
>
> **Urbanisation**: an increase in the proportion of people living in towns

task
A Based on the Table 11.1 overleaf:

1. Draw a scatter graph to show the relationship between per cent urban population and HDI rank.
2. Describe the general relationship between the two sets of data.
3. Identify any anomalies and state whether they are developing countries or more developed ones.

The reasons why people move from the countryside to live in the towns in developing countries are many and varied. One of the main reasons is that many rural dwellers live below the poverty line and they believe life will be better in the towns. It is estimated that the urban population will be larger than the rural one in developing countries by 2025.

Table 11.1 Population data for selected countries (2010)

Country	Urban Population (%)	HDI Rank	Major City & Population (millions)	Second Largest City's Population (millions)	Net Migration Rate (Migrants/1000 Population)
United States	82	4	*New York* 19.3	12.7	4.2
Mexico	78	56	*Mexico City* 19.3	4.3	−3.2
Brazil	87	73	*Sao Paulo* 20.0	11.8	−0.1
Argentina	92	46	*Buenos Aires* 13.0	1.5	0
United Kingdom	80	26	*London* 8.6	2.3	2.6
Mali	36	160	*Bamako* 1.6	N/A	−12.6
Angola	59	146	*Luanda* 4.5	1.0	0.8
Kenya	22	128	*Nairobi* 3.4	1.0	0
South Africa	62	112	*Johannesburg* 3.6	3.4	−6.2
Sierra Leone	38	158	*Freetown* 0.9	N/A	−4.25
India	30	121	*New Delhi* 21.7	19.7	−0.1
China	47	89	*Shanghai* 16.6	12.2	−0.3
Indonesia	44	108	*Jakarta* 9.1	2.5	−1.2
Australia	89	2	*Sydney* 4.4	3.9	6.0

Source: https://www.cia.gov/library/publications/the-world-factbook/index.html
http://hdr.undp.org/en/statistics/

The following case study considers the reasons for the growth of Nairobi and the characteristics of Kibera, a shanty town that has grown up on the outskirts of the city to accommodate the growing number of people who have moved to live there.

Although the details of this study are specific to Nairobi, the general principles apply in many places in the developing world. The historical background will vary from country to country but it is important to consider the past to be able to understand the present situation.

🌍 Nairobi, Kenya

History

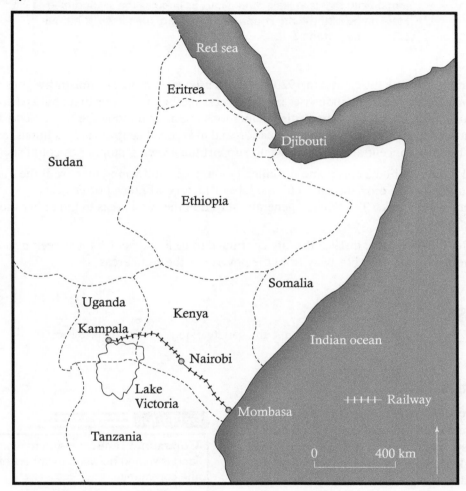

Figure 11.1   Kenya and the Horn of Africa

In the 1880s, British companies wanted to exploit the raw materials of Africa and so built a railway from Mombasa through Nairobi to Kampala in Uganda which is shown in Figure 11.1. Nairobi became the focus of the engineering works and so a town became established. In 100 years, Nairobi has grown from nothing to be the largest city in Kenya. It is now a primate city being considerably larger than the next urban area in size. This uneven development where one city completely dominates the others is a common legacy of the colonial era and after independence these cities continued to grow at the expense of smaller towns. Table 11.1 shows this feature in selected countries.

task B
1. List the countries together with their HDI rank from Table 11.1 which have a main city that is at least three times as large as the second biggest city.
2. How many of these are countries with a very high level of human development (rank 1–42)?

Nairobi became the capital in 1920 which focused even more administrative jobs into the town. Manufacturing industries set up processing the food crops that could easily be transported by rail from the British plantations inland and along the coast. Service industries such as finance, health, education and also social centres such as hotels, golf clubs became concentrated in the town to support the growing number of colonists.

All these required a cheap and unskilled labour force and young men from the surrounding areas moved there to fill the jobs of factory workers, porters, cleaners, gardeners and cooks. The women generally stayed in the rural areas to look after the home.

After independence in 1963 the city continued to be a magnet for those seeking a job and hoping for a better life away from the poverty of the rural areas.

task C

In your own words describe the variety of jobs available in Nairobi.

Politics

Before 1900, land in Kenya was farmed under a system of communal tenure. The different indigenous groups did not realise they had to make a claim for the land they had always regarded as their own. So the British took over the better land and pushed the local people into reserves on the poorer land. The white settlers set up huge plantations and Nairobi was in the centre of an area known as 'The White Highlands'. People from different ethnic groups came from all over rural Kenya to work there.

> **Definition**
>
> **Communal tenure**: a system where land is shared between members of the community
>
> **Plantation**: a large commercial farm often owned by companies and growing one crop for export

After independence many white farmers left and some of the land came into the hands of well organised groups and politicians. In the 1970s, a 'Back to the Land Policy' resettled people from the crowded urban areas on land that had been owned by white settlers. However, this land was probably originally farmed by people of another ethnic group who themselves had been displaced by the colonists.

Ethnic tensions grew because groups wanted to reclaim land that was traditionally theirs. Many people who thought they had obtained land legally were evicted and farm workers fearing ethnic violence moved to Nairobi for safety.

task D   Explain why it is difficult to know who owns the land around Nairobi.

Economics

Low prices for food in the world market affect incomes of workers in the rural areas. In more recent years food prices have soared due to increased demand. This has benefitted landowners but rural workers have had to use more of their income to purchase food to eat. For those already living on or below the poverty line, this may not be possible and another reason to seek 'better conditions' in the towns.

Apart from farm work there has traditionally been little employment in rural areas surrounding Nairobi compared with the availability of jobs in the town. As well as food processing, there are also heavy industries refining oil and making steel and cement etc.

Each manufacturing industry generates employment in associated service industries such as the refineries need workers in construction, maintenance, the docks, transport and finance. Tourism is now a very large employer.

task E
1. Draw a spider diagram to show at least ten jobs that are associated with a steelworks.
2. Draw another diagram to show ten jobs in the tourist industry that could be found in Nairobi.

Family and culture

In many societies, the land is divided up between sons on the death of the head of the family. These smaller units may be too small to provide enough food to eat or sell which means some family members have no choice but to migrate to town.

The patriarchal system of inheritance means that if a woman is widowed and she has no sons, her land would go to her husband's brothers. She would then be landless and be likely to migrate to the nearest town in order to survive.

> **Definition**
>
> **Patriarchal**: a society in which men hold the power and land is passed to male children

Women who have become pregnant before marriage are usually shunned by their family and community.

These women may migrate to the towns where they could 'disappear' and start a new life for themselves often funded by the oldest trade in the world, prostitution.

Today, changing attitudes and greater freedoms for women mean that if they have an entrepreneurial spirit and good networking abilities, they are often successful in running their own businesses in the informal sector in the towns. In the past, it was mainly the men who migrated to the towns. Now the genders are more evenly balanced.

> **Definition**
>
> **Entrepreneurial:** capable of setting up a business
>
> **Networking:** connecting and interacting with people

task F Give four reasons why women migrate to towns from the rural areas.

Social

The provision of services in rural areas is usually much poorer than in the urban areas. Often the settlements in rural areas are small and people are spread out over vast areas so connecting them all to electricity, mains water and improved sanitation services is not only very expensive but also a very lengthy process. There is also the problem that high levels of poverty in the rural areas mean that even if these services were provided, many people would not be able to afford them. Absence of proper roads means transport of goods to market is difficult. Daily journeys to schools in the urban areas are often impossible as are visits to hospitals in town.

Entertainment such as cinemas, restaurants and clubs are usually non-existent in rural areas and young people often want to experience the 'bright lights' they have heard about. Activities in villages are usually small scale and run by community members and sometimes do not appeal to young people.

Governments are always looking towards the next election and the need for votes. It makes sense to keep the largest number of voters happy by providing them with services. This is another reason governments focus their expenditure on urban rather than rural areas.

task G Choose three forms of infrastructure from the paragraph above.
Explain how the quality of life of people is improved if they have access to these services.

Table 11.2 shows the proportion of the population in rural and urban areas with access to an improved water source and improved sanitation in Kenya and other selected countries in 1990 and 2008.

Table 11.2 Access to improved sanitation and an improved drinking water source in selected countries

Country	Proportion of population using an improved sanitation facility (1990 estimate)				Proportion of population using an improved drinking water source (1990 estimate)			
	Urban		Rural		Urban		Rural	
	1990	2008	1990	2008	1990	2008	1990	2008
Angola	58	86	6	18	30	60	40	38
Bangladesh	57	55	28	52	88	85	76	78
Bolivia	29	34	6	9	92	96	42	67
Brazil	81	87	35	37	96	99	65	84
China	48	58	38	52	97	98	56	82
Indonesia	58	67	22	36	92	89	62	71
Kenya	24	27	27	32	91	83	32	52
Mexico	80	90	30	68	94	96	64	87
South Africa	80	84	58	65	98	99	66	78
Thailand	93	95	74	96	97	99	89	98

Figure 11.2 is a chart representing the data for access to an improved drinking water source.

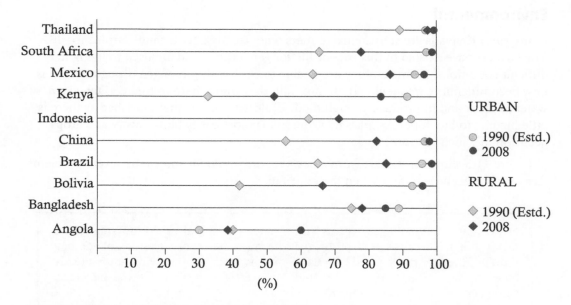

Figure 11.2 Access to an improved drinking water source

Source: http://unstats.un.org/unsd/mdg/Default.aspx, http://data.worldbank.org/indicator

task H
1. Describe the main trends shown in Figure 11.2.
2. Draw a similar chart to show the changes in the proportion of people with access to improved sanitation for the countries in the table.
3. Describe the main features of the chart.

Target 7C of MDG 7 is to halve, by 2015, the proportion of people without sustainable access to safe drinking water and basic sanitation. Considering the figures for Kenya, in 1990, 68 per cent of the rural population did not have access to a clean water supply. To meet Target 7C for these areas it will be necessary to reach a figure of 66 per cent access to clean water by 2015 [32+34 (half of 68)].

task I
1. Do a similar calculation to obtain a target percentage for access to improved sanitation by 2015.
2. Do you think Kenya is likely to meet these targets in rural areas if you consider the figures for 2008?

Environmental

Many rural Kenyans are subsistence farmers who usually have a small surplus to sell. The farmers have existed in this way of life for generations and are used to living in difficult conditions. However, they are unable to cope with prolonged drought which is now becoming more frequent. When rains fail, they find it hard to find enough clean water to drink and to produce enough food. Children become malnourished as there is little income to buy food. As grass dies, the soil is more easily blown away and crops need soil in which to grow.

Figure 11.3 shows an extract from a news report which illustrates the severe problems Kenyan farmers have to face when the rains fail.

> More than one million Kenyans risk facing hunger because of a prolonged drought, the UN has warned. The lack of rains has caused crops to fail and cattle-herders are also struggling to keep their animals alive. Many subsistence farmers are reported to be abandoning rural areas...and moving into already congested slums in the towns and cities.
>
> **Source**: Extract from http://news.bbc.co.uk – 2009-08-20

Figure 11.3 Media report on the 2009 drought in Kenya

task J

The reasons why people move from the rural areas are often called 'push' factors and the reasons that they are attracted to the towns are called 'pull' factors.
1. Make a list of all the 'push' factors that make people want to leave the rural areas.
2. Describe what you think people's perceptions are of life in the towns.

Definition

Perception: understanding and awareness

Characteristics of Kibera, Nairobi

As people flock to an urban area, there are not enough proper houses to live in and in any case many people cannot afford the rent. There are not enough jobs for everyone. Huge slums grow up to accommodate these migrants.

These shanty towns are usually set up in parts of the town that are difficult to build on, such as steep hillsides or areas likely to flood or suffer from landslips. Otherwise they are in areas where people would not choose to live, such as next to noisy transport corridors and

Figure 11.4 Part of Kibera

factories or next to rubbish dumps. Figure 11.4 shows part of Kibera, a large shanty town on the outskirts of Nairobi.

task K

Describe the main features of the housing shown in Figure 11.4.

The main features of the area are:
- high population density
- each small dwelling may house more than 10 people
- the people make their own dwellings from whatever materials they can find

- people are from many different ethnic groups such as the Luo, Kikuyu, Kamba and Luhya
- crime rates and levels of ethnic violence are high
- half of the residents are under 15 years old
- few residents can afford electricity but some tap illegally into power-lines
- some NGOs provide schooling and health care
- many shacks share one hole in the ground for sanitation
- toilets cost money to use and are closed at night
- waste is dumped on the streets and in the river and waterborne diseases are common
- most people have no legal right to the land and pay no rent
- some areas have water standpipes
- numerous informal activities take place but employment in the formal economy is low
- Kibera keeps growing due to high natural increase and continued in-migration.

task L

Make a list of all the things that are needed in Kibera to make life better for the inhabitants.

Government action

Shanty towns are usually illegal settlements as people have settled on land that does not belong to them, without permission. If governments provide services in these squatter settlements, it looks as if they are giving the dwellers legal rights to the land.

Definition

Squatter: someone who illegally occupies an area of land

Other reasons why governments are reluctant to provide services such as piped water and electricity are because:

- the government does not want more people to be attracted to an improved area
- it is too costly
- most people could not afford to pay for the services
- it would be impossible to provide services for all the new people that arrive each day
- if services are not put in as the city grows it is far more difficult to add them afterwards
- the houses are often too poorly built to support pipework and drains.

However, in some areas governments are working with the slum dwellers to build homes with better structures and with the provision of piped water and good sanitation.

The governments provide the materials and the people dig the trenches for pipework and drains. A sense of community spirit develops which could be useful in further projects.

The Kenyan Slum Upgrading Programme (KENSUP)

MDG 7, Target 7D is to have achieved a significant improvement in the lives of at least 100 million slum dwellers by 2020. In Kibera, this is being done with community involvement by building new housing, an Integrated Water and Sanitation Initiative, road construction and improvements in waste management. KENSUP is jointly funded by the Kenyan government and UN-HABITAT/World Bank Cities Alliance. UN-HABITAT is the UN agency for urban issues and has its base in Nairobi. Figure 11.5 shows the laying of sanitation drains.

Figure 11.5 Part of KENSUP

Source: http://americancity.org/buzz/entry/2247/

The main problems of these schemes are:

- upgrading slums is not a priority for government
- people have to move elsewhere while work is done
- homes have to be demolished with no compensation
- new migrants take over the space that is left
- the population of Kibera continues to increase
- residents sell their rights to a new dwelling and become squatters somewhere else
- powerful landlords are happy with the situation as it is
- the schemes are 'top down' rather than 'bottom up'.

The efforts governments are making around the world and the challenges they face are summed up in this extract from the UN MDG Report, 2010. 'The fact that more than 200 million slum-dwellers have gained access to either improved water, sanitation or durable and less crowded housing shows that countries and municipal governments have made serious attempts to improve slum conditions, thereby enhancing the prospects of millions of people to escape poverty, disease and illiteracy.

However, in absolute terms, the number of slum-dwellers in the developing world is actually growing, and will continue to rise in the near future.'

A different approach in Mathare Valley 4A

In Mathare Valley, another shanty town in Nairobi, The Catholic Archdiocese of Nairobi (NGO) purchased properties from landlords and installed infrastructure such as street lighting. The properties were then rented out at cheaper rates on a non-profit basis.

In return, residents were asked to make improvements to their homes at a scale they could afford. This is more of a 'grass roots' approach and is more likely to succeed.

NGO action

NGOs work to improve the standard of living of people in shanty towns around the world and there are many initiatives in Kibera ranging from providing schools and health care to setting up recycling facilities.

Sport

Community programmes such as those run by 'Carolina for Kibera', an NGO based in the US, keep young people away from crime and encourage racial harmony and friendships. An annual soccer tournament is organised in which teams must include youths from different ethnic groups. Players learn teamwork and make different friends. They also learn about HIV/AIDS prevention in an initiative called 'Caught Offside'.

Tabitha Clinic

A widowed mother of three children, Tabitha was given US$26 by a co-founder of 'Carolina for Kibera', to start a vegetable selling business. With the money she earned she set up a clinic in her own home which is now based in a new thirteen roomed facility with two full-time physicians, x-ray services, a clinical laboratory, a pharmacy, HIV/AIDS counselling services and a youth-friendly reproductive health clinic. These are all run in partnership with the US Centers for Disease Control and Prevention.

Tabitha Clinic offers healthcare to all residents on a sliding-fee scale and over 40 000 patients visit this remarkable clinic in the heart of Kibera every year. Specialising in maternal health, the clinic offers primary care services to residents twenty-four hours a day, seven days a week.

The informal economy

One of the main attractions of the urban area is the hope of a job with enough money coming in regularly to provide adequately for a family. Unfortunately, the perceptions of the towns do not always match the reality. In Nairobi, the few jobs in the formal sector usually require skills and the competition for each one is huge.

In 2005, 90 per cent of all businesses were in the informal sector and the success of these small income-generating activities continues to attract people to the town. The chance to run a business with a huge number of potential local consumers is more attractive than farming. This informal economy in Nairobi is called Jua Kali and includes such enterprises as hairdressers, pubs (with TV football), shops of all sorts, computer services. Whatever the activity is, the income earned helps to improve the lives of the people who live there. Toilet emptying is relatively well paid and parents do this job to earn enough money to send their children to school.

Sack gardens

Sacks filled with earth growing vegetables are a common sight on roofs and on doorsteps as seen in Figure 11.6. The French Government provides the funds and an NGO runs this project which not only provides fresh food containing important vitamins and minerals vital for a balanced diet but it is also a source of income. Money that used to be spent on buying vegetables can be used for something else. One sack can grow 50 seedlings of kale or spinach and 20 tomato plants which are provided by a plant nursery where people are shown how to grow and harvest the crops.

Figure 11.6 Sack gardens in Kibera
Source: http://hopebuilding.pbworks.com

Mary Anyango, who has 'six gardens' or six sacks, uses what she harvests from three sacks and sells the rest. Her family of five feeds on one sack of sukuma wiki for three days whenever the harvest is ready. The other three sacks earn her about $1.90 a week, enough to buy charcoal and cooking fat.

task
M
Explain how the sack gardens may help Kenya to meet targets for certain MDGs.

Cash for trash

Recycling centres have been set up by NGOs which are multipurpose as they:

- remove thousands of tonnes of rubbish per year from the dump
- increase public awareness of the importance of recycling
- create jobs for young people and gives them skills in teamwork, leadership, marketing
- reduce air and water pollution and therefore disease
- develop craft industries with the waste
- reduce crime.

Kibera's community cooker

Rubbish from dumps is collected by the community and brought to the community cooker where it is exchanged for tokens. The collected rubbish is then burnt in the cooker and the tokens used to purchase time for cooking food. A community cooker can solve many problems such as it gets rid of rubbish and creates jobs for young people.

A cooker feeds the poor and provides hot water and so improves community health. It also helps to protect the river systems and stops destruction of woodlands.

task Explain how cooking food with rubbish helps to look after river water and forests.

Other recycling initiatives

Elsewhere in shanty towns around the world people are also collecting waste and making it into something that they can sell. Some of these businesses can be seen in Table 11.3. The slums in Dharavi, Mumbai are a hive of industrial activity as described in Figure 11.7.

Table 11.3 Recycling initiatives

Place	Initiative
Nairobi, Kenya	Recycling plastic bags to make handbags, hats, footballs, baskets
Chennai, India	Recycling polyethylene and plastic wire to make baskets and bags
Chennai, India	Pencil cases, bags, wallets, cooking aprons, umbrella covers, beach mats made from recycled advertising billboards
Kampala, Uganda	Necklaces, earrings, bracelets and bags made from recycled magazines and newspapers
Nairobi, Kenya	Greeting cards made from recycled paper
Mumbai, India	Soap thrown away from hotels is melted down to reform soaps for resale
Nairobi, Kenya	Recycling plastic bags into fencing poles
Mumbai, India	Reforming metal cans and drums for resale

Sustainable settlements

Although living conditions in these sorts of settlements are very poor they are a good example of a sustainable way of life. Housing is made of locally produced materials and built with local labour. Most people have their own business run from home. People support the local markets and shops which sell local products. There is a sense of community that is lacking in many of the vast housing estates of the developed world. Many young people in Kibera have hope and a determination to overcome the problems they face from living in the slums but the following are urgently needed to help the slum dwellers to help themselves:

- the provision of clean water and good sanitation for all
- cheap access to medical care and education
- well educated community leaders with a vision for a better way of life
- security of ownership of the land their house stands on.

Dharavi may be one of the world's largest slums, but it is by far its most prosperous - a thriving business centre propelled by thousands of micro-entrepreneurs who have created an invaluable industry – turning around the discarded waste of Mumbai's 19 million citizens.

All along Apna St hundreds of barefoot street children, human recycling machines, scurry back and forward, hauling bundles of waste – plastic, cardboard or glass – retrieved from Mumbai's vast municipal dumps. From every alley comes the sounds of hammering, drilling and soldering. In every shack, dark figures sit waist-deep in piles of car batteries, computer parts, fluorescent lights, ballpoint pens, plastic bags, paper and cardboard boxes and wire hangers, sorting each item for recycling.

Walking through Dharavi, home to an estimated 15,000 single-room factories, it becomes difficult to conceive of anything that is not made or recycled here. Most of the workshops are constructed illegally on government land, power is routinely stolen and commercial licences are rarely sought. There is just one lavatory for every 1,500 residents, not a single public hospital, and only a dozen municipal schools. Taps run dry most of the time and tankers bring in potable water once in a fortnight.

But Dharavi remains a land of recycling opportunity for many rural Indians. The average household in Dharavi now earns between 3,000 and 15,000 rupees a month (£40–£200), well above agricultural wage levels.

Source: Extract from http://www.guardian.co.uk/environment/2007/mar/04/india.recycling

Figure 11.7 Industrial activity in Dharavi, Mumbai

task

1. Find out the name of a shanty town within your country or region.
2. Describe the conditions in the shanty town.
3. Describe what is being done to help improve the quality of life of the slum dwellers.

Effects on rural areas

The effects of rural to urban migration on rural areas can be summarised as follows:

- women, children and elderly are left to look after the land
- farms lose their male workers so less crops are grown
- there is more room in dwellings and less mouths to feed
- women become decision makers and take more responsibility
- remittances can be used to improve standards of living
- families are broken up and those left behind may become stressed
- fewer services are provided in villages.

Ways to reduce rural to urban migration include improving the economy of the rural areas and improving people's quality of life there by providing adequate services. If efforts to reduce rural poverty have results then the rural areas may become areas where young people want to live and work and so pressures on the shanty towns will reduce. Some of the ways rural areas can be made better places are considered in Chapter 13.

task P

Describe the advantages and disadvantages for rural areas of people migrating to towns.

Practical Research Investigation

Aim   To investigate some features of migration to an urban area.

Objectives

1. To determine the origin of families at the school
2. To determine their length of residency in the town
3. To investigate their reasons for leaving their original home
4. To consider the levels of satisfaction of living in an urban area
5. To assess the disadvantages of using parents/guardians as a source of data.

Methods

- questionnaire for parents/guardians and teachers, including the use of a 'pilot'
- collection of data on migration from local authorities.

For students at rural centres, a similar study could be undertaken but focused on perceptions of urban life and whether migration may be considered. A perception chart could be drawn up with elements such as job availability, entertainment, health facilities, pollution levels, housing quality etc. rated according to how they are perceived on a scale ranging from excellent (5) to poor (1).

Source: Adapted from Appendix to 'Scheme of work, Cambridge IGCSE Development Studies 0453'

- Reasons why people move to towns are many and varied
- The perceptions of migrants are sometimes different from the reality of life in towns
- Measures are being taken to improve conditions in the shanty towns
- There are advantages and disadvantages of migration for rural areas.

Summary

International migration

12

Learning Objectives

⮞ To understand the different types of migration
⮞ To consider the problems for refugees and their effect on the country of destination
⮞ To assess the solutions to the refugee problem
⮞ To understand why people migrate to work overseas and the effect this has on the countries and people involved
⮞ To understand that economic migrants can help countries to develop and meet MDGs.

🌐 Types of international migration

When people move from one country to another it is called international migration. This may be a movement from one country to its neighbour or it can be movement between countries across the world. Whatever form it takes, it has a major impact not only on the migrants themselves but also on the countries of origin and destination.

The net migration rate of certain countries is shown in Table 11.1 together with other statistics about the population of selected countries. Some of the terms used in this chapter are defined in Figure 12.1 below.

Immigrants: people who enter a country to live there

Emigrants: people who leave a country to live somewhere else

Net inward migration: more people enter a country to live there than leave it

Net outward migration: more people leave a country to live somewhere else than enter it

---

Figure 12.1 Migration terminology

There are different types of international migrants.

1. People are forced to migrate to another country to save their lives after a natural disaster or because there is a civil war in their own country. If people move in huge numbers it is usually obvious why they have fled and these people are given asylum in the destination country and classed as refugees with refugees' rights.

2. Economic migrants make a personal decision to move which is often based on wanting to improve a family's standard of living by finding a job or a higher income in another country. This is voluntary migration.

3. People may migrate if they fear persecution due to their political or religious beliefs or race and they are looking for a country where they can live safely with freedom. They are asylum seekers and they may or may not be granted asylum after a lengthy period of interviews. If a country will not allow them to stay, they may have to return to their homeland to face possible death.

Definition
Persecution: suffering caused by others
Asylum: protection given by a country
Expatriate: someone who lives outside their native country

4. Illegal immigrants enter and stay in a country without making themselves known to the authorities. They usually disappear into parts of towns where there are communities of similar cultures to themselves. They do not seek asylum.

5. Many young people across the world apply for places at well-known universities in the US and in Europe and stay on after their studies in the hope of finding highly paid jobs. Children from China also attend many secondary schools in the UK.

6. On retirement, elderly people often go abroad to live such as in places that may be warmer than their homeland. In Spain, for example, there is a large expatriate community of British people.

task
A   Use Table 11.1 to answer the following questions.
1. Which country had the highest inward migration rate?
2. Which country had the highest outward migration rate?
3. In which country was there no net migration?
4. To what extent is there a relationship between HDI rank and net migration rates? Draw a scatter graph to help you answer this question and explain your answer.

Refugees

A decision to move as a result of a natural disaster is often taken quickly with few plans being made. If fighting comes too close to a village and the people fear for their safety, they may then move in a hurry. The numbers of migrants are often huge and the people are desperate. Refugee camps are supposed to be temporary places where families can stay until the natural disaster or war is over. Many thousands of people arrive on foot and the only possessions they have are what they have been able to carry.

The UN refugee agency co-ordinates international action to help the refugees themselves and tries to solve the problems large numbers of them cause to the host country.

It also helps to organise camps for people who have had to move within their own country. This is done to find a place safe from danger such as those who lost their homes in the Indian Ocean tsunami in 2004. Huge sums of money are needed to help support the aid agencies in their work to help those suffering in these camps and requests for donations appear in all the media.

task B

What is money needed for in these camps? List your answers in what you consider to be an order of priority.

Many people and governments respond to emergency appeals worldwide but as time goes on and the drought and wars continue, these camps are not news anymore and it is hard for aid agencies to keep the funds coming in. As more people migrate here the infrastructure in the camps cannot cope, and cholera and disputes over limited water add to the stress of living there. Enrolment of children in primary school is low.

However, life in the camps is usually better than the life that has been left behind. Governments sometimes close their borders as they are overwhelmed by these refugees, but desperate people still usually find a way across.

Somalia to Kenya

Somalia has suffered civil war for decades. Since the 1990s several hundred thousand people have fled their home and country to seek safety in Ethiopia, Djibouti and Kenya. To escape civil war people have to cross an international boundary. During this period, Somalia has also suffered from drought which has made people's lives even more difficult. Drought knows no political boundaries so refugees fleeing drought will not escape from it over the border.

Dadaab refugee camp, Kenya

A large refugee camp in Kenya at Dadaab, part of which can be seen in Figure 12.2, was created in the early 1990s to help people escaping from the war and drought in Somalia. The camp was designed for 90 000 people.

Today, it is home to many times that number. The journey here is long and dangerous. The people carry whatever belongings they can as well as children who are too weak to walk. There is a constant fear of wild animals, criminal gangs and running out of water.

The drought affecting East Africa is a very serious humanitarian crisis.

Figure 12.2 The Dadaab refugee camp in East Kenya
Source: http://www.worldvisionreport.org/Stories/Week-of-April-2-2011/Waiting-in-Dadaab

The conditions in the camp are described in the newspaper report in Figure 12.3.

The old as well as the young arrive tired, hungry and thirsty but the sight of the camp offers them some hope. But hope rapidly turns to despair as they join hundreds of other families all heading in the same direction as they all have to register as refugees. Then at least they can receive some food and shelter but this process can take hours and they are all weak and worried. The shelters are just flimsy plastic sheets tied over some branches which they make themselves out of whatever they can find; but there are so many people here already, there is not much left to find of any use. The smell of human waste is overwhelming and disease is everywhere as there are not nearly enough latrines. All around them they see malnourished children and anxious parents. They see queues from taps and food stations – hardly surprising as there are nearly half a million people living here now.

Figure 12.3 Hundreds more refugees arrive at Dadaab

task C

Many of the people who live in the refugee camps are young children. Describe what it must be like for these children who have left almost everything behind and now live in these camps.

Effect on Kenya

Kenya itself is experiencing the same drought. The government of Kenya has a problem in supporting its own people especially at a time of crisis – it cannot cope with looking after tens of thousands of people from a neighbouring country as well. If it was able to provide funds to the camp to give people there a good quality of life, the camp would probably attract even more people.

The camp dwellers are coming into conflict with local people as they go out to search for wood and water. These are in short supply in the surrounding area and the local Kenyans regard these resources as their own and they themselves are struggling to survive the drought. The nomadic pastoralists can no longer wander across the areas where the camps are now situated.

There are three options, none of which are likely.

1. Acceptance by a developed country – but this is a very long process and people may have to spend over 10 years in these camps before a country might be found to take them.

2. Stay in Kenya and move to the towns but Kenyan towns are already overcrowded.
3. Go back to Somalia but this is unlikely while the civil war and drought continues.

Problems with finding long term solutions

If people stay in a country as refugees, then pressure is put on the receiving country's government as the numbers of migrants increase. The local people fear their culture could be diluted by too many foreigners and pressure on land and services is seen as a real problem. The government may need to take out loans to provide services for the extra people but this increases the country's debt. The government may try to control immigration as it will be looking to be re-elected at the next elections.

The UN is reluctant to get involved in conflicts between opposing groups especially if these conflicts have been going on for decades. However, it can help to negotiate cease fires and resolve differences providing the groups involved co-operate. Attempts to reduce the effects of climate change such as drought need a global solution but there are difficulties in reaching agreements, as described in Chapter 17.

Afghanistan to Pakistan

When the Soviet Union forces invaded Afghanistan from the North in 1979, many Afghans fled to Pakistan in the south-east. Since then civil war and foreign forces fighting terrorism have resulted in more migration as people flee to safety. Since the year 2000, there has been about 2 million refugees from Afghanistan living in Pakistan.

To add to this problem there are many people being displaced within Pakistan itself due to conflicts between different tribal groups near the border with Afghanistan and because the Pakistani military conduct operations in the area to remove extremists. Although these displaced people are not refugees, they put pressure on a government's funds. With many

> **Definition**
>
> **Extremist**: a person who holds political views which are far from moderate
>
> **Terrorism**: the act of using violence to achieve political aims

of its own people to look after, the country has little to offer the huge number of people fleeing to it from a neighbouring country. Pakistan is ranked 125 in the HDI for 2010.

Figure 12.4 shows two media reports about the situation.

UN agreement with Pakistan allows Afghan refugees to extend their stay

The Pakistani Government today reached an agreement with the United Nations refugee agency allowing some 1.7 million Afghans to continue sheltering in their country until the end of 2012.

The pact sets out measures relating to the temporary stay of Afghan refugees in Pakistan, their gradual and voluntary repatriation, and international support for hosting one of the largest refugee communities in the world.

Source: UN News Centre (13/03/2009)

> **Half a million flee Swat valley as Pakistan faces months of fighting**
>
> Up to 500,000 terrified residents of Pakistan's Swat valley have fled or else are desperately trying to leave as the military steps up an operation using fighter jets and helicopter gunships to "eliminate" Taliban fighters.
>
> As the military intensified what may be its most determined operation to date against militant extremists, the UN said 200,000 people had already arrived in safe areas in the past few days while another 300,000 were on the move or were poised to leave.
>
> **Source:** The Independent – 09/05/2011

Figure 12.4 Media articles about Pakistan's refugees and displaced people

task D

Why did the Pakistani government make sure it would have international support to host the refugees?

🌐 Economic migrants

The movement of people from one country to another in search of jobs is nothing new. They contribute to economic development in both the country of destination and in their country of origin.

Not all migrants from developing countries seek work in developed countries, although many of them do. Many migrate for tertiary education and graduates are often allowed to stay once they have finished their degree course. Skills learnt, therefore, do not benefit the developing country from where these people originally came. Many health professionals are encouraged to migrate to fill posts in developed countries and this prevents these people from improving the health services in their own countries where the need is greater.

task E

If you have access to the internet, find the migration information for your country in the Migration and Remittances Factbook published by The World Bank at http://data.worldbank.org/data-catalog/migration-and-remittance.

On a blank world map show the migration flows into and out from your country. Describe the main features of the map in terms of the origin and destination countries of migrants and state whether these countries have a lower or higher level of development than your own using the map in Figure 5.1.

Mexicans to the US

For decades, Mexicans have crossed the border to work, often illegally, in the hotels and restaurants of Los Angeles, in transport industries and on commercial farms where seasonal fruit picking jobs are readily available.

By 2010, over 11 million Mexicans had migrated around the world with the US being one of the top destination countries. However, there is evidence that in the last decade the return flow of migrants back to Mexico was actually greater than the number migrating to the US. The reasons for this are complex and accurate data on the issue is hard to obtain.

The US economy benefits from the Mexican migrants as they often do the poorly paid jobs that Americans do not want to do. The US society may benefit from being open to a variety of cultures such as the Mexican music and food that the migrants bring with them.

However, the border controls have been increased to try to reduce the large numbers of people wanting to find a new life in the States. People smugglers pay corrupt border guards to look the other way. Many die trying to cross the Arizona desert on their own and any who are caught are returned to Mexico. Table 12.1 shows certain facts about Mexico and the US.

Definition

Smuggler: person who moves people or goods into or out of a country illegally

Table 12.1   Selected data for Mexico and the USA

Country	Urban population %	HDI Rank	GDP per person US$	Internet users (per 100 people)	Population 0–14 %	Adult Literacy rates (%)	Under 5 mortality rate (per 1000)	Life expectancy
US	82	4	46,702	78	20	99	8	78
Mexico	78	56	9133	31	29	86	17	77

Source: https://www.cia.gov/library/publications/the-world-factbook/index.html;
http://hdr.undp.org/en/statistics/;
www.worldbank.org

task F

Explain why migrants from Mexico are likely to have an easier journey to the US than those wanting to go from Sudan to the UK.

task G

Describe the main differences between Mexico and the US as shown in Table 12.1.

Why Mexicans want to work in the US

There are many reasons why so many people migrate from Mexico to the US:

- almost half of Mexicans live below the poverty line
- there is a huge difference in GDP per person between the two countries
- the 'American Dream' of a higher quality of life
- more jobs available and a greater choice of work in the US
- farmland is degraded through overuse
- many rural dwellers do not own their land
- the United States is close
- living conditions in the shanty towns are very poor
- remittances can be sent back home
- money may be saved to be able to set up a business on return
- informal jobs and farmwork are poorly paid and unreliable.

task H

1. Describe the push and pull factors that lead to migrants moving from Mexico to the US.
2. Describe what you think is meant by the 'American Dream'.

Figure 12.5 shows four brief emails that may have been sent from a migrant worker in the US to his home in Mexico.

Here at last. Found this internet café where I've met up with another guy looking for work like me. Trying to find place to stay but people can't tell what I'm saying. I don't seem very welcome. I've heard there are jobs at a new factory so need to find out how to get there. Don't worry I'll get sorted soon and send you money to help the kids.

Got a job fruit picking – guess it's not very legal as some of us have to hide when the farmer has visitors. Mustn't get caught or they'll send me home. Missing you all loads. Got a rash but sure nothing to worry about. Not much money left when I've bought some food and paid a bit for a place on a floor to sleep. How are you managing without me?

Guess what – I've met someone from the next village to ours. He's been here ages and works in a hotel. He's going to try to get me a job. My rash is getting worse – we think it's something they've sprayed on the fruit. They won't give us gloves though. Don't ever let my sister come over here. Awful stories about girls being promised a better life but they end up prisoned in brothels.

Got job as a porter! Very smart uniform (and I get loads of tips). Hope extra money reaches you soon. Are you getting some each month or is it getting lost? May be able to save up enough to come home and start my own business....or do you all want to come over here if I can fix it? Love you all.

Figure 12.5 Emails to home

Definition

Tips: extra money given by a customer to a worker who has given good service

task
I

Write 4 short emails that may be written as replies to the above. Compare your mails with others in the class and make a list of all the worries that migrants and their families may have.

Effects on origin and destination of migrants

International economic migration obviously crosses political boundaries so it is, by its very nature, a global issue that does not only affect individual countries. The countries of origin and destination of migrants receive gains but also losses from this movement of people. Achieving an acceptable balance is needed if it is not to become a major global problem.

The people who are left at home gain certain benefits from this economic migration but they may also experience problems. Some of the effects on the community the migrants leave behind are:

- remittances (US$23 billion in 2010) help increase household income and may be spent on better variety of food, health care, education
- change in demand for local services may increase or decrease
- change in role for women left with new responsibilities
- new skills, ideas and technologies brought home
- loss of workers and skills may affect food production on family farm
- break up of family
- worry for family members if migrant fails to find work or loses contact
- less pressure on water supplies, food
- more employment for those left behind.

Definition

Remittances: A sum of money sent to someone

The effect on local services can be either positive or negative. If local people have more money to spend, this may encourage more businesses to set up in the area which in turn will provide more jobs. This may cause less people to leave. This is called a positive multiplier effect.

If large numbers migrate away from a village, the use of local services will fall and they may close. This may cause more people to leave. This is called a negative multiplier effect. In a similar way, the destination of the migrant workers gains some benefits but also some problems as shown in Figure 12.6.

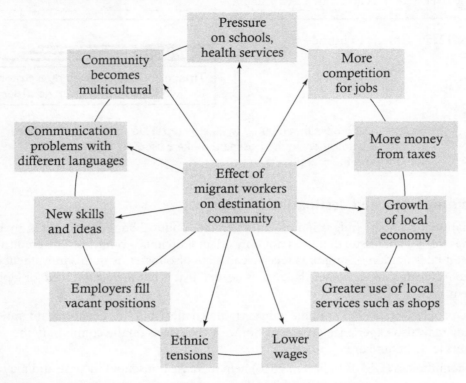

Figure 12.6 Effects of migrant workers in a community

task J

1. Describe the advantages and disadvantages of economic migration for the people left behind.
2. List the effects of migrants on a community in two columns headed 'benefits' and 'problems'.

A global challenge

In his address to the Global Forum on Migration and Development in 2009, The Secretary General of the United Nations, Ban Ki-moon said, 'Together, our goal is to harness the power of migration to reduce poverty and inequality – to help more people share in the world's prosperity – and to achieve the MDGs.'

Mexico's inward remittance flow of US$23 billion in 2010 shows how economic migration may improve living standards and so help poorer countries to achieve the MDGs.

task K

Explain how remittances can help a country meet some MDG targets.

The global challenge is to improve conditions for migrant workers and reduce barriers to migration if it is to help reduce poverty in the world. Migrant workers do not want to risk losing their job by complaining about health and safety standards or poor pay. It is likely that even if the pay is poor, it is several times that which they could earn back home.

Better health and safety measures and higher wages may mean fewer jobs are available and laws to prevent exploitation of migrant workers are not a priority for governments. Barriers to migration need to be reduced but countries will not adopt 'open-door' policies.

task L

What do you think is meant by 'open-door' policies and why do countries not usually have these?

Summary

 - International migration can cause problems but it can also bring benefits
 - Large numbers of refugees put huge strains on poor countries which need support from the global community
 - Solutions to the problems caused by refugees are difficult to find
 - Economic migrants provide remittances that help their families to improve their quality of life but problems exist for the migrant, their family and the country of destination.

Questions

Question 1

Study Figure 1 which shows information about population growth in three countries.

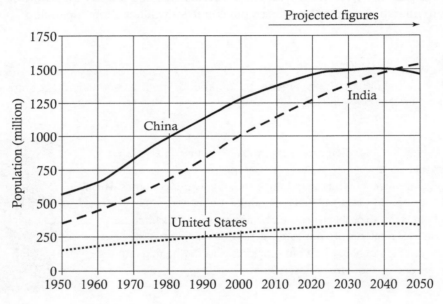

Figure 1

(a) (i) What was the total population of India in 2000? [1]

    (ii) How did the rate of growth of the population of the USA and India differ between 1950 and 2000? [1]

    (iii) Identify **one** similarity and **one** difference in the pattern of population growth which is expected in India and China between 2010 and 2050. [2]

(b) Study Figure 2 which shows birth and death rates in India during the twentieth century.

    (i) Between which years was the birth rate in India 46 per 1000 and the death rate 37 per 1000? [1]

    (ii) Calculate the natural population growth rate of India between 1981 and 1991. You must show your calculations. [2]

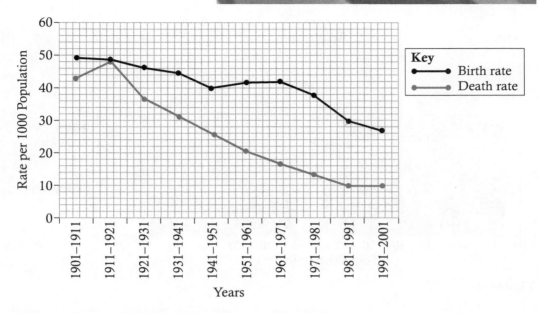

Figure 2 Birth and death rates in India 1901 to 2001

    (iii) Suggest possible reasons for the high birth rates in India during much of the twentieth century.   [5]

(c) Study Figures 3A and 3B which are population pyramids for India. Figure 3A shows information about the population in 2005. Figure 3B is based on projected figures for 2050.

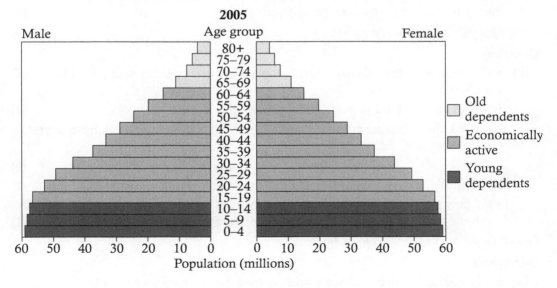

Figure 3A

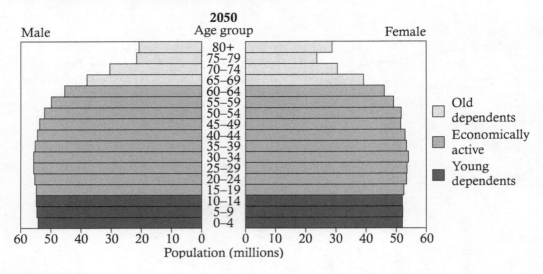

Figure 3B

    (i) Which **age group** in 2005 had the largest number of both males and females? [1]

    (ii) What evidence in the population pyramids suggests that:

        A people will have a longer life expectancy in 2050 than they had in 2005;

        B there will be a lower birth rate in 2050 than there was in 2005? [2]

    (iii) How is the dependent population of India expected to differ in 2050 from what it was like in 2005? Support your answer with figures. [3]

  (d) Suggest how the life expectancy is expected to change in developing countries during this century. Give reasons for your answer. [4]

Cambridge 0453 P2 Q1 Oct/Nov 2008

Question 2

  (a) Study Figure 4 which shows information about cities in India with a population of 2 million or more.

    (i) Estimate the total population of Bangalore. [1]

    (ii) Rank the following cities in order of their population size. Rank from largest to smallest.

        Kolkata   Ahmadabad   Nagpur   New Delhi [1]

    (iii) Identify the city with over half of its population living in slums. [1]

    (iv) Many people who have migrated to urban areas in developing countries, such as India, still end up with a poor quality of life. Suggest **three** reasons for this. [3]

Cambridge 0453 P2 Q2 b Oct/Nov 2008

Question 3

  (a) Study Figure 5 which is about a study carried out in Jaipur, a city in India.

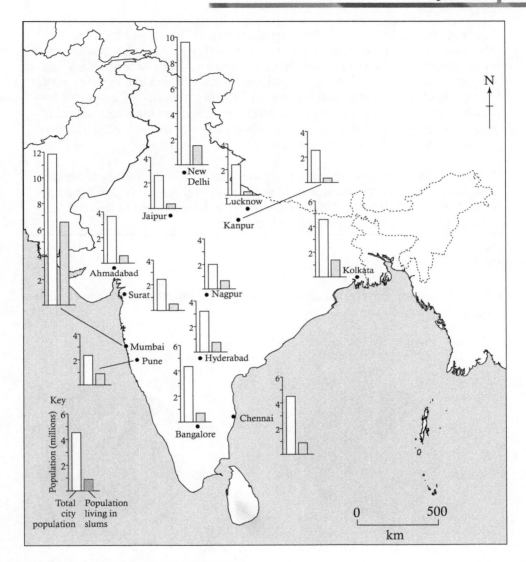

Figure 4 Population of cities of India

(i) In which city was this research carried out? [1]

(ii) Use the information in Figure 5 to explain why many new migrants to this city live on pavements, or next to roads and railways. [1]

(iii) Suggest reasons why interviews were used for this investigation. [2]

(iv) What is meant by a *10 per cent sample*? [1]

(v) Give **three** different ways by which the sample of 296 families could have been chosen. [3]

(vi) Describe and explain any difficulties which you think the researchers might have had in carrying out these interviews. [4]

In many cities in India, slums have grown wherever there was space. Many have by now become so crowded that there is no longer room for new migrants to the towns or cities to buils their homes. Therefore many new migrants line on pavements, or next to roads and raliways. Most of them live in home-made shelters made of polythene sheets, cardboard, cloth or blankets, supported by tree branches or bamboo poles. A tap in the street is often their only source of water: a nearby street lamp the source of light and any unused space becomes a place to throw rubbish and human waste.

A piece of research was carried out to investigate the lifestyle of these people, who live on pavements and alongside roads in Jaipur. A total of 296 families were studied, which was a 10% sample. Interviews were used to find out information about the people and their families.

Figure 5

(b) Study Figures 6, 7 and 8 which show some of the results of the research carried out in Jaipur.

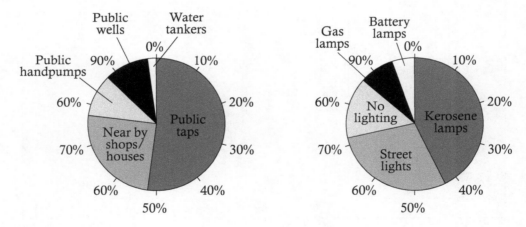

Figure 6 Main sources of water and lighting

    (i) What percentage of the families use water from public taps? [1]

    (ii) What percentage work as blacksmiths? [1]

    (iii) Name the method of presentation which has been used in each of Figures 6 and 7. [2]

    (iv) The main conclusion of this research was that the quality of life of these new migrants to Jaipur was very low. Explain how the information shown in Figures 6, 7 and 8 supports this conclusion. [5]

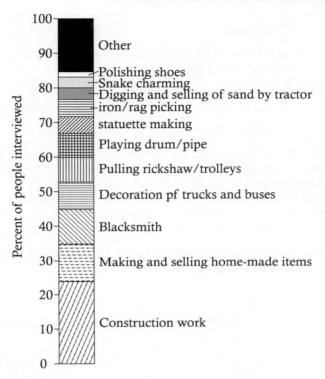

Figure 7 Main type of work done by head of family

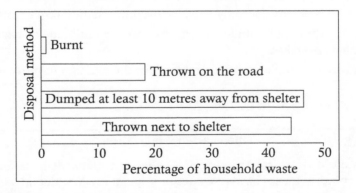

Figure 8 Disposal of household rubbish

(c) Study Figure 9 which shows information about four possible schemes being considered by the authorities of Jaipur to solve the problem of people living on pavements, or next to roads and railways.

Choose the scheme which you think will be most likely to solve the problem of people living on pavements, or next to roads and railways. Explain your reasons for choosing this scheme. You should do this by describing the advantages of the scheme you have chosen and the disadvantages of the schemes you rejected. [7]

Cambridge 0453 P2 Q3 a, c and d Oct/Nov 2008

Scheme 1	Scheme 2
Provide low-cost housing with basic amenities on the edge of the city.	Give an area of land to these people with a public washroom, piped water and toilets.
Scheme 3	**Scheme 4**
Employ more police to prevent people from living on the pavements, and teams of council workers to clear rubbish.	Give grants to farmers in the countryside so they can buy tools, fertilisers and irrigation pumps.

Figure 9 Schemes under consideration by Jaipur Metropolitan Authority Planning Department

Question 4

Study Figure 10 which shows information about international migration.

(a) (i) What is meant by *globalisation*? [1]

    (ii) What term is used to describe migrants who leave their own country to find jobs? Choose **one** of the following: asylum seekers, economic migrants, immigrants, refugees. [1]

(b) (i) Give **two** problems faced by newly arrived international migrants. [2]

    (ii) Describe the benefits and problems for those left at home of having family members overseas. [3]

(c) Explain, using examples, why migrants make the decision to move to another country. [6]

Cambridge 0453 P1 Q1 a, b and d Oct/Nov 2009

International migration

One of the results of globalisation has been the change in global demand for labour. Many of the high income countries have low rates of population growth and labour shortages, whilst changes in demand for goods and services have created new work opportunities.

Developments and education in some low and middle income countries has resulted in a labour force which is willing and able to emigrate. As farming in these countries has modernised, millions of people have left the rural areas and sought work in the cities. But the cities have become overcrowded and high unemployment levels have forced people to look for work outside their own country. Often people travel many thousands of kilometres to take advantage of the new jobs, to earn money and join other members of their family.

Figure 10 Information about international migration

Unit 4

Environment and development

Traditional farming and rural development projects

13

Learning Objectives	● To understand the main features of traditional farming
	● To appreciate the problems involved in increasing output
	● To appreciate the need for partnerships in rural development schemes
	● To understand the causes of soil erosion and possible solutions.

🌐 Main features of traditional farming

In early societies men hunted and fished and women gathered berries, nuts and plants from the wild. As animals became domesticated and plants were grown as crops, there was often still a division of labour. Farmers provided food for themselves and their families to eat. This is called subsistence farming. In good years when harvests were plentiful there was some surplus to sell. Traditional subsistence farming still takes place in many societies today as most people in the less developed countries live in rural areas.

The main features of traditional farming are:

- mainly family labour with little capital input
- simple tools such as hoes, wooden ploughs with oxen
- small areas of land
- low yields
- staple crops such as rice, beans
- small numbers of different livestock
- nomadic pastoralism in some areas.

> **Definition** ═══════════
>
> **Staple crops**: the dominant food in people's diets
>
> **Nomadic pastoralism**: a system where people (nomads) continually move in search of water and grazing for their livestock

Figure 13.1 shows shepherd boys in Lesotho looking after their cattle. This has always been a role for boys in this country. These boys are not nomads as they do not wander all their lives across vast areas setting up temporary homes. They are pastoralists as they keep livestock but they live in permanent settlements from which they take their animals to graze each day.

Figure 13.1 Shepherd boys in Lesotho
Source: Wendy Taylor

task
A
1. List the main roles of the male and female members of your household. Is this division of labour fixed or flexible or changing?
2. List the uses of cattle in societies around the world.

Appropriate technology

Traditional farmers have usually maintained a sustainable farming system for generations on the same land. A mixed farming system allows manure from the livestock to be used as fertiliser for the crops. Waste leaves and stems from the crops feed the animals. Local water supplies have usually been enough for the small quantities grown and simple tools do not require fuel. Seeds are kept from one harvest to be sown the next year. The tools and technology used are appropriate to the farmer's situation.

task
B
Make a list of the tools a traditional farmer might use. What does a farmer need to consider before replacing his ox with a tractor to pull a plough?

Land tenure and reform

In many societies, the land is divided up between sons following the death of the head of the family. These units may be too small to provide enough food to eat or sell and this increases rural poverty and hunger. It is very difficult to increase the size of the land that the family owns due to lack of capital, ownership of land is not always clear and often land is under communal tenure. It is generally thought that in order to improve output and reduce poverty in rural areas, land reform and security of tenure are essential.

Figure 13.2 Farmland ownership

Figure 13.2 shows some forms of land tenure. Sometimes people took over land illegally in the past but have farmed it for generations and so regard it as their own even though they are unlikely to have the paperwork to prove ownership. Some of the problems of land ownership in Kenya are described in Chapter 11. If a government does want to reform

land holdings to ensure a fairer distribution, then ownership needs to be established. Governments are not likely to consider land reform if politicians themselves own large areas of good farmland. If land does become available it is usually bought by companies who will grow crops commercially for export.

If families can be sure that land they regard as their own will not be taken from them, then they have security of tenure. This means they will look after the land more responsibly knowing that any improvements will benefit their family in future and not someone else.

Risk management

Many farmers already grow more than one crop and keep livestock so that if one fails, there is something to fall back on. Some members of the family work outside agriculture so if farming is in trouble they have another source of income.

They build up their assets in 'good years' so they have something to sell in 'bad years.' When the unexpected occurs, it is people who are closest to the poverty line that find it hardest to cope. Drought could mean poor families have to sell their livestock or fall into debt which makes it even harder to recover when times improve.

task C

Explain how governments can help smallholders to reduce the following risks.
1. Catching malaria at harvest time.
2. Losing a crop to theft by criminal gangs.
3. Food going bad before it reaches market.

Problems of obtaining credit

In order to improve farming techniques, capital is usually needed in the form of loans from banks. To obtain these, farmers usually have to put their land forward as security. This means that if their plans fail they may have to sell their land to pay off the loan. This is a huge risk. For many farmers it is impossible to get a loan because:

- tenant farmers do not own land
- communal farmers do not own land
- many women farmers do not have rights to own land.

Many women rely on land for food and income, especially those whose husbands have migrated to towns. Land rights are held by men and if a husband dies, the land will pass to the male relatives.

Governments can:

- set up agencies to give loans at fixed low interest rates
- encourage the formation of co-operatives
- encourage gender equality in land ownership through education and laws.

task D

Describe the various uses of a loan for a traditional farmer who wants to improve output from his farm.

🌐 Rural development projects

Improvement in services

Rural development programmes aim to increase output from traditional farms and improve people's quality of life. Service provision in rural areas is not usually as good as in the towns.

Electricity supplies are not connected to remote areas, sanitation is usually poor and roads are usually dirt tracks that are impassable in bad weather. Many people are too poor to afford transport even if there was a tarred road to town. PHC is likely to be present but not hospitals and there are primary schools but few secondary schools in many rural parts of developing countries. Jobs outside farming are few and so there is little alternative income to rely on when crops fail.

Refer back to Table 11.2 which shows the proportion of the population with access to improved sanitation and an improved drinking water source in rural and urban areas of selected countries in 2008. With two exceptions, the rural areas have a smaller proportion of people who benefit from these improved services than the urban areas and this applies to many services in rural areas. They are more scattered and more difficult to reach than concentrated urban areas where costs are therefore less.

Partnerships between governments and aid agencies working together with communities will help to improve agricultural output and standards of living of rural people. There are many ways this can be done and sometimes a small project can provide different benefits to a rural community.

There needs to be links between every organisation involved in rural development projects. Too often, different government departments act in isolation and have little contact with local organisations as illustrated in Figure 13.3.

Figure 13.3 Different views on a new road

task E

Write down what you think the farmer and mother with baby might say about the road.

Small-scale irrigation

Irrigation works can make the difference between a farmer being able to feed his family and malnourishment or even starvation. Irrigation means the artificial watering of crops and may be needed if the rainfall is less than normal or comes late. It can take many forms and in traditional farming areas may simply be a bucket used to carry water from a stream. Sometimes animals do the work and systems with levers can also reduce the manual labour involved. Water from tube wells and pumps is used in areas with no surface water.

Mwembe is located in a dry region of Tanzania. In recent years, even the traditional rainy months have not brought enough rain which meant crops died. Rain that did come ran quickly off the hills taking with it much precious soil and nutrients.

The United Nations Development Programme (UNDP) supported a local NGO in constructing a micro-dam to collect this water. The dam is owned and maintained by a group of community members who clean out the mud from the pool and manage the channeling of the water to the farm plots that serve up to 150 households. These new irrigation works have meant that farmers are now not only feeding their families but also earning extra income from selling their produce at local markets. Their children can attend school, they can afford to keep poultry and cows and their houses have been improved with iron sheets replacing hay roofs.

Grass roots sanitation project

A worldwide programme called Community Led Total Sanitation began in Bangladesh and is now supported in many countries by Plan International, UNICEF, The World Bank and Water Aid. With guidance from trained health workers, all members of a community discuss the issue of open defecation as shown in Figure 13.4.

They map where the main areas are for this around their village and consider the impacts it is having upon them all. They then decide, as a community, whether or not they want to stop this practice. If the majority decision is 'yes', the villagers are then helped by charity workers to construct latrines made out of local materials and soap and water is supplied nearby for washing hands. Once a community can state that it is ODF (Open Defecation Free),

Figure 13.4 Community discussion

Definition

Defecation: the discharge of solid matter (faeces) from the body

there is often a celebration. Kenya has set itself the target of making all rural areas ODF by 2013.

task F

Describe the many benefits for rural people of irrigation and sanitation projects such as those detailed in the previous page.

Co-operatives

Farmers often join together to form co-operatives which are organisations that help farmers in a number of ways:

- bulk buying of fertilisers etc. reduces costs due to economies of scale
- new technology can be shared amongst members
- credit is easier to obtain as a member of a group
- skills can be shared and training given
- group storage and marketing saves money
- help for each other at harvest time.

Figure 13.5 shows how a co-operative in Kenya helped farmers market their crops.

In Kenya, farmers had no way of storing their onions and so had to sell them all at once after harvest when prices were low. Local traders forced down prices knowing the farmers had little choice but to sell to them.

FARM Africa has helped the farmers set up marketing associations whose members decided together on a fair price for their crop. The traders would then have to pay the same price to everyone. FARM Africa has also set up a demonstration storage site where the groups received training on how best to store their produce. Farmers are now receiving almost three times as much for their onions.

Source: www.farmafrica.org.uk

Figure 13.5 Help for farmers from FARM Africa

task G

Make a list of the sort of information you think the co-operative members would find useful to obtain from the internet.

Renewable energy supplies

These are sustainable forms of free energy such as from the sun and wind and may be the only form of clean power in many villages. The electricity grid often does not extend beyond towns and most villagers use firewood.

One of the main problems with these renewable supplies is that the solar panels and micro wind turbines are easy to steal.

task H

What is another problem of generating electricity from the sun or wind?

The Lighting Africa programme in Kenya helps to provide solar light. The World Bank supports private industries who supply these products. Only a very small percentage of rural Kenyans can afford electricity from the grid but millions now benefit from this renewable energy which is made during the day and released when darkness comes as shown in Figure 13.6.

The programme offers many benefits:

- less money has to be spent on kerosene
- the home has no fumes so the family has better health
- small businesses can be set up using renewable energy
- systems are low cost to buy and solar power is free.

Figure 13.6 Solar lights for homework
Source: http://www.lightingafrica.org/

task I

Draw a poster to advertise all the benefits of solar powered lights as shown in Figure 13.6.

🌍 Soil erosion

Seventy per cent of the world's population live in rural areas and the world's population is growing dramatically. Rural communities depend on farming to survive and farming depends on the soil. Population growth has put huge demands on the soils. More crops take more nutrients out of the soil and overgrazing results in less vegetation cover. Soil degradation occurs and erosion takes place more easily.

Soils are held in place by the roots of vegetation. If the vegetation is removed the soils are more easily eroded. Plants also slow down the movement of water through the soil. Without plants, water passes quickly into the soil or runs off the surface. Moving water takes the soil with it or leaches the nutrients.

Definition
Degradation: loss of quality
Erosion: removal by wind or water
Leach: the action of water flowing through the soil and removing substances from it

This leaves thinner and infertile soils in which even less can grow. Poverty is increased as crop yields fall and livestock go hungry. Soil erosion occurs for a number of reasons:

- trees are felled for firewood or to make more farmland
- more animals cause overgrazing
- overuse of paths
- drought causes plants to die
- poor farming practices.

Firewood

When other fuels cannot be afforded or obtained, firewood is used for cooking in many parts of the developing world. Usually this comes from trees that have grown naturally and have not been planted for this particular use. Collecting this firewood is unsustainable as the tree dies and is not replaced.

The job of collecting firewood falls on the women and children of a household as shown in Figure 13.7. Many hours each day can be spent on this activity

Figure 13.7 Woman carrying firewood

and the time women spend will get longer as local supplies run out and they have to walk further to find their fuel.

In Sub-Saharan Africa, 28 per cent of all deaths are attributable to fumes from solid fuel use and women are more affected than men. Fire damage to property is always a further risk from open fires. Table 13.1 shows the share of the population of this part of Africa that relied on different types of cooking fuels in 2007.

task J

Why do you think women are more affected by the smoke than men?

Table 13.1 Cooking fuels used in Sub-Saharan Africa (2007)

Cooking fuel	Percentage (%)
Wood and charcoal	80
Kerosene	7
Electricity	6
Others	7

Source: http://www.who.int/indoorair/publications/PowerPoint_Energy_Access_paper-lr.pdf

task K

1. Draw a divided bar chart to represent the data shown in Table 13.1. Draw one bar 10cms long so 1mm represents 1 per cent.
2. Describe the main feature of the chart.
3. Describe the problems for the environment and people of this dependence.

Methods to reduce soil erosion

Soil erosion is a serious problem in many rural areas. Water flowing off unprotected slopes can carve huge channels in the land and precious soil can be lost from large areas. There are several ways this can be reduced.

> **Definition**
>
> **Hedges**: lines of closely growing shrubs

1. Reduce the need to fell trees by using more efficient stoves or alternative fuels.
2. Plant trees, especially on slopes.
3. Reduce the number of livestock kept or use fences to control grazing.
4. Hire advisers to train farmers in better techniques.
5. Use bio-engineering such as planting hedges.

task L

List all the possible benefits to a community of planting trees.

More efficient stoves

Aid Africa's Rocket stoves consist of 6 bricks made by local brickmakers from local clay, tied together with wire. They are more efficient than open fires so they use half as much wood, produce 75 per cent less fumes and yet produce more heat. They cost US$10 and can easily be carried home by the women who use them. Two sets of bricks are then covered with mud.

task M

Describe the many benefits of these stoves for women in particular.

Access to a reliable electricity supply for rural dwellers will help developing countries achieve the MDGs but governments do not regard this as a priority because the infrastructure is very costly and poor communities are unlikely to be able to afford the power. In its place, more efficient stoves provided by aid organisations are making a huge difference to many communities.

task N

Explain how using modern stoves will help countries achieve MDGs 2, 3 and 4 in particular.

Better farming techniques

Soil erosion can be reduced by using better farming techniques which can be demonstrated to farmers by trained agricultural advisers. Crop rotation means different crops are grown each year on a plot of land. The soil does not then get exhausted as some plants such as beans put goodness back into the soil. Contour ploughing means planting along the slopes instead of down them so water is less likely to run off down the furrows and take the soil with it. Use of compost and ploughing in of crop remains adds goodness and substance to the soil which makes it more difficult for the wind and rain to remove it.

Vetiver hedges

Many plants have been used over the centuries to control soil erosion and stabilise slopes and in the last few decades, the Vetiver plant has become widely used. As an example of bio-engineering, it is a sustainable method and has many benefits as shown in Figure 13.8. Its roots can grow 3m in a year, but they grow downwards and so do not take much water and goodness from surrounding crops. It is often planted in low hedges along the slope and there may be several rows of hedges down the hillside.

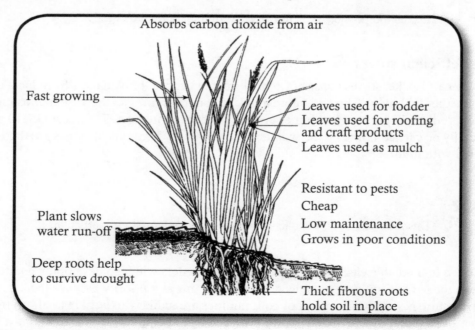

Figure 13.8 The Vetiver Plant

Community composting

Composting is a natural process that takes place when vegetation dies. Leaves and trees fall and rot into the ground and in so doing provide nutrients for the new growth of plants. It is a completely sustainable cycle as shown in Figure 15.5 (Chapter 15). Rainwater falling on bare soil not only washes the soil away but also the nutrients in it that are vital for crops. Mulching solves these two problems. For centuries people have made compost to use on their small plots from rotten fruit and vegetables, leaves, bark, paper, eggshells, fur, crop residue, manure, grass etc.

> **Definition**
>
> **Mulching**: putting organic matter on the soil to protect and enrich it

Buhlebemvelo Community Garden

Instead of sending food waste to landfill sites, Unilever factories in South Africa are sending it to be made into compost. This is then used in gardens to fertilise vegetables that provide an income for poor communities. Unilever saves on costs of waste disposal, the Buhlebemvelo community sells more produce and less waste is dumped in landfill sites. This is a project where everything wins – the company, the community and the environment.

Practical Research Investigation: Soil erosion

Aim

To determine the causes of soil erosion around a school or village and possible solutions.

Objectives
1. To find out what people think are the main causes of soil erosion
2. To investigate how serious people think the problem is
3. To determine what people feel can be done about it.

Methods
- devise a suitable questionnaire
- decide upon a reasonable sample size and choose an appropriate sampling technique
- represent the data in a variety of ways
- analyse the findings
- decide how the community could best reduce the problem of soil erosion.

Summary

- Increasing production from traditional farms is difficult due to problems of land tenure and soil degradation and lack of access to credit
- Improvements to living standards in rural areas require partnerships between the communities and outside organisations
- Small projects can make huge differences to people's lives
- There are many ways to reduce soil erosion.

Commercial farming

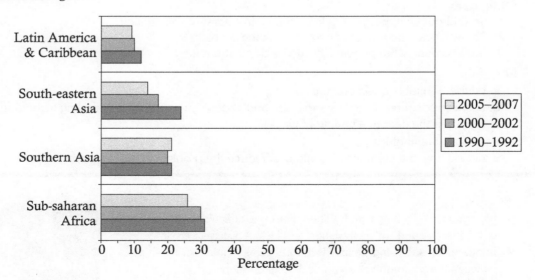

14

Commercial farming and MDG 1

MDG 1 is to eradicate extreme poverty and hunger. Figure 14.1 shows the changes in the proportion of undernourished people in selected regions between 1990 and 2007. Target 1C of MDG 1 is to halve between 1990 and 2015, the proportion of people who suffer from hunger.

Figure 14.1 Proportion of undernourished people in selected regions (%)
Source: http://www.un.org/millenniumgoals/poverty.shtm

Describe the progress being made towards achieving Target 1C.

The world's population continues to grow which makes it all the more difficult to make progress towards meeting the MDG targets. Traditional subsistence farming cannot supply adequate nutrition to the millions of urban dwellers in the developing world. It cannot produce large quantities for export, the income from which can be used to improve standards of living. Commercial farming, which produces huge quantities of food for sale, is the only way to reduce hunger in the world but the methods often used are not sustainable. Growth in the commercial agricultural sector will create further jobs in processing, transport, storage, marketing and in the supply of inputs such as fertilisers. When people have jobs they have an income which enables them to improve their standard of living and so reduce poverty and hunger.

Rice in China

Rice has always been a very important subsistence crop and the staple food for millions of people. It is grown in tropical and subtropical regions and is primarily concentrated in China, India, and Southeast Asia where most is still produced by small-scale farmers. In 2009–2010, China produced 134.8 million tonnes of rice, imported 1.2 million

Definition

Food security: the situation where a country can produce enough food to feed its own population

tonnes and exported 0.7 million tonnes. This shows that rice is produced mainly for consumption within China and also that China has reasonable food security with regard to its staple food.

In China, rice is grown both traditionally for subsistence and also commercially on terraced hillsides as well as on flat lowlands where it grows in flooded areas called paddy fields. These can both be seen in Figure 14.2.

Figure 14.2 Terraced mountains and lowland rice growing in China
Source: Amy Oakley

Figure 14.3 is a blog written by a visitor to the famous terraces of Yuanyang, shown in Figure 14.2. Hillsides such as these cover vast areas and the terraces produce rice which farmers sell to help feed China's very large population. Although some of the farming methods used are modern, many traditional practices remain.

High in mist covered mountains reside the Hani people. It is their ancestors who began constructing the terraced rice paddies over one thousand years ago and who diligently, by hand, continue the tradition of planting rice every spring, harvesting in the fall, and tending to the terraces year round. No easy task, as the hillside is steep, stretches for miles, and the only assisted labor comes from the docile and sure-footed water buffalo.

Breathtaking beyond belief, the interconnected rice terraces are flooded from the mountain top each December. A small trickle of water runs throughout the valley connecting each paddy.

Hani villages are constructed from limestone found in the mountainside. The bottom level of the small dwelling units is left open for raising chickens and pigs, while the family resides in the unit above.

Photographers trek to this corner of the world in hopes of capturing the flooded paddies at sunrise and sunset. As hundreds of photographers set-up their equipment, local women villagers, dressed in their colorful traditional dress, sold boiled eggs and offered to pose for pictures. No strangers to capitalism, it will cost you "yī yuán".

I found the entire experience a fascinating intersection of East and West, of urban and rural, and of traditional and modern. There is evidence all around of western influence. Walking through the village after sunrise, I saw the alleys littered with Coke cans, candy wrappers, bottles. A sad reminder of the powerful effect of marketing and sugar.

Source: A Oakley – China blog

Figure 14.3   China blog – February 2010

task B

Explain in your own words how traditions are found alongside modern influences in the mountains of Yuanyang.

Increasing production

As populations continue to grow, some land has been degraded through overuse. More rice can be grown either by increasing yields or by increasing the area under production. Other demands on land, water and labour from housing, industry and other commercial crops mean it is difficult to increase the area for rice cultivation.

The dependence of humans on the natural world is well shown by the fact that all food for humans was originally to be found as wild plants and animals. Over centuries, selective breeding has produced what we now trade, buy and eat. All the rice grown in the world today belongs to the species *Oryza sativa* which is a descendent of a wild ancestor.

For centuries, farmers have selectively bred varieties of rice that best suited their conditions and gave the highest yields. If one plant in a crop grew smaller but stronger than the rest, the seeds would have been collected. This plant showed a mutation that farmers saw might be useful. The seeds sown

Definition

Mutation: change in a living thing that produces a different variety

the following year produced more plants that were able to withstand strong winds, produce more seeds and be ready for harvest more quickly. Other farmers may have found a plant that survived with less water than the rest.

task C

Describe how other plants or animals have been bred for particular characteristics.

The green revolution

In the 1960s, researchers developed varieties of rice that gave high yields (HYVs). For example, they bred crops that could make the best use of fertilisers to produce grain rather than stems and leaves. There was nothing very different with this technique except for the fact the breeding was done scientifically in research stations rather than by farmers. The planting of these HYVs across the paddy fields of India, China and beyond became known as 'The Green Revolution'. Increased production helped reduce malnourishment and child mortality.

The fear of famine diminished but the green revolution was not without its problems which were:

- difficulty in getting farmers to adopt the new techniques
- higher costs for farmers
- increased use of fertilisers caused environmental problems
- fewer types of rice were grown which meant they could be wiped out by pests and disease
- increased use of pesticides caused environmental problems.

Fertilisers in the environment

Fertilisers can either be natural, organic ones such as manure or artificial ones that are made in factories. Different plant requirements such as nitrogen, phosphorus and potassium can be made into pellets that are put on the soil by the farmers. When it rains or the field is irrigated, the nutrients are taken into the soil and then absorbed by the crops.

Fertilisers increase yields but when rainwater falling on the soil carries them into rivers the effects can be damaging for wildlife. This is shown in Figure 14.4.

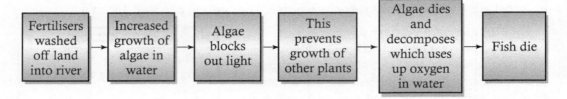

Fertilisers washed off land into river → Increased growth of algae in water → Algae blocks out light → This prevents growth of other plants → Algae dies and decomposes which uses up oxygen in water → Fish die

Figure 14.4   Effect of fertilisers in rivers

Pesticides in the environment

Insects and fungi can do serious damage to crops and reduce yields but chemicals that kill one type of pest can also kill harmless and even beneficial ones. Insects play a major role in the food chain and loss of insects means loss of birds that eat them. Bees pollinate many food plants and ladybirds eat aphids that eat the crops. Pesticides can kill both of these which can be seen in Figure 14.5.

Figure 14.5   Beneficial insects – bees and ladybirds
Source: Wendy Taylor

The yield gap and the role of governments

There is always a big difference between the yield the researchers manage to get from their plots and the yield the farmers get from theirs, using the same seeds. To increase food security and reduce poverty and malnutrition governments have to try to reduce this gap by:

- promoting research into varieties suitable for the different conditions in different parts of the country
- providing government advisers to introduce the latest techniques to farmers.

task D

Identify some of the climatic conditions found in your country and the main commercial crops grown in these different regions.

Genetically Modified (GM) crops

Genetic engineering results in a change in the genetic structure of a plant or animal and is not something that would ever happen naturally.

The scientists work towards growing a plant that will produce an even higher yield than was possible in the 'green revolution'. They take a gene with the particular characteristic that they want from one species and insert it in another. For example, some soil bacteria are toxic to insects that eat plants. If plants can contain these bacteria then they should be safe from being eaten by the insects and the farmers will get a higher yield and will not have to spray insecticide. The GM crop would contain genetic material from an organism belonging to a completely different species.

GM Golden Rice contains beta-carotein which gives carrots their orange colour. This increases the Vitamin A content of the rice. Vitamin A helps people to fight infection and so Golden Rice could prevent many children from dying.

Crops compete with wildflowers for sunlight, water and nutrients and this competition reduces yields so farmers remove the wild plants by spraying with herbicides as shown in Figure 14.6.

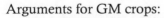

Figure 14.6 A crop being sprayed with herbicide

A GM variety of rice has been developed by a chemical company which also produces a herbicide that will kill all other plants in the field. However, many of these wild plants would attract beneficial insects and good farming practices allow some wild plants to grow, if only around the edge of the field.

Arguments for GM crops:
- they are the only way to feed the growing world population
- the genes being transferred all occur naturally and are safe for humans
- use of pesticides and herbicides will be reduced
- GM crops that need less water will provide food in dry areas
- the method used is not very different from conventional breeding methods
- the possibility of increasing nutrient levels and removing allergens
- GM crops could be made with better storage quality

- an increased yield could mean land can be left for wildlife
- biofuels based on GM plants could replace fossil fuels
- the possibility of developing crops that absorb nitrogen from the air and so fertilise themselves.

Arguments against GM crops:

- insect resistant plants may harm insects that are beneficial to plants
- new varieties can breed with native plants with unknown effects
- once a GM variety is released, it cannot be stopped from spreading to wild populations
- effects on biodiversity may not be known for years
- human trials have not taken place to determine the effect on people of eating genes that would not normally be eaten
- people may not want to eat GM food but it will be impossible to know what products contain GM strains once they are released into the environment
- organic farmers are worried that cross-pollination will result in their crops becoming contaminated by GM strains
- a limited variety of crops may be grown which may encourage more pests.

The role of governments

As there are many arguments both for and against GM crops, it is the governments who have to decide whether or not to allow research into GM crops, field trials and later full production as well as the sale of GM crops in their country. Governments also have to set the regulations for all these stages to ensure public health safety and biosafety.

> **Definition**
>
> **Biosafety**: the protection of biodiversity by the careful use of biotechnology

task E

As Minister for the Environment, you have listened to all the arguments about GM crops which are summarised below.

Environmental activist – 'We cannot take the risk of damaging our wild plants and insects for ever.'

NGO official – 'We must stop people dying from hunger and disease.'

Chemical company director – 'Our new wonder plant will increase your exports and save farmers money.'

Consumer – 'I won't buy food with GM ingredients.'

You have to decide whether to allow production of GM crops on your country's land. Write a report explaining your decision. Compare your decision with others in the class and organise a debate on the issue.

Cocoa production in Ghana

Rice is grown commercially in China but mainly for the home market. Cocoa is grown commercially in Ghana mainly for export. The cocoa tree grows naturally in the shade of the Amazon rainforest where rainfall is heavy and evenly distributed throughout the year and temperatures range from 18–32 degrees Celsius. The main producers of cocoa are now the Cote d'Ivoire and Ghana in Africa. Ghana's export of cocoa comes second in value to gold and its trade is therefore very important to the country.

Problems for the cocoa industry

A fast growing oil industry with huge potential revenues from oil exports is taking foreign investment and government attention away from farming, but cocoa production is an important means of income for thousands of families. Soil degradation is a major problem for these farmers but a sustainable cocoa industry will survive far longer than oil production

Slash and burn: a method of clearing forests by felling and burning the vegetation before sowing seeds

and it is essential not to neglect it if Ghana is to achieve the targets for the MDGs.

Traditional varieties of cocoa trees were grown below the canopy of the rainforest as this protected the forest soils and the young cocoa trees from heavy rain and strong sunlight. In the 1980s, sun-loving varieties were introduced which produced more pods per tree and were ready for harvest in three years instead of five. They did not need the shade of the rainforest which was therefore destroyed.

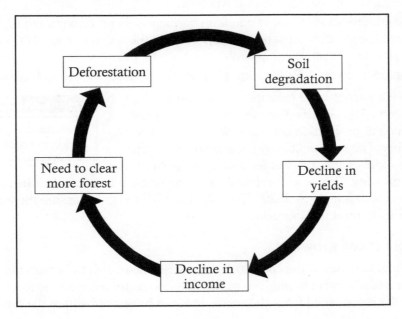

Figure 14.7 A vicious circle of deforestation

People could claim ownership of land by the process of 'slash and burn' and the planting of new crops. The nutrient cycle that gives life to the forest, as shown in Figure 15.5 (Chapter 15), was broken and the soil became degraded as shown in Figure 14.7. Without the tree cover, the forest's soils soon became exhausted. The farmers could not afford the application of the large amounts of fertilisers and pesticides needed to get good yields from the new crops. They had little assistance in the form of training in better techniques. Younger family members saw no future in farming and left to work in the towns. There was more poverty and hunger and more forests were cleared.

The Sustainable Agriculture Network (SAN) and the Rainforest Alliance (RFA)

In the 1990s, a number of organisations were concerned about the destruction of the rainforests for agriculture and set up SAN. Principles were developed which would protect the biodiversity of the rainforests and also help communities have a sustainable future. Most of the cocoa farms in Ghana are only about 3 hectares and if these disappeared, the land would probably be taken over by huge oil palm plantations. Cocoa demand is growing by about 100 000 tonnes a year but this needs to be met by improving farming practices and not by clearing more rainforest.

The standards SAN sets are based upon the following.

1. Conservation of ecosystems with no deforestation or pollution of water resources. Protection of endangered species and their habitats.
2. Reduction of water use and prevention of soil erosion. Promotion of the use of organic fertiliser and mechanical weeding.
3. Good conditions for workers and fair treatment with no discrimination. Concerns for health and safety must be met, especially in the use of chemicals with the provision of protective equipment.
4. Emphasis is on the 3 Rs for managing waste – Reduce, Re-use and Recycle.

Farmers who adopt these principles of sustainable farming become RFA certified and receive a higher price for their cocoa as production costs are more and quality usually higher. The RFA encourages businesses to source sustainable supplies and demand for cocoa produced in this way is growing. People are prepared to pay a premium for this. Mars Inc. aims to certify all its cocoa supply by 2020. The task of the RFA is to make sure there are enough certified farms to meet this demand.

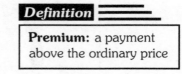

Definition

Premium: a payment above the ordinary price

Sustainable cocoa growing

The traditional varieties of the cocoa tree depend on shade. It is these varieties that are used by farmers who wish to produce sustainable cocoa. By thinning the forest carefully to preserve the more useful trees, the cocoa trees can be planted within the forest with lasting and varied benefits.

Some of these are shown in Figure 14.8. With this method, biodiversity, soil and water are conserved. By providing good conditions for workers and managing waste properly, farmers are well on the way to becoming RFA certified.

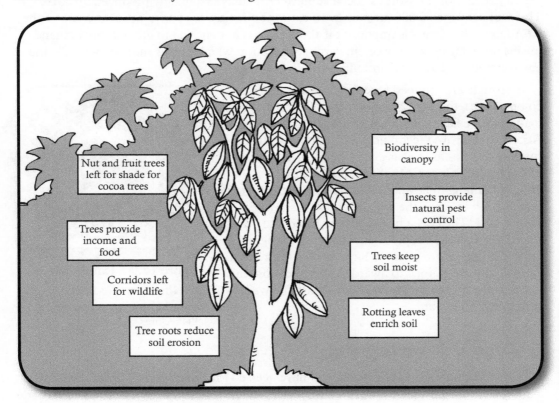

Figure 14.8 Traditional, sustainable cocoa growing

task F Describe the benefits to communities and to the environment of growing cocoa in a sustainable way.

Public-private partnerships

MDG 8 promotes the idea that development is a global partnership. 'Greening the Cocoa Industry' is a project run by the RFA, the United Nations Environment Programme (UNEP) and the Global Environmental Facility (GEF). The GEF includes governments, UN agencies, Development Banks, NGOs and private sector with the aim of providing grants to address global environmental issues. The aim of 'Greening the Cocoa Industry' is to extend the area of cocoa production under sustainable management. This will:

- improve incomes of rural areas
- supply the cocoa industry with a sustainable product

■ retain and increase biodiversity.

Together with two of the world's largest chocolate companies, this project hopes to get 10 per cent of the world's cocoa supply certified as sustainably produced by 2016. This will involve 250 000 farmers in 10 countries. Increasing consumer awareness of the RFA label – the frog – is important if the market is to continue to grow. More demand means more farmers will work towards certification which means more benefits for the environment and local communities.

If farmers are grouped together in associations or co-operatives, then providing a range of services is made much easier and local knowledge can be spread. Access to improved technology, local training and support services as well as credit facilities are all part of the project. Cocoa Abrabopa, became the first group in Ghana to be audited for Rainforest Alliance certification in 2009, the logo of which is shown in Figure 14.9. The cocoa beans have to be able to be traced through the supply chain back to the original grower if people are going to have trust in the system. People who are trained to award the certification must not be open to corrupt practices and bring the whole system into disrepute.

Figure 14.9 Rainforest Alliance Certified seal
Source: http://www.rainforest-alliance.org/

🌐 Organic crop farming

Many traditional farms are organic and have been so for generations. Production costs are higher and so prices for organic products in the shops carry a premium, like Fairtrade products. The main differences between organic farming and the more conventional system are shown in Table 14.1.

Table 14.1 Main differences between organic and conventional farming

	Commercial Organic System	**Commercial Conventional System**
Size	Generally small/medium	Very large
Labour	Labour intensive	Highly mechanised
Products	Variety of crops and livestock	Monoculture
Fertilisers	Natural, organic manure, compost from local supplies	Artificial chemical pellets of nitrogen, potassium and phosphorus made by industrial process
Weed control	Manual hoeing and mulching	Spraying with chemical herbicides
Pest control	Crop rotation, biological control	Spraying with chemical insecticides and fungicides

Table 14.1   Main differences between organic and conventional farming (Continued)

	Commercial Organic System	**Commercial Conventional System**
Soils	Soils enriched with organic materials hold moisture	Soils often degraded and eroded
Water	Mulching holds water in soil	Irrigation often used
Environmental impact	Natural predators encouraged	Loss of biodiversity

Figure 14.10 shows some organic and artificial fertiliser and a crop of potatoes that had been sprayed with acid to kill the tops before harvest.

Figure 14.10   Manure, artificial fertiliser and potato crop sprayed with acid to kill tops before harvest
Source: Wendy Taylor

Answer the following questions:
1. What problem might be caused by introducing an insect such as a beetle to control a pest such as blackfly on an organic farm?
2. How can crop rotation help to reduce pests on an organic farm?
3. Why do some consumers prefer to buy food from organic farms?

Organic and free-range pig rearing

Pigs are naturally sociable animals and on organic and free-range farms spend most of their lives outside where they are free to dig in soil and wander around in groups. They are never confined

> **Definition**
>
> **Welfare**: health and happiness

in crates. These animals are under less stress and require less medication, but they do take more looking after which is why organic and free-range pork is more expensive. A high emphasis is put on animal welfare.

Livestock

There is a growing demand for meat from countries such as China as increased standards of living mean people can afford to buy meat and they want a more varied diet. However, diets rich in meat and dairy products are not sustainable as livestock need over ten times more inputs to provide the nutrients that humans can obtain directly from plants. As the world's population continues to grow and more people want cheap meat, the demands placed on the earth's resources by the rearing of livestock mean that meat will be made in factory farms which are more like industrial systems than farms. Vast areas of rainforests are cleared to provide space to keep large numbers of cattle in small pens or to grow crops for them to eat.

Factory farmed animals

Pigs are kept in conditions that make it easier for the farmer and make the most profit for him. They are kept in crates so they cannot turn round and in crowded sheds with concrete floors where diseases spread rapidly and use of antibiotics is high. They cannot go digging or exploring and are fed artificially produced feedstuffs. They become stressed and frustrated and end up harming each other. It is not just pigs that are kept in such conditions. The welfare of chickens and cattle is a serious problem when they are kept in totally unnatural conditions to supply humans with cheap meat.

Breeding and cloning

As with plants, farmers have bred animals over centuries to select the best qualities but often the animals end up suffering if this selective breeding goes too far. Animals bred for high milk yield, for example, may not have strong enough legs to support the extra weight.

Cloning is a technique whereby farmers can create exact copies of their best animals but as with GM crops, this would not happen naturally. Many die, are deformed or suffer from a variety of health problems.

The role of consumers and governments

Governments can pass laws that ban the sale of food from cloned animals. They can ban the use of crates and insist on low stocking densities in sheds. Consumers can buy free-range pork and chickens and only drink milk that has come from cows that graze outside on grass. Farmers will supply what the consumers demand.

Fairtrade products

Consumers in developed countries can help reduce poverty in developing countries by buying products with the Fairtrade label. More people are making this choice, as can be seen in Figure 14.11 which shows the growth in sales of Fairtrade coffee in the UK.

Buying Fairtrade products means consumers are supporting:

- fair wages for reasonable working hours

- no child labour and no discrimination
- health and safety considerations and freedom to join unions
- environmental protection and improvement.

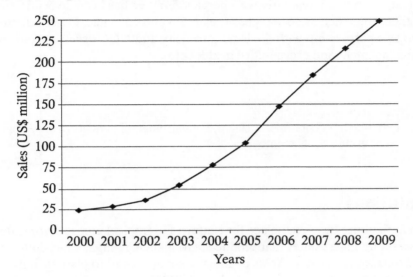

Figure 14.11 Fairtrade coffee sales in the UK

Source: http://www.fairtrade.org.uk/what_is_fairtrade/facts_and_figures.aspx

Fairtrade bananas in Colombia

Asoproban is a co-operative in N.W. Colombia established in 1984 and Fairtrade certified in 1998. It has 133 members and a democratically elected committee that manages the daily running of the banana co-operative. 15 000 boxes are produced each week, 4000 of which are Fairtrade, from farms which average 3ha in size. The co-operative also organises co-ordination of the harvest, quality control, transport logistics and sales.

task H Why are quality control and transport logistics so important?

The Fairtrade premium has been used for many things including:

- cash payments to producers to improve living standards
- irrigation system; as well as computer systems and software
- re-building of village square, chapel and two sports fields
- canteens and toilets at packing stations
- reforestation of riverbanks of the Orihueca River
- training programmes such as in soil and water management
- waste collection with plastic sent to the Asomura women's co-operative for recycling.

The co-operative has been working towards more sustainable production in many other ways as well. It has reduced spraying to protect workers and the environment and some pesticides have been completely eliminated. Workers now hoe manually to remove weeds instead of spraying regularly with herbicide. There has been diversification into growing other crops such as cocoa, guava, plantain and coconuts. Other schemes have been set up as a partnership with the local university and NGOs such as courses in financial management and preventative health care.

task I

Describe the economic, social and environmental benefits of the Asoproban co-operative to its members.

Plantations

Plantation agriculture has taken place for centuries in tropical and sub-tropical regions. Colonialists set up huge estates that produced crops such as sugar cane, coffee, tea, rubber and tobacco for export. Areas of forest were destroyed to plant usually just one type of crop and the process continues today – by MNCs.

Although much of the work is mechanised, local people are provided with jobs and the country earns foreign exchange from exports. As with most large-scale commercial farming methods, chemicals are used in vast quantities but outputs are high.

Palm oil production

Palm oil trees are native to Africa. They require high temperatures and a heavy rainfall evenly distributed throughout the year. Seeds grow in clusters which are usually harvested by hand. The trees are now being planted in areas such as Indonesia and Malaysia which supply over three-quarters of the world's palm oil. Some plantations are 10 000 hectares in size and are usually monocultures. Nearly half of the 100 best-selling products in British supermarkets contain palm oil and it is found in the following:

- food
- cosmetics
- soaps
- biofuels
- engine oils.

> **Definition**
>
> **Monoculture**: a farming system where only one crop is grown

task J

Find out some of the types of food that contain palm oil.

Companies prefer to use forested land for their plantations as the soil has not yet been degraded and they can generate more income by selling the timber before they plant the oil palms. The forests contain a rich biodiversity and as the trees are felled, habitats are lost. Figure 14.12 shows Orangutans who are losing their habitat to palm oil plantation and as a result are close to extinction.

Figure 14.12 Orangutans or palm oil?

Biofuels can be made from a number of different crops such as sugar cane and maize as well as palm oil. Biofuels therefore use land, water and other resources that could otherwise be used for food production. As demand for biofuels increases, prices of these crops rise. Indonesia plans several million more hectares of oil palm plantations for biofuel production by 2015.

task K

Debate the motions:
1. Countries should make sure their own people have enough to eat before they export crops.
2. It is wrong to use land to grow fuel instead of food when so many people in the world are hungry.

Practical Research Investigation

To consider the links between a commercial farm and activities in other sectors of the economy. This is described in detail in the appendix.

Summary

- Products of commercial farming help countries meet MDG 1
- New techniques to increase yields are not without problems but may be necessary to feed the world's growing population
- Commercial production in tropical zones needs to be sustainable and protect the forests
- Co-operatives give economic and social benefits to their members.

Exploitation and conservation of resources

» To appreciate the importance of biodiversity
» To understand the causes of deforestation
» To understand the impacts of deforestation on communities and wildlife
» To evaluate conservation methods
» To study the different forms of energy production
» To understand the dependence on oil and its possible impacts
» To appreciate the importance of water as a resource.

The importance of biodiversity

Biodiversity means the variety of plant and animal life. It is vital to conserve it in all areas of the world and not just in the tropical rainforests where the most diverse ecosystems on the planet are to be found.

Maintaining biodiversity is important to human life because:

- all plants and animals are part of planet Earth on which all life depends
- plants give oxygen for us to breathe
- insects pollinate our crops
- micro-organisms aid decay
- plants and animals provide food
- it promotes economic activities such as ecotourism
- it adds richness to our experiences
- ethically it should not be destroyed for our own greed

Deforestation in the tropical rainforests

The main areas where tropical rainforests are found are in Brazil, Peru, The Democratic Republic of the Congo and Indonesia. In these areas, the climate is hot and wet all year round. Tropical rainforests cover only 5 per cent of the earth's surface but contain half of the earth's biodiversity. They are under threat from many activities which are summarised in Figure 15.1.

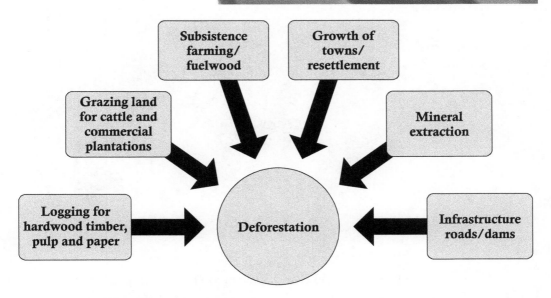

Figure 15.1   Causes of deforestation

Often the only way to claim ownership of land was to clear forest and plant crops. In the past, local communities used the technique of 'slash and burn' to clear small forest areas for subsistence farming.

Today, global companies clear huge areas of rainforests to supply the global demand for a variety of products. In the Amazon rainforest, about 75 per cent of the deforestation takes place to clear land for cattle ranches and commercial crop farms. Soya farmers in Brazil, for example, can earn several thousand US$ per hectare. The loss of these forests between 2005 and 2010 is shown in Figure 15.2.

task A

Answer the following questions based on Figure 15.2.

1. Use an atlas to help you name the countries where over 250 000ha of forest were lost.

2. What was the average loss per year of forests in Brazil? How many hectares does this work out at each day on average?

3. 225 ha is 1.5 km X 1.5 km. Try to picture the area of rainforest lost each day just in Brazil.

Illegal mining and logging in the Amazon rainforest

The Trans-Amazonian Highway was planned in the 1970s as a way of opening up Brazil's rainforest to exploit timber and minerals and so promote economic growth and also to provide land for people suffering from drought in the crowded north.

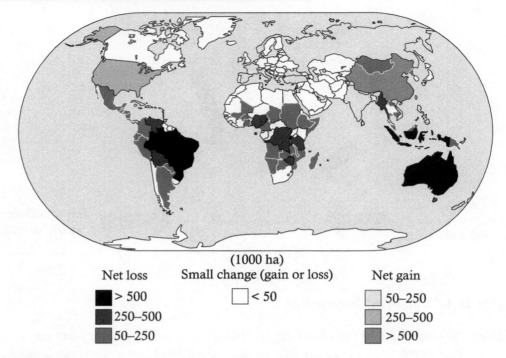

Figure 15.2 Changes in forested areas by country 2005–2010
Source: http://www.fao.org/forestry/fra/62219/en/

The road has since been continued across Peru as shown in Figure 7.4 (Chapter 7). A once inaccessible area of rainforest is now accessible. Figure 15.3 shows two different views of the impact of the road and Figure 15.4 describes activities in the mining areas, many of which are illegal.

Figure 15.3 Different views on the Trans Amazonian Highway

The road now stretching from the Atlantic to the Pacific has meant that illegal loggers and miners can exploit the rainforests along its route. Once they have shipped valuable hardwoods such as mahogany off to the developed countries to be made into expensive furniture, they mine for gold. A single mahogany tree can fetch US$4000 and even a small lump of gold is worth even more. Meanwhile the indigenous communities of Amazonian Indians are driven from their homelands through fear or hunger. They have hunted the wild animals sustainably for generations but now those in the logging camps are after the same food. The hundreds of people who travel there in the hope of finding jobs bring diseases which the Indians cannot fight. Child trafficking is common as there is no law here, just widespread corruption. Workers use mercury to extract the gold from the rock which then goes into the rivers and no-one in authority seems to care.

Figure 15.4 Illegal logging and mining in the rainforest

task

B Use Figure 15.3 and 15.4 to describe, in your own words, the problems for local communities in the mining areas of the Amazon rainforest. What could the government do to make sure the natural resources are used to benefit the people of the country?

Palm oil production and the Orangutans

Orangutans used to live across much of SE Asia but now are only to be found in the wild on the islands of Borneo and Sumatra. Due to loss of their habitat, as well as the demand from the pet and bush-meat trade, they are in serious danger of becoming extinct. Their rainforest habitat is being destroyed by logging and palm oil companies. The roads built to export the timber and oil make it easier for poachers to hunt in previously inaccessible areas while corrupt officials look the other way.

The World Wildlife Fund is working to try to protect the few Orangutans that remain. The island of Borneo belongs to three countries – Indonesia, Malaysia and Brunei so inter-governmental co-operation is needed to protect large areas of prime rainforest.

In 2004, 2.5 million hectares of the tropical rainforest of Sumatra were designated as a World Heritage Site by UNESCO for its biodiversity. It is home to over 200 mammals, 15 of which are only found in the Indonesian region, one of which is the Sumatran Orangutan.

However, in spite of having such high international protection, in 2011 it was placed on the List of World Heritage in Danger. It is suffering from 'threats posed by poaching, illegal logging, agricultural encroachment, and plans to build roads through the site.' (*Source: http://whc.unesco.org/en/news/764; http://whc.unesco.org/en/list/1167/*)

task C

What can (a) governments and (b) citizens do about the likely extinction of Orangutans in the wild?

Wildlife trade

Wildlife trade is worth billions of dollars and some of this trade threatens to push some species to extinction. The Convention on International Trade in Endangered Species (CITES) aims to make sure that the trade in wild plants and animals does not threaten their survival in the wild. International co-operation is needed to solve a global problem. Further loss of endangered species cannot be allowed to happen for a number of reasons.

1. Many of the poorest people in the world depend upon their local wild plants and animals for survival and for generations have harvested them in a sustainable way.
2. Removal of a species can have a negative impact on the food chain.
3. As species become rarer they become of greater value to criminal gangs. Usually with the help of bribes they remove large animals from National Parks where they were a major tourist attraction that brings huge benefits to local communities.

task D

Undertake research into large mammals that are in danger of extinction in your continent. List the species and describe the human activities that are putting their future at risk. Evaluate some of the strategies that have been put in place to protect them.

Services provided by the forests

Scientists believe that over 100 species become extinct each day as forests are felled at an average rate of over 40 000 hectares each day. (1 hectare = 100 metres × 100 metres). It is likely that species are being lost before we even know about them. Although we do not fully understand the role rainforests play in other global systems, we do know they undertake many vital environmental as well as social and economic services such as:

- releasing billions of tonnes of moisture every day through transpiration some of which is carried to water farmland thousands of miles away
- binding the soil and preventing soil erosion with their roots
- preventing flooding

- preventing soil degradation by contributions to the nutrient cycle
- providing homes, medical plants, food and other materials for local communities
- providing habitats for biodiversity
- absorbing carbon dioxide.

Figure 15.5 shows how trees help to add nutrients to the soil which keeps it fertile.

Figure 15.5 A nutrient cycle

task E Describe the effects of deforestation on the natural environment.

Possible solutions to the problem of deforestation

Payment for environmental services

The rainforests have to be worth more alive than dead. One way of doing this is for developed countries to pay developing countries to preserve their forests on the basis of the global services that they provide which are listed above. Logs can only be sold once but a forest can provide a service forever. However, it is difficult to get international agreement on how to do this.

Similarly, a country's government could pay its own local communities to protect the forests. For example, over US$2 billion is estimated as reconstruction costs resulting from the 2011 floods in Pakistan. If communities had been paid to preserve forests along the upper reaches of the river, these floods may not have happened or been so severe.

Afforestation

As shown in Figure 15.2, Asia has managed to actually increase its forest cover by afforestation. Whilst this has many benefits, these secondary forests can never replace the original forest which has taken thousands of years to develop the huge

Definition

Afforestation: the planting of more trees

variety of plants and animals found in them. However, if enough large areas of prime forest are left they can act as sources of biodiversity for the new forests.

task F

Find out about any local tree planting projects – what the main purposes are, what sort of trees are being planted and by whom. Undertake a study to see if it is possible to plant some trees in your school grounds and prepare a report, including the benefits of afforestation, to give to your head teacher.

Selective felling, licences and quotas

Governments may allow a limited amount of legal deforestation in order to bring in some revenue from timber but not to destroy the forest completely. Sometimes it may be that only a few valuable trees are worth felling, such as mahogany or teak. However, it is much easier to get these trees out if everything else is cut down as well. Instead, helicopters could be used to lift these trees out of the forest and so leave the rest unharmed. These forms of selective felling keep some of the forest so wildlife habitats remain and are hopefully linked up with corridors of remaining forest.

Only companies that respect the country's laws and pay taxes to the government should be given licences to fell so that the income from the sale of timber goes to help improve the country's infrastructure. Companies granted a licence will be given a quota which will only allow a certain number of logs to be removed.

Timber certification system

The Forest Stewardship Council (FSC) is an international NGO that set up a wood labelling scheme. Some trees can grow quickly and in that sense they are renewable so a forest can produce timber for generations if the forest is well managed. Timber showing the FSC logo has not been logged illegally and certain criteria have been met. When people buy FSC timber, they know that:

- national, international laws and rights of indigenous people have been respected
- land has not been obtained illegally
- the economic and social situation of workers and local communities is improved
- biodiversity, soils and water are conserved.

In 2010, the European Union (EU) voted to ban the import of illegal timber and this will come into force in 2012. A trusted certification system is therefore essential in order for people to know where the wood has come from.

task
G Why do you think it has taken the EU so long to bring in this law when the contribution of illegal logging to tropical rainforest destruction has been known for some time? Do you think it will make much difference to the amount of illegal logging that takes place?

National Parks

Figure 15.6 shows the percentage of forest area under protection in different regions. Protected areas may be large national parks or smaller forest reserves. These can have an important role to play in ecotourism which benefits local communities. Hunters become forest guides and communities sell crafts instead of practising 'slash and burn'. If their livelihood depends on the forest, they will try to protect it. If local people protect the forest, then the biodiversity it supports is also protected.

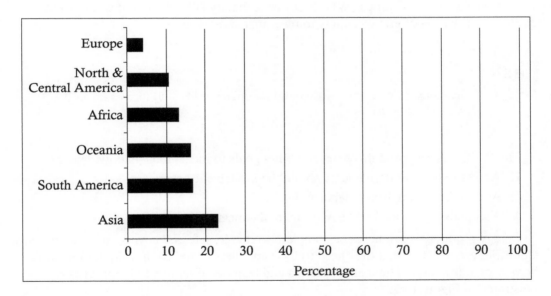

Figure 15.6   Percentage of forest area in protected areas (2010)
Source: http://www.fao.org/forestry/fra/62219/en/

task
H

1. Describe the main features of the chart in Figure 15.6.
2. Find out the names of the National Parks within your own country. Identify why they are protected areas and how successful this protection is.
3. Describe the human activities that take place in your National Parks.

The role of governments

Governments have a major role to play in protecting the world's forests and the tropical rainforests in particular.

They need to:

- control the illegal loggers
- increase support for the policing of National Parks
- make laws that are enforced
- support companies that produce timber more sustainably.

🌐 Energy supplies

Daily living, industrial production, transport and trade all depend upon the use of energy. This may be directly in the form of firewood and petrol or indirectly in the use of electricity generated by fossil fuels, nuclear energy or renewables.

The World Energy Council (WEC) estimates that by 2050 the world will need to double today's level of energy supply to meet increased demand.

task I

Give two reasons why the demand for energy is likely to increase over the next few decades.

The WEC has proposed three sustainability goals to meet global energy demand.

1. Accessibility – modern energy should be available for everyone.
2. Availability – supply is reliable and safe.
3. Acceptability – social and environmental concerns are met.

Energy production can never be completely reliable, safe and environmentally friendly. Countries are realising that they need to have an 'energy mix' so they do not rely too heavily on one source. There are problems and benefits of all the different types as illustrated in Figure 15.7.

task J

Decision making exercise

Undertake some further research into the eight forms of energy shown in Figure 15.7 and draw up a table to show the advantages and disadvantages of each of them.

Select four that you think would make a good energy mix for your country. Explain why you have chosen these and why you have not chosen the other four.

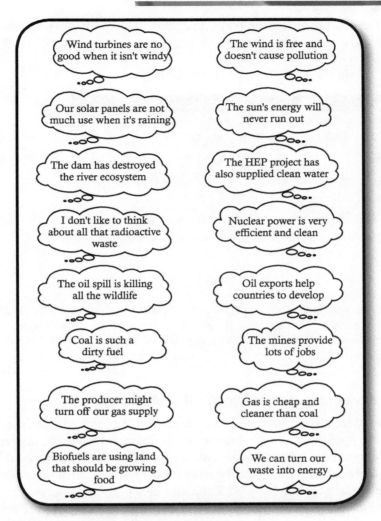

Figure 15.7 Different views on forms of energy

To limit climate change (see Chapter 17) it is essential to reduce carbon emissions from burning fossil fuels. This can either be done by burning smaller amounts or by burning them more efficiently. There are many ways individuals in these countries can reduce their own personal use of fossil fuels such as by not leaving computers on stand-by and by turning down the heating. Higher prices will force research into new technologies so that less fuel is needed to produce the same amount of energy.

Oil

Oil is not only used to generate electricity in oil-fired power stations, it is used to lubricate machines and keeps transport on the move. It may be regarded as the most important commodity to industrialised nations.

Table 15.1 shows the oil consumption on a daily basis of the top six consumers. (1 barrel = 0.16 cubic metre / 160 litres.)

Table 15.1 Main oil consuming countries (2009)

Country	Oil consumption (million barrels/day)
US	18.7
China	8.2
Japan	4.4
India	3.0
Russia	2.7
Brazil	2.5

Source: http://www.nationmaster.com/graph/ene_oil_con-energy-oil-consumption

task K

What measures could individual Americans take to reduce their daily consumption of oil so that there will be some left for future generations? Draw up a class list of all the ways energy can be conserved by individuals around the world.

Social and environmental effects of oil production

Oil production is highly mechanised and once the drilling rigs and pipelines have been constructed, the operations provide little local employment. However, tax revenues from the oil companies do provide governments with funds that can be used to develop a country so there can be some social benefits if the money is spent on improved healthcare and more schools. Oil production and transportation is a risky business and spills can have disastrous effects on the natural environment. Habitats are ruined and biodiversity is lost as vegetation becomes covered in oil and animals suffocate or are unable to move. Local communities that depend upon their natural environment for food and water will suffer serious health problems and people may even have to migrate from their homeland.

The most accessible sources of oil have been used and exploration is now going ahead in remote wilderness areas where even a small oil spill could have devastating consequences for local communities and wildlife. The statements in Figure 15.8 are extracts from Shell's website, an oil company that already operates in the Arctic.

> **Respecting our neighbours** – The Arctic is home to around 400 000 native peoples who have close ties with the land, sea and wildlife. We recognise the importance of listening to these communities before moving ahead carefully with our activities.
>
> **Source:** http://www.shell.com/home/content/innovation/meeting_demand/arctic/respecting_neighbours/

Protecting biodiversity – The Arctic is rich in biodiversity and contains ecologically-sensitive areas. The health of plants and animals depend on the survival of their habitat. We work with scientists to better understand the Arctic's ecosystems. We have policies in place to assess environmental risks and we closely monitor the impact of our activities.

Source: http://www.shell.com/home/content/innovation/meeting_demand/arctic/protecting-biodiversity/

Figure 15.8 Shell's web statements on Arctic oil exploration

task L Use the internet to undertake research into recent oil spills either on land or at sea, and describe their impacts on local communities and the natural environment.

Case study – Ogoniland, S Nigeria

Half a century of oil production has caused devastation to the natural environment and communities in Ogoniland. In 2011, the UN Environment Programme (UNEP) published a report highlighting the following causes of oil spills in the area.

1. The oil company did not follow international best practices and ignored local regulations.
2. Government agencies lacked resources and expertise to monitor the oil operations and spills.
3. Local authorities did not enforce regulations.
4. Illegal operations.

> **Definition**
>
> **Best practice**: the most suitable way of doing something

The effects of many oil spills were damaging in the following ways.

1. The heavy rainfall meant oil was washed across farmland and into rivers and oil was found in soil at depths of 5m. At Nisisioken Ogale, an 8cm layer of refined oil floated on groundwater supplying community wells.
2. Crops became stressed and died. Roots in mangrove swamps were coated in oil and fires had destroyed all vegetation in their path.
3. Wetlands are now highly degraded. Destruction of habitats meant loss of fish spawning grounds with impacts on the food chain. Fishermen have lost traditional fishing grounds.
4. At Nisisioken Ogale, wells were contaminated with carcinogens at levels 900 times WHO guidelines. Waste from operations was dumped in the environment.

> **Definition**
>
> **Carcinogen**: a substance that is capable of causing cancer

UNEP made a number of recommendations.

1. A fund of US$1 billion to be provided by the oil industry and Nigerian government.
2. New staff to be trained for the Ministry of the Environment.
3. The oil industry must review and improve its procedures.
4. An Environmental Restoration Authority to be set up to clean the soil and river systems, replant mangroves, run danger awareness campaigns and provide clean water supplies and health monitoring in local communities.

Nigeria facts and figures

Nigeria is the tenth largest oil producer in the world producing 2.5 million barrels/day. Table 15.2 shows some facts about the country.

Table 15.2 Nigeria facts and figures (2010)

Exports	US$83 billion
Imports	US$44 billion
Life expectancy	48 years
Population with improved drinking water	58%
Population with improved sanitation	32%
Literacy rate	68%
Petroleum and petroleum products as % exports	95%
HDI rank	142

Source: https://www.cia.gov/library/publications/the-world-factbook/geos/ni.html

task M

Answer the following questions:
1. Does Nigeria have a trade surplus or a trade deficit?
2. How much money does Nigeria earn from its exports of oil and oil products?
3. Do the social statistics suggest this money is being used to benefit the population?

🌐 Water resources

Water is the key to all life but this most precious resource is under pressure from:

- increasing populations
- increased industrial production
- pollution from farms, industries and settlements
- climate change and drought.

task N

Make three lists to show the different types of pollution that could come from farms, industries and settlements.

Chapter 19 considers in detail the Lesotho Highlands Water Project. Multi-purpose projects such as this bring a variety of benefits to communities and the economy but they can also have negative impacts on local people and wildlife.

China's rapidly growing economy has put its water supplies under enormous pressure. Industries require vast quantities in production processes as well as in the cooling of machinery. Rivers are accessible means of disposing of an industry's waste. China's Three Gorges Dam project had three main aims which were to control flooding on the River Yangtse, improve navigation and generate hydro-electric power. The discussions about the advantages and disadvantages of this huge construction project continue as China undertakes another scheme to alter the natural water flows. Its water crisis is described in Figure 15.9.

Cities such as Beijing, which now has over 20 million people, require huge amounts of water each day but parts of northern China are suffering from drought. The use of underground sources of water is clearly not sustainable as these supplies have taken thousands of years to fill up and have now been seriously depleted. Rivers such as the Yellow River are often too polluted to use and as they dry up, the pollution becomes even more concentrated.

The South-North Water Transfer Project will see water from the River Yangste diverted north. The financial and environmental costs are huge, and whole communities have to move to make way for the canals that transfer the water from one river system to another. The people of the south wonder if their rivers will still be able to water their crops and supply their towns as they have done for generations.

Figure 15.9 China's water crisis threatens economic production

task O

1. Describe the many uses of water.
2. Describe in your own words the problems facing China with regard to its water supplies as described in Figure 15.9.

Water footprints

In the same way a person's carbon footprint can be estimated, so it is also possible to work out a water footprint – the water that a person uses directly for household use as well as that used to produce the food they eat and the clothes they wear.

The water footprint per person per year in the UK is 1.7 million litres. 1 million litres of this is water used in other countries to make goods for the UK citizen. The following list shows the litres of water needed to make certain products.

2500 → 1 kg rice
10 000 → 1 kg cotton
1800 → 1 kg cane sugar
1000 → 1 litre milk
1600 → 1 kg wheat bread
15 400 → 1 kg beef
17 000 → 1 kg chocolate
214 → 1 kg tomatoes
5060 → 1 kg cheese
11 400 → 1 litre biodiesel (soybean)

Source: http://www.waterfootprint.org/?page=files/home

Water resources need careful management if they are going to be sustainable and not be a cause of 'water wars'. Water security is going to become as important as food security for governments. Building more dams across rivers and digging deeper wells is not sustainable.

As more water is pumped to supply urban populations, ponds and rivers dry up with devastating consequences for wildlife. Declining water supplies for humans and loss of biodiversity in wetlands are linked together in what is another serious global problem.

Practical Research Investigation: Water supply

Aim
To assess the sustainability of the school's water supply.

Objectives
1. To find out from where the school gets its water
2. To consider the reliability of the supply
3. To observe the uses made of water during the school day
4. To determine the best ways to conserve water
5. To increase awareness of the need to conserve water.

Methods
- interviews to establish sources of water supply
- observation of the reliability of supply over a week/month/year
- recording of water meter data, number of bottles, tanker deliveries etc.
- observation of water use and water waste
- questionnaires to determine possible conservation methods.

Source: Adapted from Appendix to 'Scheme of Work, Cambridge IGCSE Development Studies 0453'

Practical Research Investigation: Biodiversity

Aim

To assess the biodiversity of a local site.

Objectives
1. To identify a local area of natural vegetation that may be under threat
2. To undertake a study of the wildlife of the site
3. To investigate the present use made of the area and possible future use
4. To consider local residents' concerns about habitat destruction.

Methods
- observation in the field/study of local records
- line/quadrat survey to identify plant diversity
- interview with local ranger/wildlife official
- questionnaire of local residents.

Source: Adapted from Appendix to 'Schemes of Work, Cambridge IGCSE Studies 0453'

- Biodiversity is essential to all life on the planet but it is under threat from many human activities and many species are in danger of extinction
- Deforestation is a global issue of extreme importance as forests play many roles in global systems
- Deforestation can be reduced with support from governments around the world
- Oil production is essential for modern economies but causes problems in the environment
- Energy and water conservation will become more important as pressure on supplies increases.

Summary

Tourism

16

Learning Objectives

» To appreciate the negative impacts of mass tourism
» To understand that a more sustainable approach is possible
» To appreciate the problems of dependence on the tourist industry
» To understand how eco-tourism can protect the natural environment and cultures.

🌐 Sustainable tourism

Tourism is a main source of income for many developing countries and as one of the world's top job creators it can play a major role in improving local people's quality of life. The tourist industry pays taxes which can be used by governments to improve roads, build schools and hospitals. Governments determine the regulations and laws by which the tourist industry operates.

Sustainable tourism is seen as a way to relieve poverty and improve living standards now and at the same time protect a country's culture and natural environment for the future. The challenge is to develop an industry that benefits the local economy and people without spoiling what the tourists have come to see. The inter-relationship between economic, political, social and environmental issues is very important.

Table 16.1 shows the negative impacts tourism can have on an area and how these could be managed to make it more sustainable.

Table 16.1 A more sustainable approach to tourism

Negative impacts of mass tourism	A more sustainable approach
Natural vegetation and biodiversity destroyed to build airports, hotels	Natural areas have a value with ecotourism
Wildlife disturbed and cultural sites eroded by large numbers of visitors	Restricted areas and licences for responsible guides, promotion of other attractions
Loss of culture due to tourists bringing new ideas/clothing/customs	Traditions promoted as tourist attraction
Lack of respect for local traditions	Education of tourists in local culture
Overuse of resources	Notices to conserve water in hotels

Table 16.1 A more sustainable approach to tourism (Continued)

Negative impacts of mass tourism	A more sustainable approach
MNCs run hotels and profits go abroad	Small scale businesses run by local people
Mass produced, cheap souvenirs imported	Traditional craft industry encouraged
Visual impact of hotels	Regulations to restrict height and design
Exclusive use of facilities for tourists	Local use of facilities at off-peak times
Foreign food imported to provide meals for tourists	Business links between hotels and local producers to increase the market for farmers and fishermen
Rubbish and human waste causes water pollution	Limited tourist numbers reduce pollution
Cruise ships and airports cause visual, noise and air pollution	Limited arrivals due to high prices

How tourism can protect a forest

What is a forest worth? How do you put a value on its peacefulness or its value to a group of gorillas that live in it? It may be worth US$ 20 000 to a logging company for its timber. This would be a short term 'win' for the economy but long term 'lose' for wildlife and everything else that depends on the forest.

If a forest can be of value as a tourist attraction and is worth more in the long term than it is in logs, then it may not be destroyed for timber. This is a 'win-win' result for the economy, communities and the environment over the long term.

task A

Draw two sketches and use labels to show:
1. A forest cleared and trucks carting away the logs. Value = US$ 20 000.
2. A forest protected for tourists with lodges, cycle hire etc. Value = US$ 2000 per year.

Education of tourists

It is important to educate tourists about the need for sustainable tourism when they book their holidays. As developing countries try to create sustainable tourism, tourists from developed countries must play their part. MDG 8 states the importance of a global partnership for development.

These may be some of the comments overheard on a tropical holiday:

'Why can't I have a shower everyday like I do at home?'

'I'm going 4X4 driving over the dunes tomorrow.'

'We've spent so much on our hotel we won't be going shopping while we're here.'

'I've heard the guides can be bribed to give us a better view of the lions from the jeep.'

'I'm going diving to collect some coral to take home.'

task B Draw up a Tourist Charter – a list of ten things that tourists need to do to help tourism be more sustainable.

The problem of sewage

Many tourist resorts are on the coast as sea, sun and sand are the most popular holidays. The disposal of huge amounts of sewage from the tourist hotels is a major issue for local authorities. Sewage should be treated and piped far out to sea. Often it is not treated and it is washed back near the shores with the waves and tides. Where there are no proper sanitation systems, sewage passes through the ground into rivers and then into the sea by the beaches.

If popular beaches become contaminated by sewage, people are advised not to swim or fish in the waters. Not only is it very unpleasant to look at, it is also a health problem as it can cause diarrhoea and skin problems. It can also damage marine ecosystems by adding too many nutrients to the water. Internet search engines quickly pick up newspaper reports and it could take years for a resort to recover from bad publicity.

Cruise liners

Cruise liners dock at islands and ports around the world. Large cruise liners travel about 3 metres on a litre of fuel. They have several restaurants where food is always available and the waste generated is substantial (Figure 16.1). They bring economic benefits to the places at which they stop as the tourists go ashore and spend money. Some places, however, do not welcome them.

Figure 16.1 Cruise liners and crowds in the Mediterranean
Source: Wendy Taylor

task C

Make a list of the benefits that cruise liners can bring to a tourist area and suggest reasons why some resorts do not welcome them.

🌐 Tourism in Mauritius

Island History

In 1598, the island of Mauritius in the Indian Ocean was uninhabited until it was settled by the Dutch and later by the French. By the late eighteenth century, 50 000 slaves worked there. The British took over in 1810 wanting a stop on their passage to India. From 1834, there was much immigration from India to Mauritius to solve the labour shortage problem in the expanding sugar industry and many never returned. After Independence in 1968, tourism and textile industries developed although the country still relied on sugar.

Main attractions

Mauritius is one of the hundreds of holiday destinations offering the following: a mix of cultures and cuisines, quality hotels, island location, sub-tropical climate, sea, sun and sand, rich history, traditions, sport including golf on 16 courses and wildlife safaris. Some of these features are shown in Figure 16.2.

Figure 16.2 Beaches, hotel and golf course in Mauritius
Source: Cynthia Tipper

A successful tourist industry may result in a country depending on it for an income. Other sectors of the economy may be neglected as investment is focused on tourist resorts. Fashions in holidays tend to change and if large numbers of people decide they want a different sort of holiday, hotels will stay empty and financial losses in all the industries associated with tourism will be considerate. Natural disasters and unstable political situations are some of the other reasons countries should not rely on tourists for an income as they can so easily go elsewhere. Some facts about the tourist industry are shown in Figure 16.3 and Figure 16.4.

2009 – 871 356 tourists

2010 – 934 827 tourists – 7.3 per cent increase

2011 – 980 000 tourists (forecast) – 4.8 per cent increase

Tourist receipts – US$1.37 billion (2010)

GDP – US$9.7 billion (2010)

Population – 1.3 million (2010)

22 per cent increase from Asia – 2009–2010

Figure 16.3   Mauritius Tourist facts and figures

Source: http://www.gov.mu/portal/goc/cso/ei878/toc.htm; https://www.cia.gov/library/publications/the-world-factbook/geos/mp.html

task D

Answer the following questions:
1. What proportion of GDP was from tourist receipts in 2010?
2. How does the number of tourists compare with the population of Mauritius?
3. How would you describe the increase in tourist numbers between 2009 and 2011?
4. Why is the national airline proposing its own flights to China?
5. Do you think the increase in the number of tourists each year will eventually mean people stop going? Explain your answer.
6. How might the upkeep of the golf courses affect the natural environment?

2006 – Outbreak of Chikungunya, a mosquito-borne disease

2008 – Start of the global financial crisis

2010 – Euro fell considerably against the US$ and Mauritian rupee

2011 – Irish Football manager's daughter murdered in hotel room

2011 – National airline's proposed flights to China

Future developments – Major golf championships, luxury wedding venues

Figure 16.4   Factors affecting the tourist industry of Mauritius

task E

Answer the following questions:
1. Why is it important for countries not to depend too heavily on tourism?
2. Why do you think it is important to ensure visitors' safety?
3. What can Mauritius do to make sure tourists return and new ones continue to arrive?

Biodiversity of Mauritius

Before 1598, Mauritius was teeming with wildlife typical of sub-tropical islands. Due to deforestation for plantations and deer ranches, hunting and the introduction of alien species, its biodiversity is now amongst the most threatened in the world. As it is an island, wildlife cannot move back in from neighbouring areas. As a result:

- good quality native forest is estimated to cover less than 2 per cent of the island
- 24 of the 52 native species of forest animals are now extinct, including the Dodo, a giant parrot and two species of giant tortoise
- only twelve species of land bird have so far escaped extinction and of these, nine are under threat
- of the 17 native reptile species, only 12 remain.

Water sports and sport fishing are popular but catches are falling in terms of size of fish and numbers. Anchors are damaging corals. Marshes and mangroves are being degraded or lost due to construction for housing or tourist accommodation.

task F

Explain why ecotourism is not likely to be very important in Mauritius.

Sustainable tourism

The following list shows some of the efforts made in Mauritius to develop tourism in a sustainable way:

- a Social Responsibility Programme helps tourist companies contribute to social and environmental projects
- locations on routes to particular attractions are developed to spread the benefits of tourism across more communities
- priority is given to hotels that provide the highest standards although these are usually operated by MNCs
- coastal landscapes are protected by hotel regulations that cover height (13–15m), area (20 per cent of plot), design (reflect tropical island) and distance from the sea (30m)

- natural vegetation is left to reduce the visual effects of hotel development
- energy saving systems are encouraged
- operators of dolphin watching boats have to be licenced and there are strict regulations such as not to approach within 50 metres of dolphins.

task G

Answer the following questions:
1. Why has Mauritius focused on high quality tourism?
2. Compare the hotels in Figures 16.1 and 16.2. To what extent do you think the coastal landscape of Mauritius is more protected than that of the Mediterranean resort.

Tourism in Belize

Tourism is the main foreign exchange earner in this small country in South America. In the past, it was diving that was the main tourist activity. Today, it is the cultural and natural environment that is attracting older and more affluent tourists, particularly from the US. Its main attractions are:

- the second longest barrier reef in the world with diverse marine life
- one third of the land is under some form of protection
- rainforests
- Maya cultural and archaeological sites
- 571 species of birds
- 163 species of land mammals
- 121 species of reptiles.

task H

Decision making exercise.
A marine environment such as a coral reef attracts tourists for boating, swimming, diving and fishing. Consider the following possible courses of action to protect it from damage and decide which would be the best strategy. Explain why you have chosen that solution and why you have not chosen the others. Suggest how your chosen strategy could be put into operation.
1. Create zones for the different activities.
2. Limit the number of boats.
3. Do not allow diving and snorkelling and only allow 'catch and release' fishing.
4. Create marine reserves where tourists are not allowed.

task 1

List the activities that can be enjoyed within a National Park that consists of rainforests and fast flowing rivers and which is home to large numbers of different forms of wildlife. Consider whether any of these activities might conflict with each other and suggest possible solutions to the problems that might be caused.

Problems for the tourist industry

If tourism in Belize is to be sustainable, pressures on the natural environment must be removed or at least controlled. If the natural environment is not protected then the tourist industry does not have much of a future. The main problems are:

- a lack of adequate sanitation systems
- destruction of beaches, mangroves and forests for housing and industry
- overfishing and illegal hunting
- lack of enforcement of protected areas.

Eco-tourism in Belize

Belize was one of the first countries to develop the idea of ecotourism. Ecotourism is an economic activity that contributes to, rather than exploits, the natural and cultural features of an area. Local communities are involved rather than foreign tourist operators and as they earn income so it improves their quality of life.

For eco-tourism to be really sustainable it needs to have a small impact and so it needs to be small-scale. The Toledo Eco-tourism Association (TEA) set up a community project that benefits the local people and conserves the tropical forests as well as the culture of the communities. Instead of 'slash and burn' agriculture, the forests are used as a natural resource for small groups of tourists who live in villages such as Laguna. The accommodation provided is simple but clean and made out of local materials. Latrines are provided but a shower is likely to be a bucket and cup.

Figure 16.5   A view of Laguna

Laguna, part of which is shown in Figure 16.5, is a village of about 300 people near the Aquacaliente Lagoon, shown in Figure 16.6. The benefits of tourism are shared widely throughout the village with different families providing the guides, food and entertainment. The description in Figure 16.6 shows some of the attractions of the area for eco-tourists.

'The hike is strenuous, dirty and definitely worth it. As you near the lagoon, wildlife increases. Turtles and fish are visible in the swamp and nearby by black creek, which the trail follows for a short way. Solitary egrets and herons hunt along the creeks edge, while flocks of ibis and wood stork roost atop the creekside vegetation. Kingfishers continuously clatter while darting above and diving into the water. The mangrove surrounding the lagoon is alive with warblers and flycatchers feasting on the plentiful insect life.'

Source: http://www.southernbelize.com/vill_laguna.html

Figure 16.6 The Aquacaliente Lagoon

task J

Bird watching and wildlife photography are growing in popularity as tourist activities. Assume a MNC wants to build a large hotel on the shores of the lake shown in Figure 16.6 and build a road up to it. The MNC has assured the Minister for the Environment that this project will protect the biodiversity of the lake and its surroundings and will employ 50 local people as waiters etc. The MNC claims that the road will allow further projects that will help the economy. In a group, discuss the advantages and disadvantages of this proposal and prepare a report for class discussion as to whether the hotel should be allowed or not.

- A more sustainable approach to tourism benefits both the natural environment and local communities
- Tourists themselves are global partners in promoting a sustainable industry
- It is important that countries do not depend too much upon the tourist industry
- Regulations can reduce the impact of tourist developments and activities
- Eco-tourism protects both ecosystems and cultures.

Summary

Climate change and pollution

17

Learning Objectives

- To understand the causes and effects of climate change and ways to reduce its impact
- To appreciate the problems caused by acid rain and its possible solutions
- To consider solutions to pollution in urban areas from vehicles and waste.

🌐 Climate change

Climate conditions have changed over the earth for billions of years. Ice ages in Europe have come and gone. Hot, humid conditions that resulted in the coal measures of China have long since disappeared from that region. Where oil is now found there were once seas.

task A

Research how coal and oil were formed and explain why:
1. They are called fossil fuels.
2. They are non-renewable.
3. They emit carbon dioxide when they are burned.

Over the last 100 years, the average temperature of the earth's atmosphere has risen by about 0.75 degrees Celsius. Many scientists believe that this warming trend is caused by human activities. Some scientists do not recognise the warming trend and point to data that shows otherwise. Some believe the warming is due to natural processes such as sun-spot or volcanic activity. We may never be completely certain one way or the other, but the human activities that might be contributing to climate change will now be considered.

Causes of climate change

Figure 17.1 shows what happens when the radiation from the sun reaches the earth's atmosphere. Within the atmosphere there is a layer of gases, mainly carbon dioxide and methane, which trap warmth rather like a blanket. As they act like the glass in a greenhouse, these gases are called 'greenhouse gases'.

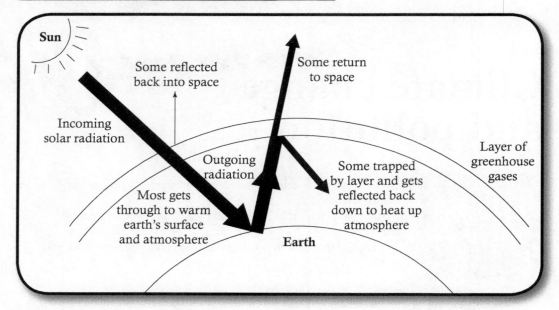

Figure 17.1 Solar radiation and greenhouse gases

These gases occur naturally, such as in volcanic eruptions and when organisms decompose, and have helped to regulate temperatures on earth for millions of years. It is generally thought that human activities are adding to this layer and so causing an increase in warming in the earth's atmosphere. This global warming is linked to climate change as it causes changes in rainfall patterns as well as in temperatures. Changes in temperature influence wind systems and any change in the global circulation of air currents will have a worldwide impact. The pie chart in Figure 17.2 shows the global proportion of greenhouse gas emissions from different sources of human activities.

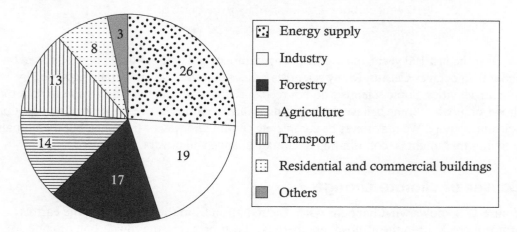

Figure 17.2 Greenhouse gas emissions (%)

Source: http://www.ipcc.ch/pdf/assessment-report/ar4/syr/ar4_syr.pdf Page 42

Burning fossil fuel releases carbon dioxide and accounts for nearly two-thirds of all greenhouse gas emissions. Livestock produce methane and when forests are burnt, the carbon stored in them is released. How much further the global temperature of the atmosphere will rise depends upon our ability to reduce these emissions and stop deforestation.

Impacts of climate change

It is generally agreed by many scientists that some of the changes that are occurring in weather and climate patterns are due to climate change brought about by man's activities. The possible effects are many and varied and include:

- warmer seas expand and cause sea level to rise
- melting ice in the Arctic and ice caps in Antarctica and Greenland cause sea level to rise
- low lying coasts and islands such as The Maldives may be submerged
- extreme weather events such as cyclones in Bangladesh and droughts in Somalia may become more severe
- people will become displaced from their homelands
- food production will be affected such as growing wheat in Russia
- species may be unable to adapt and will migrate or die
- diseases such as malaria could spread
- rainforests such as the Amazon could suffer as rainfall patterns change.

Rises in sea level of 0.5m will cause serious flooding in low-lying coastal areas. Study a map of your own continent and list the main cities that are situated on the coast. How many of these are the capital cities? Describe the likely problems for people living in these places if sea levels rise.

Explain some of the ways that food production may be affected by climate change.

Government action

Individual countries have their own ways of trying to combat climate change. These may include:

- Climate Change Act which sets a target for reduction in greenhouse gases by 2050
- promotion of the use of low carbon fuels, nuclear power and renewable energy

- promotion of energy conservation
- research into new technologies such as carbon capture – the carbon dioxide emitted from coal and oil-fired power stations would be captured and piped underground for safe storage perhaps in old oil wells
- emission trading schemes – companies are allowed to produce a certain amount of carbon dioxide. If they produce less than this, they can sell their credit to a company which has gone over its limit.

The United Nations Framework Convention on Climate Change seeks to get international co-operation as this is a global problem which has to have a global solution. Many governments have signed up to agreements to try to limit climate change at various summits shown in Figure 17.3.

Kyoto, Japan (1997) – Laws were drawn up under which industrialised countries would reduce their emissions by a certain per cent compared with 1990 levels.

Copenhagen, Denmark (2009) – The summit was supposed to decide global action after 2012 when Kyoto expires. Some countries stated their intentions as to what they were prepared to do but there was no legally binding treaty.

Cancun, Mexico (2010) – A Green Climate Fund was outlined to help developing countries reduce the impacts of climate change and introduce low carbon technology. It seems there were many disagreements and progress was limited.

South Africa (2011) – The international community decided to begin negotiations on a new agreement that would legally enforce commitments to control emissions of greenhouse gases.

Figure 17.3 International climate summits

Under the Kyoto Protocol, emissions are assigned to the country that produces the goods, not the one that consumes them. So countries which have outsourced their manufacturing to developing countries look as if they have reduced their emissions when really they have just transferred them elsewhere. The carbon dioxide emissions of selected countries are shown in Table 5.1 (Chapter 5).

Individual action

An individual's contribution to climate change comes from three main areas.

1. Use of energy in the home – heating, lighting, cooking, entertainment.
2. Means of travel – car, bus.
3. Purchase of consumer goods – food, household items, electrical equipment.

Definition

Carbon footprint: the amount of greenhouse gases emitted by the actions of a person in using fossil fuels

In order to have a reasonable standard of living, it is inevitable that people use energy and so emit carbon dioxide. However, people are being encouraged to work out their own carbon footprint and consider ways it could be reduced.

The carbon emissions for which each person is responsible do not only take place where they live. Many of the goods used by people in developed countries are manufactured elsewhere and it is in these countries that the carbon dioxide is emitted during production. Figure 17.4 shows some of the ways people have tried to reduce their carbon footprint. In most cases, money is saved by reducing consumption of energy.

Figure 17.4   Some ways of reducing carbon footprints

For each of the points 1–3 above, describe the ways people might be able to reduce their energy use.

Reducing Emissions from Deforestation and Degradation (REDD)

Forests are vital in the struggle against climate change. The leaves absorb carbon dioxide and store it and when the forests are burnt in order to clear them for agriculture, carbon dioxide is released. REDD is a system where tropical countries are paid to preserve their forests. Payment has to be greater than the economic benefits of chopping them down but many conflicting land uses have to be resolved before anything can happen. Satellite technology can be used to check deforestation rates by comparing images of an area over a period of time. You can see an example of this online at http://www.earthobservatory. nasa.gov/IOTD/view.php?id=6811.

task E Describe some of the conflicting land uses there might be in an area of rainforest that is being deforested. How might these be resolved?

REDD money could be used for:

- forest rangers and police to control illegal loggers
- better vehicles/technology to prevent crime
- alternative economic activities that take the pressure off the forests.

task F 1. What sort of new technology could be useful in helping to protect the forests?

2. To what extent do you think increasing patrols in the forests will prevent them from being felled?

🌐 Acid rain

Sulphur dioxide and nitrogen oxides are emitted into the atmosphere when fossil fuels are burnt. These gases dissolve in water droplets in clouds and fall as rain sometimes large distances away from the source of the pollution.

Winds take no notice of regional or even national boundaries. As the diluted sulphuric and nitric acids fall as rain, they affect both the natural and human environment:

- lakes become acidic and fish die which impacts on the food chain and fishermen's livelihoods
- crops become stressed and weak so cannot fight off pests and eventually die
- trees often lose their leaves and die

- acids leach the nutrients such as potassium out of the soil which reduces its fertility
- stonework on buildings and statues is attacked and crumbles and tourism suffers
- toxic metals are dissolved out of soils and enter water supplies.

In developed countries, laws to control emissions have resulted in scrubbers being fitted to chimneys of power stations which remove the gases before they are released. One of these can be seen in Figure 17.5. Lime is added to lakes to try to neutralise the acid.

Figure 17.5 A scrubber on a power station chimney

Source: Wendy Taylor

task G

1. Why is international co-operation needed to reduce acid rain?
2. What are the factors that will determine which areas around a large industry might suffer from acid rain?

Acid rain in China

China has the third largest reserves of coal in the world so coal will be its main source of power for many years to come. Coal in particular produces large quantities of gases which cause acid rain as shown in Figure 17.6. It is a problem in several parts of China as the country depends on manufacturing products for export and there are many industrial areas.

Dalian is a summer resort about 400km from Beijing. In 2007, over half of its rain was reported as acid. However, efforts have been made to reduce sulphur dioxide emissions.

Acid rain in Zambia

The major exploitation of Zambia's Copperbelt began in the 1930s. Today, copper and cobalt account for nearly two-thirds of Zambia's exports but the mining of these products comes at a cost to both communities and the natural environment as illustrated in Figure 17.7.

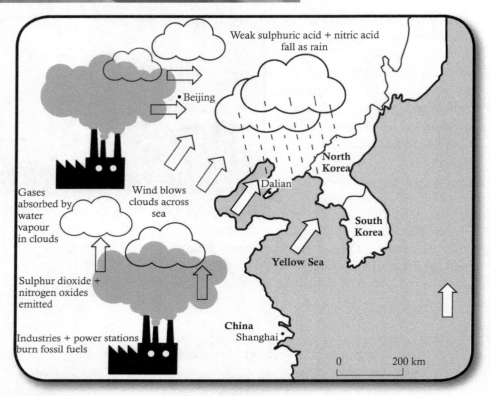

Figure 17.6 Acid rain in Northern China

In the small mining town of Mufulira in the copper belt of Zambia, people still struggle to get by on a few dollars a day. Not enough to feed families never mind buy medicines to treat those suffering from air and water pollution from the copper mines and processing works which give off sulphur dioxide. Acid used in the smelting process has spilt into the drinking water supply, clouds of sulphur make it difficult to breathe and acid rain kills crops and damages houses. The people wonder why the government does not do something about it all.

Figure 17.7 Acid rain affects small community

Figure 17.8 shows some facts and figures about Zambia. It is a country of Low Human Development on the basis of its HDI ranking.

Glencore

A Swiss company called Glencore is the world's largest trader of commodities. It produces, processes, stores, transports and trades minerals such as zinc and copper as well as energy and agricultural products. It controls half of the world trade in copper.

Main exports	Copper and cobalt (64 %)
Main export partner	Switzerland (51 %)
Exports	US$7.2 billion
Imports	US$4.7 billion
GDP (2010)	US$20 billion
GDP spent on education (2008)	1.3 %
GDP spent on health (2009)	4.8 %
HDI rank	150

Figure 17.8 Zambia facts and figures

Source: http://hdr.undp.org/en/media/PR3-HDR10-HD1-E-rev4.pdf;
https://www.cia.gov/library/publications/the-world-factbook/geos/za.html

In May 2011, the company began to trade its shares on the world market and public interest in the company grew. Glencore employs over 50 000 people in 30 countries including Zambia and its turnover for 2010 was US$145 billion. MNCs generate enormous profits and Glencore is investing in a process that will remove sulphur emissions at Mufulira by 2015.

task H

1. In what ways are the Zambian people benefitting and suffering from copper production in their country?

2. Suggest reasons why the government might not want to do anything about the negative effects of mining on communities and the environment.

3. Consider some of the facts about Zambia in Figure 17.8 and describe in your own words what they are showing about the country.

🌍 Vehicle emissions

As people's standard of living improves, car ownership increases. Emissions from each car are quite low (and getting lower with better technology) but there are millions of vehicles on the roads. Vehicle exhausts are low where people walk and live and traffic congestion makes the problems worse in urban areas. Poor air quality such as haze can irritate eyes and people may suffer breathing difficulties. Lead has largely been removed from car fuels but poisonous carbon monoxide is still given off.

Petrol engines generally produce more carbon dioxide but diesel engines give off more nitrogen oxides and small particles such as soot. Data is now published on vehicle fuel efficiency ratings as well as carbon dioxide emissions so people buying cars can compare different models.

Electric cars will reduce pollutants in town centres but the power for the batteries still has to be generated somewhere. The following list gives some ways countries around the world are trying to reduce dependence on cars:

- improved public transport with parking/drop-off points at stations – 'Park & Ride' or 'Kiss & Ride'
- cycle-ways
- cycle hire and docking points with payment by mobile phones
- motorway lanes for cars that have passengers
- car sharing schemes
- working from home
- very high car park charges in city centres.

task
I

Assume you are the official in charge of reducing traffic congestion in your town. You need to prepare a report for the next committee meeting to show:

1. The problems for residents, workers and businesses caused by traffic congestion.
2. The three solutions you propose as a priority to try to solve the problem.
3. Any problems that might occur in putting these into practice.

🌐 Domestic waste

In many developed countries households sort out their rubbish into different containers for recycling and the separated glass, plastic, paper etc. is then collected by local councils. People are encouraged to compost food and garden waste. There is still, however, a huge amount of waste sent to landfill sites. Efforts are being made to reduce the amount of packaging of goods and use biodegradable materials, but there is a long way to go. Landfill sites are not only eyesores but they attract flies and give off methane, a greenhouse gas. Some of the rubbish will contain toxic materials which can be dissolved in rainwater and washed into water supplies.

In Europe and North America, each consumer wastes around 100 kg of food each year. This works out at over 200 million tonnes of food. In a world where so many people are hungry, this is an appalling situation. It is also a complete waste of land, water and other precious resources. In developing continents, the figure is a tenth of this but a greater proportion of food is lost along the supply chain before it reaches the markets. This may be due to:

- slow delivery of perishable goods such as milk from farms in warm conditions
- unhygienic market conditions
- poor road surfaces and rough handling causing bruising and decay
- lack of refrigeration and other methods of preservation.

task J

Describe some of the unhygienic conditions that you have seen in markets and shops that result in food being thrown away.

Besides food, households throw away other rubbish such as packaging and broken goods. In countries where there is no rubbish collection, much of it is dumped anywhere in or around the settlement. This presents a serious hazard not only to the community but to the natural environment.

task K

Describe how rubbish can be a hazard to people and the natural environment.

The 4 Rs

Reduce **Re**-use **R**epair **R**ecycle has become a well-known initiative to reduce the amount of waste that has to be dumped. While it is possible to do much of this within the school or household, sometimes it depends upon local authorities setting up recycling points where items can be taken, such as drink cans.

task L

Identify within your home or school items that are or could be recycled.

Baladarshan is a Fairtrade company in South India that promotes and markets handicrafts. It works to improve the livelihoods of women by giving them training and employment in craft production. Craft workers from the slums of Chennai, shown in Figure 17.9 make baskets out of recycled plastic and pieces of wire.

Figure 17.9 Craft workers using recycled materials
Source: http://www.baladarshah.com/en/recycled-based-products.html

Local Practical Research Investigation: Waste

Aim   To assess the type of waste produced by the school, what happens to it and how the amount could be reduced.

Objectives

1. To find out the types of waste produced by different school activities
2. To find out whether this waste is collected or disposed of by the school
3. To assess the impacts of local dump sites on the community and environment
4. To assess possible strategies to reduce the amount sent to dumps
5. To determine ways to increase awareness of proposed recycling strategies.

Methods of data collection

- observation, questionnaires for students, teachers, other staff
- interview with Head Teacher
- mapping of local dump sites – official and unofficial
- questionnaire for local residents
- bi-polar impact assessments of dump sites.

To undertake a bi-polar survey, a table to show environmental quality such as the one in Figure 17.10 is completed for each site and a total mark given. The exercise could be repeated a certain distance away. The data can then be represented on the map of the sites to give a spatial dimension to the problem.

	+3	+2	+1	0	−1	−2	−3	
Visually pleasant								Visual pollution
No smell								Very smelly
Quiet								Noisy
No vermin								Many rats
No flies								Many flies
No fires								Much burning

Figure 17.10   Bi-polar survey

- Impacts of climate change will affect the development of many poor countries
- International agreements to limit the effects of climate change are difficult to reach
- Individuals are making efforts to reduce their carbon footprints
- Acid rain is still a problem in parts of the world in spite of solutions being available
- As car ownership increases in rapidly growing economies, people elsewhere are cycling or making more use of public transport
- Problems caused by domestic waste have resulted in recycling initiatives.

Summary

Natural disasters

18

- ➤ To understand the causes and effects of different natural disasters
- ➤ To study in detail the Pakistan floods
- ➤ To understand the type of emergency aid involved in a relief operation
- ➤ To realise the importance of co-ordination of the relief effort and how people's needs change over time
- ➤ To appreciate how planning for future events is vital to reduce suffering
- ➤ To assess the effect a natural disaster may have on a country's development.

Natural disasters and their causes

An event that is part of the earth's processes and has always occurred becomes a natural disaster when people who live in the area are badly affected. The impact depends on the scale of the event as well as on the development of the area that it affects. A small earthquake in a remote rural area will have less effect than a larger one that happens near a town. The tsunami on December 26, 2004 was a huge disaster as the islands and coastal areas of SE Asia were densely populated and many people were poor. The main natural disasters are shown in Table 18.1.

Table 18.1   Natural disasters and their causes

Natural disaster	Main causes
Floods	Large amounts of rain in a short time, deforestation
Drought	Unusual climatic conditions, climate change
Earthquakes, volcanoes, tsunami	Movement of earth's tectonic plates
Hurricanes and cyclones	Warm oceans generating violent storms

task A

Name places within your country that have suffered from natural disasters and describe how they have been affected.

🌐 The Pakistan floods of 2010

Some countries rarely suffer from natural disasters but Pakistan is a country that suffers from earthquakes, cyclones and floods. The River Indus has always flooded and provided fertile silt for the agricultural lands along its banks. The river provides water for irrigation, transport and drinking and over 100 million people now live along its valley. The monsoon rains have always fallen too. Each year in summer, hot air over the interior of the Asian continent rises up and draws in moist air from the Indian Ocean. This cools as it rises and condensation of the water vapour causes rainfall. Figure 18.1 shows a map of the Indus valley in Pakistan.

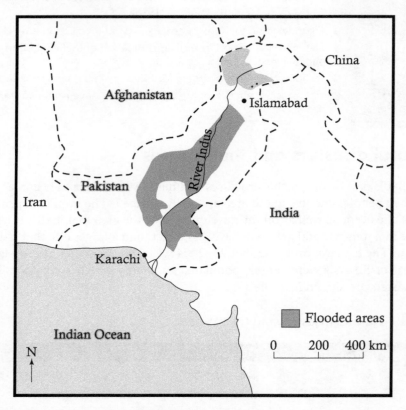

Figure 18.1   Flooded areas in Indus Valley (2010)

Causes of the 2010 flood

The main causes were as follows.

1. The monsoon rains that are usually spread over several months fell in a few weeks.
2. The beds of the Indus and drainage channels were full of soil washed from the Himalayas.
3. Deforestation had left the soil bare.
4. Flood defences were lacking or in a bad state of repair.

Results of the 2010 flood

July

When the river burst its banks, huge volumes of water rushed over the surrounding fields and villages with terrible immediate results:

- 2000 people lost their lives
- 11 million people fled their homes and many suffered distress
- over 2 million homes were damaged or destroyed together with possessions
- over 2 million hectares of crops were ruined and 1.2 million livestock killed
- 12 000 schools were destroyed
- bridges and roads were washed away with US$10 billion damage caused to infrastructure
- wildlife was drowned and trees uprooted.

Figure 18.2 A flood affected area in Pakistan

> **Definition**
>
> **Embankment:** a long mound of earth or stone often built to prevent flooding

task B

Using evidence from Figure 18.2, describe the effect of flooding on the community and natural environment.

Images of the disaster travelled quickly around the world and it soon became obvious that millions of people who had lived in poor conditions before, now had nothing. One fifth of the country was submerged. Those who had managed to escape were isolated on bits of dry land that were often just thin embankments or mounds as shown in Figure 18.2. Many charities such as World Vision and Save the Children appealed for donations. Figure 18.3 shows the sort of emergency aid that was needed immediately.

There is a desperate need for temporary shelter, clean drinking water and toilets to avert a public health catastrophe. People also need medical care and basic food items.

Figure 18.3 Emergency aid

task C

Explain some of the problems for aid workers caused by bridges and roads being destroyed and how these difficulties might be overcome.

August

Many aid agencies were working in the area and so were already there to help provide basic needs. Agency workers were able to put disaster relief operations into action quickly and efficiently as they were familiar with the local places and transport systems. However, the scale of the disaster was such that even they could not cope. There were concerns that the flood water would cause even more deaths as time went on from:

- snake bites as people struggled through the water to safety
- increased threat of malaria and dengue fever
- diarrhoea and cholera.

task D

Explain why malaria, diarrhoea and cholera were likely to become problems.

September

15 UN agencies and 100s of NGOs were all working in Pakistan to relieve the people's suffering. An Integrated Survival Strategy was put together by the World Food Programme (WFP) and WHO to make sure aid was not missing in some areas and duplicated in others. The UN has an office to coordinate humanitarian affairs in an emergency and a priority is to know 'Who Does What Where'.

Definition

Coordinate: ensure different parts work together smoothly and effectively

October

Temporary schools were established for thousands of children by various charities in the camps. Water supplies and food were still a priority with many children needing vitamin supplements. In the far north, the distribution of winter survival kits became essential as temperatures dropped and snow began to fall. The EU offered to lift import tariffs on some goods from Pakistan to help boost its income by increasing exports.

task E

Describe what might be in the winter survival kits.

November

The World Bank, Asian Development Bank and the Pakistan Government drew up a Damage and Needs Assessment. They concluded that between US$8–10 billion were needed to repair all the damage caused by the floods. Besides road and bridges, 5 per cent of health and 6 per cent of education facilities had been swept away.

December

People continued to move back to their home areas so aid agencies needed to provide shelter, food and water there as well as in the temporary camps that had been set up. Children who had become weak through malnutrition had begun to catch many diseases. A rising number of children had polio so a mass vaccination took place in the flood districts.

The world's response

The United Nations appealed for several US$ billion in emergency aid but the response was poor with only US$1.3 billion being donated. Why did people not give as generously as they had to past disasters? That is a hard question to answer but it may have been for the following reasons.

1. Corruption is well known to exist in Pakistan's public life and people could not be sure that their hard earned money would go to those who desperately needed it.
2. Many who had given to the Asian Tsunami Appeal in 2004 had found out that much of the money had not been spent on helping people re-build their lives.
3. The global financial crisis had affected people's incomes and ability to give.

Some governments were very keen to help such as by sending specialist rescue teams but they had to be invited. Equipment and expertise cannot just be sent to another country without official permission.

The Pakistan government's response

Many thought the Pakistani government was slow to act but it sent some military boats and helicopters to rescue people stranded by the flood waters like those shown in Figure 18.4.

The co-ordination of government aid and NGO's responses was not organised as well as it could have been. Suffering could have been less if the government had requested more help more quickly from foreign governments but sometimes governments are too proud to ask for help.

Figure 18.4   Flood rescue helicopters

task F

Give three reasons why it is necessary to co-ordinate relief work by the military, the government, NGOs and international partners.

Contingency planning

It is important that lessons are learnt to reduce the impacts of future natural disasters. This planning can take a number of forms:

Definition

Contingency: provision for a possible future event

- increase equipment for search and rescue operations
- set up early warning systems to notify people
- arrange for the co-ordination of the relief effort
- build a system of dams and embankments to try to control the river
- dredge the river bed and channels to make more space for the water
- remove incompetent local officials and reduce corruption
- stop illegal deforestation.

The problem is that all these cost money. For a country already deep in debt and whose development has just received a major set-back, money for contingency planning is probably not available.

task G

Decision making exercise

The government has called a meeting of interested parties who all want the same amount of money to try to reduce the effects of flooding in future. The government only has money to spare, at that particular time, for one of the following requests:

1. The Minister for the Environment – to increase security in the forests to stop illegal logging
2. The Officer from the Emergency Services – to fund inflatable boats and a helicopter
3. The Minister for Industry – to build flood defences to protect factory sites
4. The Minister for Communication – to set up an early warning system.

Prepare a report on the benefits of the different projects. A follow-up class discussion can decide which project is to be chosen.

September 2011

When more floods came in 2011, it was found that little had changed as shown in a newspaper report shown in Figure 18.5.

Few lessons had been learnt and there had been little time for any contingency plans to have been put in place even if there had been money made available.

Communities have not yet recovered after the devastating floods of 2010. Now, twelve months later, the Indus has broken its banks again and washed away crops that were ready for harvest. People are stranded on rooftops and the rescue effort on the ground appears to be unorganised and lacking in urgency. This is in spite of the fact that aid agencies are already warning of a rapid spread of disease from the floodwaters and are asking the world for donations.

Figure 18.5 The people of Pakistan suffer from floods again

Effect of flood on development

The floods washed away much of the existing water and sanitation supplies. Many schools and health services were destroyed. Girls became increasingly at risk of being married at an early age because then there would be less people to feed in the family. Child labour became more of a problem as people had lost everything. Food had to be imported as crops had been ruined and industries trying to export goods found communication lines had been damaged. Figure 18.6 shows some information about Pakistan.

HDI rank	125
GDP	US$177 billion
GNI per capita	US$1050
Child mortality rate	74 per 1000
Life expectancy	65
Measles immunisation	86 %
Primary school age children not attending school	5.1 million
Adult literacy rate (over 15)	56 %
Access to improved sanitation	48 % total population
Access to improved water source	89 % rural population

Figure 18.6 Pakistan facts and figures (2008–2010)
Source: http://data.worldbank.org/country/pakistan

task
H

1. What do the facts shown in Figure 18.6 tell you about the country of Pakistan before the floods?
2. Describe how you think the floods will have affected Pakistan's ability to meet the MDGs 1, 2, 3, 4, 5 and 6.

Deforestation and flooding

In the hills where the Indus begins its journey, deforestation is taking place at a rapid rate. The forests are a valuable natural resource for Pakistan, and if managed sustainably could provide revenue for the government to spend on reducing poverty amongst its people for many years to come.

However, illegal logging means the forest's wealth is being exploited now by a few criminals and local officials who are bribed to allow it to happen. Flooding is now more likely because:

- trees use up some of the rainfall and also allow it to soak slowly into the ground
- bare soil is easily washed into rivers by rain and settles on the river bed
- more rainwater is getting more quickly to the river and the river cannot hold as much water as it did when the valley slopes were covered in trees.

One year on from the Haiti earthquake

In the event of a natural disaster, the response by the various agencies usually takes the following format.

1. Rescue teams find survivors and remove bodies. Emergency aid is delivered into temporary camps.
2. Survivors move back to their place of origin and temporary homes are set up with basic facilities. Cash hand-outs may be given so people can begin to take more control of their lives.
3. More permanent solutions such as proper houses and training for new jobs are provided.

On January 12, 2010 an earthquake of magnitude 7.0 killed 230 000 people in and around the capital of Haiti, Port-au-Prince. However, in 2011, there were still over a thousand camps and over 1 million people lived in them. Another million people lived on any small space they could find – often alongside the roads. Even in the camps there were few proper sanitation facilities. Dead bodies still remained buried under the rubble.

Figure 18.7 Destruction caused by the Haiti earthquake

Haiti has a HDI rank of 145. Even before the earthquake Haiti had a low literacy level and high child mortality rate. In a country classed as a one of low human development, the government certainly did not have money to spend on rescue equipment and large numbers of trucks that might never be used. So the land people may once have owned in the town is still covered in rubble in spite of the US sending thousands of troops to help its neighbour. Although the Red Cross is able to construct more sanitation facilities, no land has been made available by the government to dispose of the waste.

Many government buildings were destroyed and officials killed which has not helped decisions to be made to start the re-building process. The effect of the earthquake on buildings is shown in Figure 18.7.

1. Describe the scene in Figure 18.7 and suggest some of the many problems for local people that result from this sort of destruction.
2. Describe the difficulties, the aid agencies have had in Port-an-Prince.

Choose another example of a natural disaster, perhaps one that has affected your country. Briefly explain its cause. Describe how the government and NGOs responded to the impacts of the disaster and whether or not these methods were successful.

Summary

• The world's natural disasters vary in scale and effect
• Different forms of aid and levels of response are provided by governments and NGOs
• The response to a disaster depends on a number of factors
• Natural disasters usually have a negative effect on development
• Planning for future events costs money but can save lives and property
• Deforestation makes floods worse.

Questions

Question 1

(a) Study Figure 1 which gives information about Antigua, a tropical island in the Caribbean.

Tourism is big business in Antigua. When a jumbo jet arrives from Britian, Germany or the USA it is the biggest thing on the island. The vast cruise ships which dock in the part of St. John's dwarf the surrounding buildings. More than half a million tourists visit Antigua each year.

Antigua is a small island of only 280 square kilometres, with a permanent resident population of 66,000. It was originally settled by South American tribal peoples and was named by Christopher Columbus, who sighted the island in 1493. In 1794 the English Admiral Nelson supervised the construction of the famous Dockyard. Sugar plantations were developed by the British in the seventeenth century and most of the population is descended from African slaves, who were shipped here to work in the sugar industry.

The sugar industry declined, but in the last fifty years tourism has taken its place. Infant mortality is 18 per 100 live births, life expectancy is 75 years and literacy is 95%. Many of the major international tourist companies operate in Antigua and they have brought work and prosperity to the island.

Figure 1

(i) Suggest **three** different reasons why Antigua is a successful tourist destination.

[3]

(ii) What evidence is there to show that tourism has brought prosperity to Antigua? Justify your answer.

[3]

(iii) More than half a million tourists visit Antigua each year. Suggest some environmental problems for places such as Antigua that may result from mass tourism. You may refer to examples you have studied.

[5]

(b) Suggest some of the social and economic disadvantages of a country relying on tourism as a major source of income.

[6]

Cambridge 0453 P1 Q1 b, c Oct/Nov 2008

Question 2

(a) Study Figure 2 which is about coffee growing in Guatemala.

Figure 2

    (i) Why do governments want farmers to grow coffee for export?   [1]

   (ii) Two huge companies control over half of the world's coffee sold in shops. Explain why this causes problems.   [2]

  (iii) Give **three** reasons why the price of farm products like coffee is always going up and down.   [3]

 (b) Describe some of the ways that the incomes of farmers might be improved with the help of their governments.   [4]

 (c) Explain why increased commercial crop production may result in environmental and social problems.   [6]

Cambridge 0453 P1 Q3 b, c and d Oct/Nov 2008

Question 3

 (a) Study Figure 3 which shows background information about the environment of the Philippines.

    (i) Suggest **three** of the problems that the Philippines may experience after an earthquake or volcanic eruption.   [3]

   (ii) Explain why some of the natural disasters and man-made problems occurring in the Philippines are likely to become worse over the next few years.   [4]

(b) With reference to a natural disaster:
- state the type of natural disaster.
- name the place where it happened.
- describe the way the government and NGOs dealt with the impact of the disaster. [6]

The environment of the Philippines

Natural disasters

- Since 1975, there have been twelve earthquakes and six volcanic eruptions.
- Over one million people were affected by floods in 2000.
- The Philippiness has many tropical storms each year, causing flash floods.

Biodiversity

- The islands have the richest biodiversity on earth. There are 510 species of mammals, birds, frogs and lizards that are only found in the Philippiness.

Man-made problems

- In the 1950s, three quarters of the Philippines were covered by tropical forest. By the year 2000 forests covered only one third of the land.
- Soil erosion is occurring on the hillsides.
- There is air and water pollution in urban areas.
- There is pollution of coastal mangrove swamps and degradation of the coral reeefs.

Source: Global Eye 2001 www.globaleye.org.uk/secondary_autumn2001/eyeon/land. html)

Figure 3

Cambridge 0453 P1 Q2 b and c Oct/Nov 2009

Unit 5 — Large scale case studies

The Lesotho Highlands Water Project (LHWP)

🌍 The reasons for the project

It has been several decades since the suggestion for a large scale water project in the mountains of Lesotho was first made. The reasons for such a project can be summarised as following.

1. For Lesotho:
   - few natural resources apart from water
   - high rainfall in catchment of the Orange/Senqu River in Drakensberg Mountains
   - high water quality as away from urban/industrial/agricultural area
   - small household water consumption with plenty to spare for export even in the future
   - income generation from the sale of water to South Africa
   - hydro-electric power for industrial and domestic use.
2. For South Africa:
   - Johannesburg industrial area is not on a main natural water supply
   - nearby Vaal River cannot supply the huge water needs of the area
   - uneven distribution of rainfall with droughts.

> **Definition**
>
> **Catchment**: the area on which rain falls and flows into a river

The politics

The LHWP is a major transnational project with co-operation between the governments of Lesotho and South Africa to construct a series of dams and tunnels to transfer water to South Africa and generate hydro-electric power (HEP) for both countries. The first dam at Katse in Lesotho was completed in 1997 and the project should be completed in 2020.

> **Definition**
>
> **Transnational**: extends across national boundaries

The project is run by public companies and is funded by the governments of both countries involved, The African Development Bank, European Development Fund, The World Bank and others. The World Bank tries to make sure there is no corruption in the form of bribes to secure contracts and that everyone benefits from the project. The purpose is to stimulate economic growth and improve the livelihood of the people of Lesotho and South Africa by reducing poverty. The general location can be seen in Figure 19.1.

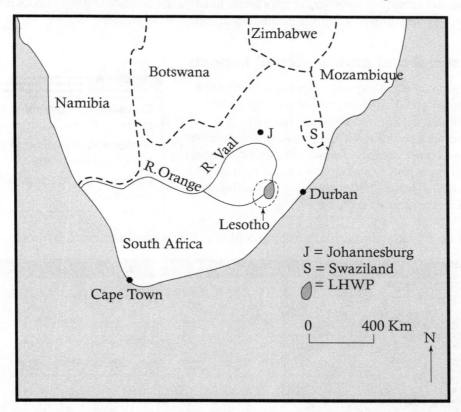

Figure 19.1 Map showing the location of the LHWP

If South Africa had used the water from the stretch of the Orange River which flows through the country, it would have had to pump the water uphill to the Johannesburg area which would use large amounts of energy. By creating a short tunnel through the mountains near the source of the river in Lesotho, the water can flow by gravity down to where it is needed. The project consists of a series of dams and tunnels. The Mohale dam is shown in Figure 19.2.

Figure 19.2 Mohale Dam
Source: Wendy Taylor

The economics

The project provides the Lesotho government with considerable revenue from selling water and electricity. In August 2010, these figures were US$4.7m and US$0.6m respectively. An estimate for the year would be US$64m. GDP for Lesotho in 2010 was US$2 133m so direct revenue from the project was about 3 per cent of GDP. However, the indirect economic benefits are impossible to calculate considering the impact it has had on so many different aspects of life and industry in the country.

The social and environmental impacts

Most projects these days are required to undertake studies to consider the impacts of a development project on local communities and the natural environment before work can proceed. The possible negative effects are called constraints and developers have to show how these impacts can be reduced by mitigation. The LHWP made a detailed assessment which is summarised in Table 19.1.

Definition

Constraints: something that may restrict development

Mitigation: a method to make something less severe

Endangered: in danger of extinction

Table 19.1 Constraints and mitigation of social and environmental factors

Constraints	Mitigation
Loss of homes, communities, burial grounds, traditional meeting places etc.	Compensation for loss of property and a disturbance allowance. Resettlement with improved water and sanitation facilities.
Loss of farmland	Compensation for loss of land, training in new jobs.
Loss of jobs	LHWP employment policy states first preference for unskilled work is for people from local communities. Ecotourism opportunities such as walking and wildlife guides, work in visitor centres, hotels, craft shops etc., running cycle hire, pony trekking, campsites etc.
Loss of cultural heritage	Interpretation of San art and early Basotho history at Liphofung Cave, one of the reserves created to protect local cultural sites. Displays of traditional dancing and singing at reserves. Traditional crafts sold have to be locally made and not imported.
Loss of medicinal plants and plants of cultural value	Compensation for losses at community level and training in the growing of these plants.
Flooding of land	149 plant species were removed from project sites. Katse botanical gardens set up.

Table 19.1 Constraints and mitigation of social and environmental factors (continued)

Constraints	Mitigation
Loss of habitats and biodiversity and disruption of food chains	Nature reserves were set up such as The Bokong to conserve rare wetland sponges, the Bearded Vulture and Vaal Rhebuck. Ecosystems would be regularly monitored.
Endangered Maloti minnow under threat as dams would prevent migration and populations would become isolated	Movement to areas of the river system where their relocation would not cause problems to other river life.
Effect of water control on ecosystems elsewhere	Flow from dams into rivers to be maintained. The Senqunyane from Mohale dam always has water flowing into it.

Source: www.lhwp.org.ls/

task A

1. Describe the problems families may face from having to move from their homes and land.
2. Describe the advantages and disadvantages for local people of putting on cultural displays for tourists.
3. Explain how it might be possible to enable some people to enjoy watching wildlife in the mountains while others want to create a lot of noise in 4X4s.
4. The mountains of Lesotho at the moment are wild and unspoilt. Tourist brochures advertise it as a place...' just waiting to be discovered'.

   Suggest ways it might be possible to prevent any further loss of wildlife, such as to the Vaal Rhebuck and Bearded Vulture, as tourist numbers increase.

task B

Decision making exercise

The LHWP has made the highlands more accessible through the construction of tarred roads. If you were Minister of Tourism, consider the advantages and disadvantages for the people and the environment of Lesotho of the following:

1. An expensive high altitude training centre for sports people worldwide.
2. Several ski resorts.
3. A series of low quality hotels for tourists around the reservoirs.

Decide which one development you would allow giving reasons for your choice and reasons why you did not select the other options.

Provision of services

While some communities had to be resettled, others gained an improvement in services. The Water and Sanitation programme provided a piped water supply to local communities who decide where a standpipe should be put in the village. Materials for latrines are supplied to households and local people are trained to build them as well as lay water pipes and maintain them. The skills learnt in this way may result in jobs in other construction projects.

The private latrines of a village situated above the reservoir at Mohale can be seen in Figure 19.3.

Figure 19.3 Village above Mohale dam
Source: Wendy Taylor

Katse Botanical Gardens

The gardens at Katse were created to provide a place where the plants that would be flooded by the reservoirs could be planted. They try to preserve the unique flora of the high mountainous kingdom by having collections of plants that are found in all the main ecosystems of Lesotho. If these plants become lost in the wild, some specimens are therefore safe for possible introductions back into their natural habitat in the future. The collections are displayed in such a way as to increase people's understanding of the importance of plants to all life on earth.

Katse conserves threatened plants such as the Spiral Aloe and Berg Bamboo. This plant is a host plant to an endangered butterfly and is of significant cultural importance to the Basotho people. Training in the growing of plants used in traditional medicines is given to local communities so that the sustainable use of plants continues.

The benefits of the LHWP

The flow chart shown in Figure 19.4 gives a summary of the possible benefits to the economy and quality of life of the people of Lesotho. For each vertical flow, it is possible to link each of the nine areas of benefit of the LHWP shown in Row 3 to the MDGs.

For example, water supplied to villages could be used for irrigation to grow better quality crops on small vegetable gardens. There may be a surplus to sell which will provide a small income. This could be used to buy a greater variety of foods and these, together with the home-grown ones will provide the family with a better diet. This leads to improved health. This will help eradicate hunger (MDG 1), reduce child mortality (MDG 2), and improve maternal health (MDG 5).

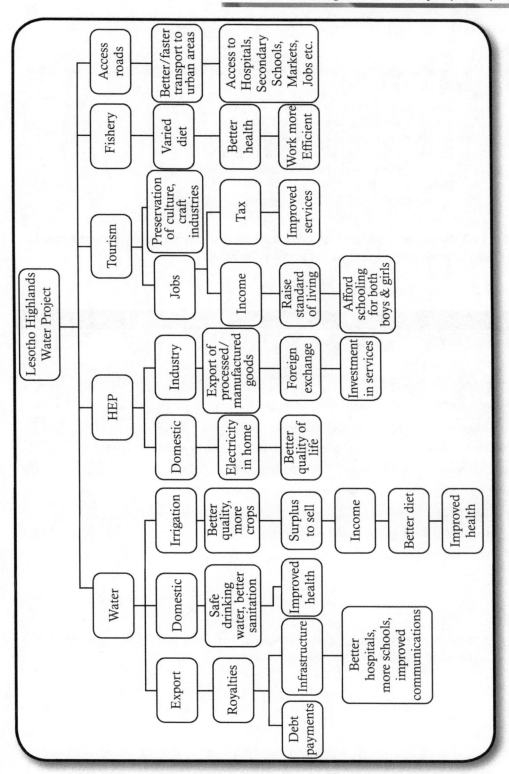

Figure 19.4 Flow chart showing the benefits of the LHWP

In a similar way, show how the LHWP has helped Lesotho to work towards the following MDGs.

1. The export of water → MDGs 2, 4, 5, 6
2. Clean water in the home → MDGs 3, 4, 5, 6, 7
3. Electricity in the home → MDGs 3, 7
4. Electricity for industries → MDGs 1, 2, 4, 5
5. Jobs in tourism and craft industries → MDGs 1, 2, 3, 4, 5
6. Fisheries → MDGs 1, 4
7. Access roads → MDGs 1, 2, 3, 4, 5, 6

Table 19.2 shows some selected statistics for Lesotho which give the progress that is being made towards meeting certain targets for the MDGs.

Table 19.2 Selected statistics for Lesotho

Indicator	2000	2008/9
2.1 Net enrolment ratio in primary education %	76	72
2.3 Literacy rate (youth) %	91	92
4.1 Under five mortality rate (per 1000)	117	96
4.3 Proportion of 1 year-old children immunised against measles %	74	85
5.2 Proportion of births attended by skilled health personnel %	60	62
6.3 15–24 year-olds with comprehensive correct knowledge of HIV/AIDS %	18 ('04)	29
7.8 Population with access to improved water source (rural) %	76	74
7.8 Population with access to improved water source (urban) %	94	92
7.9 Population with access to improved sanitation (rural) %	22	24
7.9 Population with access to improved sanitation (urban) %	37	33

Source: www.worldbank.org

Use Table 19.2 to suggest what progress, if any, has been made towards meeting some targets for MDGs 2, 4, 5 and 7

Rural Roads – A Lifeline for Villages in India

The following account of a development project in rural India has been adapted from 'Rural Roads – A Lifeline for Villages in India' written by The World Bank.

🌐 The need for rural roads

In 2000, around 40 per cent of the 825 000 villages in India lacked all-weather access roads. This made it difficult to bring in the inputs for economic activities and distribute any products that were made. It was difficult for people to reach essential services such as hospitals, and other services such as electricity were often not connected to remote areas.

Government-led project

In 2000, the Government of India launched a nationwide programme, the Prime Minister's Rural Roads Programme under the Ministry of Rural Development and supported by The World Bank. The programme aimed to provide new links to about 180 000 settlements through the construction of about 372 000 kms of roads, and to upgrade large stretches of the existing rural network. Wherever the road network has come, the rural economy and quality of life has improved.

Selection process

Population size was the factor chosen to decide which settlements would be connected under the programme, in order to rule out preference being given to settlements where officials might live.

Village representatives and members of some of the affected households walk the entire stretch of the proposed route so that they can state any concerns. Suggestions of alternative routes can be made wherever the community feels a natural or cultural heritage site, an important water supply or an extremely poor farmer's land was being acquired for road construction. Those who understood that the value of their land would go up with a road by its side were very eager to be included in the scheme. This 'Transect-Walk' was introduced by the World Bank and conducted for the first time under this project and has resulted in better cooperation by the community.

Green standards

An Environmental Code of Practice makes sure top-soil is preserved, trees are planted, soil erosion is controlled and construction sites are re-developed once the work is complete. Natural and cultural heritage of villages is protected.

Better markets – better incomes

Cheog, a small centre in Himachal Pradesh with around 60 mountainous villages, is now bustling with activity. It has become the hub for truck drivers to rest before their onward journey to the big cities. Roads in this area now connect remote hamlets making it possible for trucks to collect fresh vegetables and fruits from farmers in the whole area who stack them up on the side of the newly built roads next to their fields. Cabbages are now taken directly to market, in Delhi. In order to cut transportation costs further, some villagers have got together to hire trucks.

Up in the Shimla mountains, farmers are pleased with their extra earnings this year. It is the first time up to 80 per cent of their vegetables did not perish because of a lack of proper transportation facilities. The 2 km stretch of road from village Talai to Khadharab has linked their village to the main road leading to Cheog. Some farmers have earned enough to buy cars and can now drive people to hospital if necessary. Some farmers are also experimenting with organic farming in the hope of supplying directly to big hotels in the cities.

Mushrooming dairies

In Rajasthan many farmers rely on dairy farming for their livelihood. The roads have brought large refrigerated milk tankers to their farms each day, saving them a long hot trek carrying the milk containers on their backs to the highway and the uncertainty of catching the milk collection vans in time. The State's Milk Cooperative brand, has set up a milk producers' cooperative society, managed by local people, which provides a cold storage tank and fat content measurement equipment.

One local man bought a jeep after the road was built to ferry milk collection from three hamlets. A real businessman, he runs the jeep as a taxi on the return journey.

Family bonds

As villages are easier to access, visits between family members become more frequent. People are earning more and travel is less time consuming. According to one happy mother, "Even our sons, working in big cities, are visiting us for festivals as just three days leave is enough for a home visit."

In Rajasthan, a young girl is happy with the road. Busy working in her fields, she smilingly said that she could easily go to the next village to chat with her mother.

For villagers of Thooni Ahiran, rural roads have meant better marriage offers for their children. Before the road came, few people were willing to give their daughter in marriage into a village where access was difficult and time consuming.

Schooling

An overcrowded government school had been operating from a dilapidated building in village Khadharab. With a 4 km road now connecting the village to the nearest town, Fagu, some farmers have started a car pool to take their children to school there. Another big advantage of the roads for schooling is explained by a resident of village Karansar, "On days when it rained or was too hot, we would just keep the children at home, knowing well that the teacher too would have taken the day off as walking through dirt-tracks or crossing fields was impossible", he said. Now the teacher arrives on time as there is a direct bus from his village.

The headmaster of a primary school at Swami Ka Bas has said that there had been a 20 per cent rise in the enrolment rate since the road came to their village and 60 per cent of these students are girls.

Road to earning

In the villages around Dedkiya, people lived under conditions of extreme poverty with poor lands and high unemployment. Now they take the bus to reach work at building sites in Udaipur. They try not to miss a single day unlike in the past, when they would often turn around to go home from sheer exhaustion and hunger. At least now they can afford to get some food for their family every day even though they have to pay a bus fare.

Medicine in time

The PHC at Thooni Ahiran is bustling with activity. The road has joined the neighbouring villages and, as a result, more mothers come for their ante-natal check-up. Dr Singh is pleased that women are able to come to the PHC for their delivery as well. Complicated cases can now be referred quickly to the Community Health Centre or to the District Hospital.

The PHC is not facing shortages of polio vaccine anymore and children are being immunized at regular intervals. Roads have also helped with better follow-up of TB patients with some coming to the centre each day to take their tablets in the presence of the medical staff. Accidents are also being attended to at the PHC itself.

Work for local contractors

Access to finance and a promise of continuous work for 3–4 years to recover costs has helped people invest in the purchase of machinery in Rajhastan. Small contractors can now support their families with a regular income from this equipment.

Skills are learnt in building the road and now many contractors are bidding for larger projects in other parts of the country either individually or by forming a consortium.

task A

Using examples where possible, explain in detail how the rural roads development project has:
1. Helped to reduce poverty amongst farmers.
2. Improved social life in villages.
3. Helped India meet targets for MDGs 2, 4 and 5.
4. Improved employment opportunities.

task B

Roads bring many benefits to local communities but many problems occur during the construction phase.
1. What do you think the impact on communities might be of large numbers of construction workers camped in the local area?
2. What do you think may be some of the effects on people and their homes of blasting rock with dynamite and heavy trucks and equipment moving huge amounts of material nearby?
3. How do you think some of these negative impacts could be mitigated?

task C

Decision making exercise

The administration offices for part of the road project are in a village called Khublai. The main office will be left behind for community use once the roads are finished. You need to find out what sort of facility the community would like. It may be for a clinic, a youth club etc. You need to:
1. Draw up a questionnaire
2. Decide upon an appropriate sampling method
3. Identify the four most popular suggestions
4. Decide which project to put forward to the local council with an explanation of why it has been chosen and why the others are not as suitable.

Appendix

🌐 1. Practical research investigation: Relationship between different indicators of development

Aim

To describe and explain the relationship between two indicators of development.

Objectives

1. To select a sample of countries at varying stages of development
2. To choose appropriate indicators of development that may show a relationship
3. To represent the data in an appropriate form
4. To determine to what extent there is a positive/negative relationship
5. To give reasons for the relationship
6. To attempt to explain anomalies.

Method

- From the Internet/books find a table of GNP/GNI per person for all countries. This can be found at http://data.worldbank.org/. Alternatively, use HDI rankings which can be found at http://hdr.undp.org/en/statistics.
- Use an appropriate sampling technique to select a useful number of countries at varying stages of development.
- Choose two indicators of development and research statistics for the countries sampled – the data can be found on the World Bank site as above.
- Represent data in the most appropriate way to show the relationship between them.

Write-up

The investigation needs to include the following sections.

1. Introduction

A brief introduction might include comments such as the fact that the standard of living of a country's citizens is largely related to the country's wealth. Aspects of educational attainment, health, energy consumption etc. can be measured and statistics compared between countries. Indicators of development are often related as the more economically developed a country is, the more money it has to invest in health care, education etc.

2. Research question/hypothesis

A research question needs to be devised such as:

- Does life expectancy have a positive correlation with electric power consumption?
- Is there a relationship between percentage employed in agriculture and life expectancy?

Alternatively, a hypothesis can be made such as:

- Literacy rates show a negative correlation with child mortality rates.
- Mobile phone use shows a positive correlation with CO2 emissions.

3. Methods of data collection

In the write-up for this investigation, it will be necessary to discuss the merits of different sampling techniques and which is most appropriate for this particular task. The sample size must also be considered.

4. Data representation

A scatter graph can be used to represent the data.

5. Analysis

The analysis will include a discussion as to whether the relationship is positive or negative as well as how perfect the correlation is. There may be no correlation shown at all between the two sets of data, or there may be too many anomalies to make any firm conclusion. Reasons for the relationship need to be given.

For the second research question given above, the analysis may include an explanation such as:

Countries with high levels of employment in the agricultural sector produce primary goods which do not have a high value when exported. The country's income is therefore low and it cannot invest large sums of money in education and health services. Therefore many people are uneducated and do not know the advantages of a balanced diet and how to prevent diseases, and when they become ill there are no available medical facilities. Also farmers' incomes are low and so they cannot afford a varied diet or to send their children to school.

6. Conclusion

Reference back to the original aim and research question/hypothesis should be made, with the question answered or the hypothesis accepted or rejected.

7. Evaluation

This may consider how the method of data collection could be improved or whether or not the methods of data representation were the most appropriate. Other relationships for study could be suggested.

2. Practical research investigation: Links between different sectors of the economy

Aim

To consider the links between a commercial farm and activities in other sectors of the economy.

(This investigation could easily be adapted to consider the links between a manufacturing industry and other sectors of the economy.)

Objectives

1. To identify the different land uses on a local farm
2. To identify the inputs and their source
3. To investigate the production process
4. To identify the outputs and their destination
5. To consider the ways the inputs/outputs are delivered/distributed.

Methods

- Land use mapping and field sketches. Mapping of the farm to include the use of buildings as well as land with annotations as appropriate.
- Field sketches of anything relevant to the investigation.
- Use of secondary data/local knowledge to map transport infrastructure, local settlements etc.
- Interview/questionnaire for farmer.

Write-up

The investigation needs to include the following sections:

1. Introduction

A brief background to the topic would include a rationale for the investigation including an explanation of the need to consider links between different sections of the syllabus. Reasons for the choice of farm to study should also be made clear.

2. Research question/hypothesis

A research question needs to be devised such as:

- How important are the links between a commercial farm production and other sectors of the economy?

Alternatively, a hypothesis can be made such as:

- Commercial farm production is totally dependent on other parts of the primary sector as well as the secondary and tertiary sectors of the economy.

3. Methods of data collection

A discussion of the relative merits of interviews and questionnaires needs to be included in the write-up of this investigation to indicate why a certain method was chosen. Some of the questions for the farmer might include:

(a) What inputs are always on the farm?
(land, weather conditions, machinery, labour, manure etc.)
(b) What inputs are regularly brought in, from where and how?
(new seed, livestock, fertilisers, pesticides, herbicides, fuel, labour etc.)
(c) What inputs are occasionally brought in, from where and how?
(new machinery, advice from Rural Development Agency etc.).

(d) What are the main processes on the farm?

(e) What are the outputs, to where are they sent and for what purpose?

(crops for local processing, milk/meat/crops/for local named markets/export, waste etc.)

4. Data representation

Methods of data representation will vary depending on the data collected but may include:

- detailed farm plan with a suitable key together with some reference to scale
- larger scaled map of local surroundings to show location of farm in relation to transport infrastructure and settlements
- annotated sketches of carts, lorries, farm tools etc.
- detailed flow chart showing all the factors of production, with colour coding for the different sectors of the economy.

5. Analysis

This may be best divided into links with the three main sectors of the economy, to relate it directly to the original aim and research question or hypothesis.

Primary Sector – sources of seed/stock from other parts of the agricultural sector as well as fuel from the extractive primary industry. Farmers need food to eat themselves in order to keep healthy to work.

Secondary Sector – if the output is processed, then this is a major forward link with the secondary sector of the economy. The links may be less obvious, such as the secondary sector providing the machines/tools/buildings/irrigation pumps/pesticides etc. for the farming processes and links with factories processing the crops/livestock products.

Tertiary Sector – it may be emphasised here that production is no good to the commercial farmer unless he can sell the produce. So distribution to the points of sale relies not only on the use of road/rail infrastructure and transport services to move inputs and outputs. Communication via telephone or the Internet may determine markets. The supply of utilities such as electricity and water also need to be considered.

An extension of the analysis could include consideration of more hidden elements of the tertiary sector. The skills the farmer uses may have been learnt at an agricultural college or in workshops provided by the local co-operatives. The efficiency of his/her workers will depend on their health, which can be improved through access to local Primary Health Care.

6. Conclusion

A brief summary of the findings will lead to reference back to the original research question or hypothesis. The question can be answered or the hypothesis can be accepted or rejected on the basis of the evidence collected.

7. Evaluation

This needs to consider whether or not the aim has been achieved, the problems encountered and how these could be minimised in a future investigation. Improvements can be suggested for methods of data collection. The value of the study may also be considered.

Source: Adapted from Appendix to 'Scheme of Work, Cambridge IGCSE Development Studies 0453'

3. Practical Research Investigations – further guidance

It is important to collect primary data which is original data collected by the students from interviews, questionnaires and observation. This can be supported by secondary information from sources such as books and the Internet which has been written by someone else. Questionnaires can include structured questions to generate statistics which can then be represented in a variety of ways. Charts need a title, scale and key to explain any different types of shading.

The following suggestions given for one investigation can easily be adapted for use in another. The structure of each investigation should follow the sequence of enquiry as shown in Appendix 1 and Appendix 2 in terms of aims, objectives, methods etc.

1. The value of a clinic to a community (Chapter 2)

The frequency of bus services throughout the day could be shown on a histogram. The hours of the day are shown continuously on the horizontal axis and bars drawn up to the correct frequency shown on the vertical axis.

Due to the nature of this investigation, questionnaires could be left in the waiting area of a clinic or with the receptionist. The problem of asking people questions directly can be discussed as well as the advantages of an interview with a health care worker.

Sample questions for questionnaire	Data representation
Where have you come from?	Map with circles drawn of different radii – 1km, 3km etc.
What means of transport did you use to get here? Walk….. Bus….. Car….. Cart….. Truck….. Taxi…..	Divided bar chart
How long did it take you to travel here? Under 15mins….. 15-30mins….. 30mins-1hour….. 1-2hours….. etc.	Bar chart

2. To investigate some features of migration to an urban area (Chapter 11)

An appropriate sampling technique would need to be chosen from the following:

Random sample – Everyone has an equal chance of being selected. This can be achieved either by giving every child a number and then using a random number table to generate the numbers to be selected or by picking names out of a container that contains all the names of children in the school.

Stratified sample – This means that samples are chosen from different 'layers', in this case, different year groups. Once a sample size for each group has been determined, random samples are then taken from each one. This type of sampling avoids bias to any particular age group.

Systematic sample – A starting point is chosen at random and then people are selected at regular intervals, such as every third person on each class register.

The size of sample would depend on the number of children in the school but at least 50 questionnaires would be needed to obtain sufficient data. The larger the sample is, the more reliable the data. A 'pilot' survey of a small number of parents is needed to make sure the questions can be understood.

Sample questions for questionnaire	Data representation
How many years have you lived in this town? 0-5.... 6-10..... 11-15..... over 15.....	Bar chart
Where did you live before?	Map with circles showing 10km, 50km radius etc.
What were your two main reasons for moving to this town? Work..... Schools..... Family..... Better services..... etc.	Pie chart
Which of the following describes your level of satisfaction with living in this town? Very unsatisfied.... Unsatisfied.... Satisfied.... Very satisfied....	Tally chart
Please give three reasons why you are unsatisfied /satisfied.	General written summary of answers

3. To determine the causes of soil erosion around a school or village and possible solutions (Chapter 13)

As in (2) above, an appropriate sampling technique and sample size would need to be determined.

Sample questions for questionnaire	Data representation
How would you describe the problem of soil erosion in this area? Slight...... Moderate..... Severe.....	Pie chart
What do you consider to be the main cause of soil erosion? Drought..... Overgrazing..... Deforestation..... etc.	Pictogram
What do you think are the main effects of soil erosion on a) the community and b) the natural environment?	Table with two columns
What do you think could be done to solve this problem?	Spider diagram

4. To assess the sustainability of the school's water supply (Chapter 15)

Tally charts are useful tools to record results and the data is usually already collected into groups. A chart could be set up for the class to complete as a whole during one day.

Activity	Tally	Frequency
Washing hands	//// //// //// // etc.	17
Toilet use	etc.	
Drink from tap		
Drink from bottle		

5. To assess the biodiversity of a local site (Chapter 15)

A map showing different land uses can be drawn showing areas such as trees, grass, marsh, bare soil, buildings, paths etc. For a wildlife habitat such as the grassland, an area 1mx1m could be selected at random and the number of different plants in it counted. This would be repeated 10 times and the average number of plants calculated. This would be repeated for different habitats. On the appropriate place on the land use map bars the length of which represents the plant biodiversity of each habitat surveyed could be drawn. The number of birds/animals/reptiles/amphibians that are seen in each habitat could be counted and the sightings summarised.

In the analysis, the areas of the site that need to be protected if it is developed for housing/road building etc. can be considered as well as how this could be achieved.

6. To assess the type of waste produced by the school, what happens to it and how the amount could be reduced (Chapter 17).

Observation of the different types of waste produced by the school can be illustrated on a spider diagram with arrows then going further out to describe what happens to it. Diagram could be colour coded to show all items recycled, reused, dumped in landfill etc.

Sample questions for residents' questionnaire	Data representation
How far is your dwelling from the dump site? (i)	
On a scale of 1-5, how would you rate the overall problems caused by the waste? 1 = very severe → 5 = very slight (ii)	Scatter graph to show relationship between (i) & (ii)
What is the main problem the site causes you and your family?	Pie chart
What do you think needs to be done to reduce the amount of waste sent to dumps?	General summary of answers

4. Official list of Millennium Development Goals

All indicators should be disaggregated by sex and urban/rural as far as possible.

Effective 15 January 2008

Millennium Development Goals (MDGs)	
Goals and Selected Targets (from the Millennium Declaration)	Selected Indicators for monitoring progress
Goal 1: Eradicate extreme poverty and hunger	
Target 1.A: Halve, between 1990 and 2015, the proportion of people whose income is less than one dollar a day	1.1 Proportion of population below $1 (PPP) per day[1]
Target 1.B: Achieve full and productive employment and decent work for all, including women and young people	1.4 Growth rate of GDP per person employed 1.5 Employment-to-population ratio
Target 1.C: Halve, between 1990 and 2015, the proportion of people who suffer from hunger	1.8 Prevalence of underweight children under-five years of age
Goal 2: Achieve universal primary education	
Target 2.A: Ensure that, by 2015, children everywhere, boys and girls alike, will be able to complete a full course of primary schooling	2.1 Net enrolment ratio in primary education 2.2 Proportion of pupils starting grade 1 who reach last grade of primary

Goal 3: Promote gender equality and empower women	
Target 3.A: Eliminate gender disparity in primary and secondary education, preferably by 2005, and in all levels of education no later than 2015	3.1 Ratios of girls to boys in primary, secondary and tertiary education 3.2 Proportion of seats held by women in national parliament

Goal 4: Reduce child mortality	
Target 4.A: Reduce by two-thirds, between 1990 and 2015, the under-five mortality rate	4.1 Under-five mortality rate 4.3 Proportion of 1 year-old children immunised against measles

Goal 5: Improve maternal health	
Target 5.A: Reduce by three quarters, between 1990 and 2015, the maternal mortality ratio	5.1 Maternal mortality ratio 5.2 Proportion of births attended by skilled health personnel
Target 5.B: Achieve, by 2015, universal access to reproductive health	5.3 Contraceptive prevalence rate

Goal 6: Combat HIV/AIDS, malaria and other diseases	
Target 6.A: Have halted by 2015 and begun to reverse the spread of HIV/AIDS	6.1 HIV prevalence among population aged 15-24 years 6.3 Proportion of population aged 15-24 years with comprehensive correct knowledge of HIV/AIDS
Target 6.B: Achieve, by 2010, universal access to treatment for HIV/AIDS for all those who need it	6.5 Proportion of population with advanced HIV infection with access to antiretroviral drugs
Target 6.C: Have halted by 2015 and begun to reverse the incidence of malaria and other major diseases	6.6 Incidence and death rates associated with malaria

Goal 7: Ensure environmental sustainability	
Target 7.A: Integrate the principles of sustainable development into country policies and programmes and reverse the loss of environmental resources	7.1 Proportion of land area covered by forest 7.4 Proportion of fish stocks within safe biological limits 7.6 Proportion of terrestrial and marine areas protected
Target 7.B: Reduce biodiversity loss, achieving, by 2010, a significant reduction in the rate of loss	7.7 Proportion of species threatened with extinction
Target 7.C: Halve, by 2015, the proportion of people without sustainable access to safe drinking water and basic sanitation	7.8 Proportion of population using an improved drinking water source 7.9 Proportion of population using an improved sanitation facility
Target 7.D: By 2020, to have achieved a significant improvement in the lives of at least 100 million slum dwellers	7.10 Proportion of urban population living in slums[2]

Goal 8: Develop a global partnership for development	
Target 8.A: Develop further an open, rule-based, predictable, non-discriminatory trading and financial system Target 8.D: Deal comprehensively with the debt problems of developing countries through national and international measures in order to make debt sustainable in the long term	8.6 Proportion of total developed country imports (by value and excluding arms) from developing countries and least developed countries, admitted free of duty
Target 8.E: In cooperation with pharmaceutical companies, provide access to affordable essential drugs in developing countries	8.13 Proportion of population with access to affordable essential drugs on a sustainable basis
Target 8.F: In cooperation with the private sector, make available the benefits of new technologies, especially information and communications	8.15 Cellular subscribers per 100 population 8.16 Internet users per 100 population

[1] For monitoring country poverty trends, indicators based on national poverty lines should be used, where available.

[2] The actual proportion of people living in slums is measured by a proxy, represented by the urban population living in households with at least one of the four characteristics: (a) lack of access to improved water supply; (b) lack of access to improved sanitation; (c) overcrowding (3 or more persons per room); and (d) dwellings made of non-durable material.

4. Acronyms

AIDS – Acquired Immune Deficiency Syndrome

ART – Antiretroviral (drugs)

BRIC – Brazil, Russian Federation, India, China

EU – European Union

FAO – Food and Agriculture Organisation

FSC – Forest Stewardship Council

FTA – Free Trade Areas

GDP – Gross Domestic Product

GM – Genetically Modified

GNI – Gross National Income

GNP – Gross National Product

HEP – Hydro-electric Power

HIPC – Heavily Indebted Poor Countries

HIV – Human Immunodeficiency Virus

HYV – High Yielding Varieties

IMF – International Monetary Fund

IT – Information Technology

MDG – Millennium Development Goals

NGO – Non-governmental Organisation

NIC – Newly Industrialised Country

OPEC – Oil Producing and Exporting Countries

PHC – Primary Health Care

RFA – Rainforest Alliance

SADC – Southern Africa Development Community

SAN – Sustainable Agricultural Network

UK – United Kingdom

UN – United Nations

UNEP – United Nations Environment Programme

UNESCO – United Nations Educational, Scientific and Cultural Organisation

UNFPA – United Nations Population Fund

UNICEF – United Nations Children's Education Fund

UNIFEM – United Nations Development Fund for Women

US – United States

WFP – World Food Programme

WHO – World Health Organisation

WTO – World Trade Organisation

Sample answers

The example answers in this section were written by the author; in examination the number of marks to answers similar to these may be different as the context would be different.

🌍 Unit 1

Question 1

1. (a) (i) All children in the world receive basic schooling. [1]
      (ii) Ghana [1]
      (iii) Morocco [1]
   (b) (i) Equal treatment and opportunities for boys and girls [1]
      (ii) Venezuela [1]
      (iii) No country reached the target for goal 2 by 2005 as they all have less than 100 per cent of children in school. Only one country reached the target for goal 3 which was Venezuela. Bangladesh and Morocco had about 6 per cent less girls than boys in primary school. [3]
   (c) (i) Girls are more likely to drop out of education than boys because if the family is poor and cannot afford to educate all their children, parents will send the boys to school as they are regarded as more important in many cultures. Traditionally, women's work has been in the home and girls are often married at a young age. [2]
      (ii) Women will be able to obtain jobs such as teaching which will earn more money for the family so living standards will improve. Educated women are more aware of disease prevention and the importance of hygiene in the home and so will be able to care better for their families. Women are more likely to practise family planning so families will be smaller which will mean the mother's health will improve. If women have gender equality they will be able to contribute to making important decisions in the home that affect themselves and their children. [4]
   (d) Laws to allow women to vote as an equal right would enable their views to be heard. Women should be encouraged to enter parliament with a quota system to ensure a certain number of women were elected. The government should set an example by appointing women as ministers and these women holding important positions could act as role models for others.

   Laws to prevent discrimination in the workplace would encourage women to follow careers. Governments should help women to set up cooperatives and provide them with loans. They would then be able to share ideas and improve their businesses. They could be trained in new skills such as how to budget and achieve more independence through being able to earn more income or own their own land. [6]

Question 2

   (a) (i) High HDI = USA

Medium HDI = Brazil

Low HDI = Kenya [3]

    (ii) North America   South America   Africa [1]

(b)

    (i) A = Ethiopia

       B = Egypt

       C = South Africa [3]

    (ii) Gross Domestic Product is the total value of all goods and services produced within a country in a given time. [2]

    (iii) There is a positive correlation as the higher the GDP per person the greater the energy use.

However there is an exception as Uganda does not fit the general pattern so it is not a perfect relationship. [2]

    (iv) GDP per person is an average figure but everyone does not have an equal share of a country's income as wealth is not evenly distributed.

Development is more than just about a country's wealth. GDP per person takes no account of development issues such as the availability of health care and schooling.

Many people survive on income gained in work in the informal sector which is not taken into account in government data. Money earned shining shoes in the street, for example, may be used to buy a more balanced diet which will lead to development as people's health improves. [3]

(c)   (i) Justice and freedom of speech are difficult to measure. [2]

    (ii) Political freedoms can be measured by determining which groups of people are allowed to vote. The proportion of women in parliament and those holding ministerial jobs can measure the degree of gender discrimination in politics. The number of prisoners held due to their outspoken political views can be determined.

Freedom to join religious or other groups could be measured by assessing the variety of groups and their numbers within a certain area. If there are none, this would suggest an absence of this human right. [4]

Question 3

(a)   (i) A pilot is used to check whether or not questions on the questionnaire work. [1]

    (ii) All the names of the villages in the survey area could have been written on individual pieces of paper and folded to conceal the name. These would then have been mixed up in a container and eight selected. [1]

    (iii) One advantage would be that this would be the easiest method of choosing the students and would therefore be a quick method. A disadvantage is that the sample would not be representative of the whole school. [2]

(b)   (i) Information plotted graphically using an appropriate graph (bar or similar) with no obvious inaccuracies in plotting or graph construction. [3]

    (ii) Literacy improves if there is a library in the village as more books are read. Students living in villages without a library read on average about 7 books in a year while those who lived in villages with a library read almost double that number.

88 per cent of students use a village library regularly if there is a library in their village compared with only 16 per cent who live in villages without one. [4]

(c) (i) For Student B:

A hypothesis such as 'Literacy levels are not affected by gender' would be identified first. A sample of the village's population would be asked to complete a questionnaire about their education. A stratified sample would be chosen so each age group would be included in the study.

An interview with teachers would provide useful extra information.

Bar graphs could be drawn to show literacy levels of males and females for each age group.

Figures could be obtained from schools and the Ministry of changes in levels of literacy for boys and girls as well as newspaper articles about gender inequalities and school attendance.

The data collected could be described including whether or not different age groups show different results. Explanations of the data collected would be given.

A report could be written and sent to the local authority with suggestions on improving literacy levels for girls.

The problems encountered and how these may be overcome in any future investigation would need to be considered in the evaluation. [8]

(ii) People may not want to cooperate as they do not have enough time to answer questions and may not want to answer the questions for various reasons. Those questioned may not tell the truth but answer what they consider to be the correct answer. People who are illiterate may not even be able to read a questionnaire or there may be language difficulties with ethnic groups. Views given in an interview may be very subjective and a head teacher may be biased to give a higher literacy level for his students than the school deserves. Some secondary sources of data may be out of date or not available and it may be difficult to obtain data from schools and other organisations. A student may not have the time to carry out a proper survey or may not be able to afford transport to the study areas. [6]

🌐 Unit 2

Question 1

(a) (i) 50 per cent [1]

(ii) Bangladesh [1]

(iii) As a country develops the percentage of people employed in agriculture decreases and the percentage of people employed in industry and in services increases. [2]

(iv) Industrialisation occurs as countries develop and as agriculture becomes mechanised it requires fewer workers. Higher wages in secondary industries encourage people to move to the growing industries in the towns where the demand for services increases as workers have more money to spend and seek a higher standard of living.

New industries require development of services such as transport and banking which increases the number employed in the tertiary sector.

Governments have more income from taxes to spend on more schools and education increases the skills available for more industries. [3]

(b) (i) Services are activities such as energy supply that enable people to produce goods or are actions such as teaching that help to improve people's lives. [1]

(ii) Traditional education often took place under a tree where local culture and survival techniques were taught by village elders. As countries develop, schools with classrooms are built with books and trained teachers. A greater variety of subjects is then taught with the use of computers and access to the internet increases the information available to learners. [3]

(iii) A mixed economy. [1]

(iv) An advantage of private ownership is that competition between companies leads to a greater choice of products for the consumer to buy and prices are determined by market forces. These goods are of often of higher quality than if they are produced by the state. As there is no government control of production the owner makes all the decisions and shares in the profits. [2]

(c) A furniture factory may receive its raw materials/wood from the primary sector in the local area or from imports. The inputs will arrive by means of road, rail or sea transport and are delivered to the factory. The service sector also supplies electricity for the machinery and computers as well as water for the different processes. The skills provided by the workers will have been learnt from education and training departments that require teachers. These are also part of the tertiary sector of the economy. Marketing of the product may require promoting the brand on the Internet or printing advertisements in local newspapers. The finished products are then distributed to furniture warehouses/shops or they are exported and earn foreign exchange. [6]

Question 2

(a) (i) UNICEF [1]

(ii) A country may be given emergency aid after a natural disaster such as an earthquake. This could take the form of shelters and blankets as well as food and clean water. [2]

(iii) One type of technical aid may be hospital equipment. [1]

(b) A clinic could be provided by an NGO with Mother and Child Classes. Lessons in hygiene will help ensure that water-borne diseases such as diarrhoea do not spread and parents and children would been encouraged to keep their homes and neighbourhoods clean. By educating the family on the importance of a balanced diet, the family will be stronger and more work can be done both at school, on the farm and in local jobs. If the children are properly educated, they will learn skills that will enable them to get jobs and contribute to the economy. They will also be able to improve their own standard of living by using their income to pay for better food and services. The clinic could provide HIV/AIDS testing and supply antiretroviral drugs which would improve people's quality of life and enable them to work more efficiently for longer. [6]

Question 3

(a) (i) Land refers to natural resources or raw materials such as soil, water, fish, timber and minerals or the actual site for a building. [1]

(ii) Capital may be in the form of money or capital goods such as machinery, computers, factory buildings. [2]

(iii) Enterprise organises the land, labour and capital and uses them efficiently in the production of goods. [1]

(iv) Less labour is needed in factory production than in craft production so it is less labour intensive. Instead it uses more capital goods such as machinery. Technology in factory production is more complex as machinery and computers are used rather than simple hand tools. [2]

(b) (i) In industrialised countries.   [1]
     (ii) A. Free trade zones: areas in which companies do not have to pay import taxes and
          there are no quotas on the amount of goods traded.   [1]
          B. Specialised skills: the ability to do work which requires training and expertise.   [1]
     (iii) Gap first developed retail branches and suppliers in its home country and then
          expanded to set up sales branches in other developed countries. It began to obtain
          supplies from other countries, mostly developing ones, where labour costs were cheaper
          which meant profits were greater. It also saves money by taking advantage of free trade
          zones. However, its headquarters and its research and development remain in the home
          country. It has a strong brand which is known world-wide.   [5]
(c)   MNCs create jobs for local people who learn new skills and expertise which may allow
          them to progress to better jobs or set up their own business. There are opportunities for
          local businesses to develop as people spend their wages in food stores and on leisure
          and require banks and transport. Families would be able to afford a better diet and
          health care.
          MNCs usually pay tax to governments which can be used to improve roads and ports,
          build schools and hospitals. Export of goods brings in foreign exchange and may lead
          to a positive balance of trade. A country could pay for more imports or pay off some of
          its debt.
          However, most of the profits go out of the developing country back to the host country
          of the MNC.
          MNCs employ people on low wages who cannot therefore afford to live in good
          conditions. They employ people to work long hours which may affect their health.
          Some factories cause air and water pollution which can affect the health of whole
          communities.   [6]

🌍 Unit 3

Question 1

(a)
          ˙ˈˈˈ million   [1]
                          ᵗʰ in India was more rapid than in the USA.   [1]
                                    ᵗᵉ starts to decline in both China and India. One
                                              ˡⁱⁿᵉ from 2040 while the population
                                                                                                 [2]
                                                                                                 [1]

                                                                                                 [2]
                                                                                  ᵼg. Poor
                                                                                  ren are
                                                                                  ᵵe families are
                                                                                  rtality is high,
                                                                                                 [5]
                                                                                                 [1]

    B The wider base to the pyramid in 2005 means there is a greater numbers of children in younger age groups and so a higher birth rate than in 2050. [2]

    (iii) There are similar numbers of young dependents in 2050 and in 2005, a difference of only 20 million. However, there is a far greater numbers of old dependents in 2050, 230 million compared with 50 million in 2005. There is therefore a greater number of total dependents in 2050. [3]

(d) Life expectancy may increase due to improved health care such as new medicines and better access to clinics. Increased education means people will understand the importance of hygiene and other methods of disease prevention. Governments may increase the supplies of piped water and improved sanitation to more areas and so reduce deaths from water borne diseases. As industries develop, more people have jobs and so can afford a more balanced diet. [4]

Question 2

(a) (i) 4.2 million [1]

    (ii) Delhi – Kolkata – Ahmadabad – Nagpur [1]

    (iii) Mumbai [1]

    (iv) Many people who migrate to urban areas have to do low paid jobs as they don't have an education and so lack skills, so they cannot afford to live in good conditions. They may have large families to support and there is not enough proper food for everyone. They often live in the worst places such as by rubbish dumps and factories where polluted air causes health problems. [3]

Question 3

(a) (i) Jaipur [1]

    (ii) There is little space left to build a house anywhere else. [1]

    (iii) Interviews were used because people who live on the streets are unlikely to be able to readand write. Information is obtained straight away and if a question is not understood, it can be put in a different way and further questions asked if necessary. [2]

    (iv) The 296 families represented 2960 families of pavement dwellers. [1]

    (v) A systematic sample would have selected every tenth family.
An opportunity sample would have interviewed any 296 families that were available or willing to answer questions.
A random sample would have selected families using a random number table to identify them. [3]

    (vi) Some of the squatters may not have spoken the same language as the interviewer. People who are occupying land illegally may be suspicious of outsiders and think the researchers may be from the government who wants them to move on. People may lie as they do not want to reveal who they are and what they are doing there. It may be unsafe for the interviewer, either because there will be health risks due to the unhygienic conditions or they could be robbed as this area suffers from so much poverty. [4]

(b) (i) 52 per cent [1]

    (ii) 10 per cent [1]

    (iii) Figure 6 = Pie chart
Figure 7 = Divided bar chart [2]

(iv) They do not have water sources in their homes and many have to use public taps. Water has to be collected which is heavy work and time consuming. With limited supplies, hygiene in the home may be poor.

With no electricity, lighting is by lamps which give poor light or have a limited life. Nearly half of those interviewed use kerosene lamps which give off fumes and are a fire hazard.

Apart from the 25 per cent involved in construction work, most people work in craft businesses or in unskilled occupations such as pulling rickshaws. These are generally low paid for long hours of often strenuous work and there is little income to improve standards of living.

Over 40 per cent of household rubbish is thrown out next to the shelters. This causes a low quality of life as it smells, attracts flies and rats and looks very unpleasant. [5]

(c) Scheme 4 would be the most permanent solution to the problem of people living on pavements. Many of these families have come from the rural areas where drought and poor soils mean farming is very difficult. If rural areas were developed to include money for better farming techniques, many people would not migrate to the towns. Schemes 1 and 2 will help the people already living on the pavements and provide them with a much better standard of living but it will encourage even more people to come to the towns if they think the government is going to provide them with amenities. However, the people may not be able to afford the housing. The government will always have to provide more housing and land for them and it may not have the money to do so.

Scheme 3 is not a good choice because people have to live somewhere and there may be nowhere else for them to go. To use police to evict these families from the pavements will just mean they go somewhere else in the town. [7]

Question 4

(a) (i) The increasing organisation and interconnection of the economies of countries to allow movement of companies, people and trade. [1]

(ii) Economic migrants. [1]

(b) (i) The migrants may have difficulty understanding the language and find it hard to get a job. They may find it difficult to adjust to new customs and experience discrimination. [2]

(ii) The people at home benefit from remittances which they can use for education. There are fewer mouths to feed in the family and they are able to buy better quality food so health improves. However, the family worries about the migrant in a strange country and how they will manage without them. [3]

(c) Unemployment means poverty and people cannot buy sufficient food to eat.

In rural Mexico, educational facilities are poor. The young people therefore have few qualifications or skills and there are not many jobs anyway. They migrate into the USA where they find jobs as waiters and maids in hotels in large urban areas and some work picking fruit at harvest time. They can earn more money in a few months than they can in a year in Mexico.

Political unrest can cause people to leave their land and abandon their harvests as they fear for their safety. The political situation in Zimbabwe has resulted in serious food shortages and many have migrated to Botswana in order to be able to survive. In times of drought subsistence farmers have little or no alternative source of income and so families are in danger of starving or becoming malnourished. In Somalia, drought and civil war have meant large numbers of people have migrated to Kenya in the hope of finding a better life. [6]

🌐 Unit 4

Question 1

(a) (i) Antigua is a successful tourist destination because there is much to see of historical interest. A tropical island has sea, sand and sunshine which is a popular combination. It also has an airport and a port that can take large cruise ships.   [3]

(ii) Half a million tourists visit Antigua each year so employment in the tourist industry is high.

The infant mortality rate is low which shows that healthcare is accessible. There is a high literacy rate which means that the population is provided with a good education. Income from tourism would help to pay for these services.   [3]

(iii) Clearance of forests for tourist facilities means natural habitats are destroyed. This means wildlife loses its habitat which can affect the food chains of the forests.

Coral reefs can be destroyed by scuba divers which means species can be lost.

Tourists require huge amounts of water and produce large amounts of waste. More reservoirs have to be built which often means further loss of habitat. Waste contains plastic and toxic materials which can cause death to wildlife if it is eaten or it can pollute water supplies when dumped in the environment.   [5]

(b)   Tourism can decline suddenly if there is a world recession or a natural disaster strikes an area. If a country relies on tourism then large numbers of people will become unemployed and this leads to poverty. People can become malnourished and suffer from ill health. A government would receive fewer taxes from the tourist operators and so would have less money to spend on new roads and schools.

Large numbers of tourists may bring in unwanted cultural influences which affect local traditions. People may feel that their culture is being exploited if traditional songs and dances are used to make money.

Wealthy tourists may encourage crime as robbery is seen by many as an easy way out of poverty. Children learn to beg and so drop out of school to earn money for their parents. Crimes such as prostitution become more common in tourist areas with all the problems of disease this may bring.   [6]

Question 2

(a) (i) In order to earn foreign currency and improve the balance of trade.   [1]

(ii) This causes problems because these two large companies control the market and so can keep prices high in the shops but only pay the farmers a low price.

Monopolies make it difficult for new companies to enter the market and compete with the large companies.   [2]

(iii) Variations in world production and supply mean if there is a large amount grown but little demand, the price falls and vice versa. Changes in supply can depend on the weather and how many farmers go into coffee production. Harvests can be good or bad depending on how much rain or warmth there has been during the growing period. Changes in demand can be due to the seasons in the main coffee drinking nations as people tend to like cold drinks when the weather is hot.   [3]

(b) Governments can provide loans with low interest so that farmers can make improvements such as introduce irrigation or purchase more modern machinery. They could also subsidise the price of fertilisers and pesticides to make them more affordable. Governments can encourage farmers to join co-operatives so they can receive education in new techniques through agricultural advisers and share ideas, machines and work together at harvest. If governments improve roads and transport to market, farmers would be able to get their produce there more easily and quickly before it went rotten. [4]

(c) Forests are being cleared to plant crops resulting in soil erosion of the hills which causes silting of rivers and flooding. Destruction of wildlife habitat may mean species are lost or become endangered. Species have to move elsewhere and this can disrupt the food chain. Fertilizers run off into rivers and cause a decline of aquatic life and pesticides kill insect life which will affect numbers of birds.

Children are not being properly fed because farmers have switched from food production to growing crops for export. Malnutrition makes them too weak to work and they fail to attend school regularly.

Some traditional farmers are being turned off their land to make way for huge commercial plantations. They have no form of income which means their children may not get a proper education because farmers cannot afford the school fees. This will affect the country because it will not have a skilled population. [6]

Question 3

(a) (i) An earthquake may mean that crops cannot be taken to market as bridges may have been destroyed. People will have lost their life and families will suffer from bereavement. Water pipes can break in an earthquake which would mean disease may become a problem if people have to drink dirty water. [3]

(ii) Due to climate change, the number and intensity of storms is likely to increase. Together with a rise in sea level caused by global warming, this will mean that low lying areas will be more likely to flood.

Man-made problems such as water and air pollution will become worse as more industries are attracted to boost economic development and populations continue to grow in urban areas. A growing tourist industry worldwide will put more pressure on coral reefs and the rich biodiversity could be threatened by too many people wanting to see it.

Further deforestation is likely due to increased global demand for timber and as the population grows, more people clear the forests to grow crops. Soil erosion from this land will increase during the heavy storms and soils will become infertile quickly. [4]

(b) The government called for foreign assistance, particularly in the form of heavy lifting equipment and sniffer dogs to search for people buried under the rubble. Emergency services rescued people and took them to hospitals or temporary refuge centres where medical treatment and basic needs were supplied. Helicopters were sent to reach remote areas cut off by landslides or broken bridges. The government provided money to help rebuild settlements.

NGOs such as The Red Cross organised the supply of medicines, bandages, food, blankets and shelter, often in the form of tents to those who became homeless. Charities requested money from the international community to help ease the suffering. They ensured water supplies in the temporary camps were clean and basic sanitation was set up so that diseases like cholera did not spread. [6]

Acknowledgement

The following photographs are used by kind permission of the author and family:

Wendy Taylor: Figure 2.4; Figure 2.8; Figure 6.3; Figure 13.1; Figure 14.5 (1) (2); Figure 14.6; Figure 14.10 (1) (2) (3); Figure 16.1 (1) (2); Figure 17.6; Figure 19.2; Figure 19.3

Stephen Taylor: Figure 9.6

Cynthia Tipper: Figure 9.2; Figure 16.2 (1) (2) (3)

Amy Oakley: Figure 14.2(1) (2); Figure 14.3

The author wishes to acknowledge research and technical assistance from Stephen and Natalie Taylor, constructive advice from Claire Lovell and continuous support from Mervyn Taylor.

We are grateful to the following for permission to reproduce photographs and maps:

The Maria-Helena Foundation (www.mariahelenafoundation.org); World Vision (www. worldvision.org); www.baladarshan.com; Christine McFarlane (http://chrissymcfarlane. blogspot.com); African Studies Center, Michigan State University; Mongabay.com; Pavel L Photo and Video / Shutterstock.com, OlegD / Shutterstock.com, Asianet-Pakistan / Shutterstock. com, Hector Conesa / Shutterstock.com, arindambanerjee / Shutterstock.com, paul prescott / Shutterstock.com, africa924 / Shutterstock.com, Tupungato / Shutterstock.com, Ken Tannenbaum / Shutterstock.com, Brians / Shutterstock.com

We would also like to thank the following for permission to use their material in either the original or adapted form:

The Maria-Helena Foundation (www.mariahelenafoundation.org); UNESCO Institute for Statistics (www.uis.unesco.org); UNFPA, United Nations Population Fund; Food and Agriculture Organization of the United Nations; Farm Africa (www.farmafrica.org.uk); United Nations Publications Board; United States Census Bureau; Intergovernmental Panel on Climate Change; World Bank

The following is reproduced by permission of Cambridge International Examinations:

Syllabus Name and Code	Paper and Question Number	Month/Year	Chapter/Page in book
Cambridge IGCSE Development Studies 0453	Paper 1 Q2	Oct/Nov 2010	Unit 1 Questions Page 69
Cambridge IGCSE Development Studies 0453	Paper 2 Q1 a, b, c	Oct/Nov 2009	Unit 1 Questions Page 71
Cambridge IGCSE Development Studies 0453	Paper 2 Q3	Oct/Nov 2009	Unit 1 Questions Page 72
Cambridge IGCSE Development Studies 0453	Paper 1 Q3	Oct/Nov 2010	Unit 2 Questions Page 127
Cambridge IGCSE Development Studies 0453	Paper 1 Q4 b (i) (ii) and (iv), c	Oct/Nov 2010	Unit 2 Questions Page 128

Syllabus Name and Code	Paper and Question Number	Month/ Year	Chapter/Page in book
Cambridge IGCSE Development Studies 0453	Paper 1 Q2	Oct/Nov 2008	Unit 2 Questions Page 128
Cambridge IGCSE Development Studies 0453	Paper 2 Q1	Oct/Nov 2008	Unit 3 Questions Page 176
Cambridge IGCSE Development Studies 0453	Paper 2 Q2 b	Oct/Nov 2008	Unit 3 Questions Page 176
Cambridge IGCSE Development Studies 0453	Paper 2 Q3 a, c, d	Oct/Nov 2008	Unit 3 Questions Page 179
Cambridge IGCSE Development Studies 0453	Paper 1 Q1 a, b, d	Oct/Nov 2009	Unit 3 Questions Page 180
Cambridge IGCSE Development Studies 0453	Paper 1 Q1 b, c	Oct/Nov 2008	Unit 4 Questions Page 256
Cambridge IGCSE Development Studies 0453	Paper 1 Q3 b, c, d	Oct/Nov 2008	Unit 4 Questions Page 257
Cambridge IGCSE Development Studies 0453	Paper 1 Q2 b, c	Oct/Nov 2009	Unit 4 Questions Page 258
Cambridge IGCSE Development Studies 0453	Research Investigations 1, 2, 7, 8, 10 adapted from Appendix to 'Schemes of Work, Cambridge IGCSE Development Studies 0453'		1, 2 – In Appendix Page 271 – 274 7 – Chapter 2 Page 29 8 – Chapter 15 Page 224 10 – Chapter 11 Page 162

Index